Bismarck's Shadow

Bismarck's Shadow

The Cult of Leadership and the Transformation of the German Right, 1898–1945

Richard E. Frankel

Oxford • New York

First published in 2005 by
Berg
Editorial offices:
1st Floor, Angel Court, 81 St Clements Street, Oxford, OX4 1AW, UK
175 Fifth Avenue, New York, NY 10010, USA

Berg is the imprint of Oxford International Publishers Ltd.

Library of Congress Cataloguing-in-Publication Data
A catalogue record for this book is available from the Library of Congress.

British Library Cataloguing-in-Publication Data
A catalogue record for this book is available from the British Library.

ISBN 1 84520 033 0 (Cloth)
1 84520 034 9 (Paper)

Typeset by Avocet Typeset, Chilton, Aylesbury, Bucks
Printed in the United Kingdom by Biddles Ltd, King's Lynn

www.bergpublishers.com

For my family …

Contents

Acknowledgments

Many people provided invaluable assistance along the way to making this book a reality. Now that I can finally step out of Bismarck's shadow, so to speak, I have the enjoyable task of thanking them all. At Buffalo, Professor William Sheridan Allen introduced me to German history and (if unknowingly) planted the seed of an idea that resulted in this book. John Naylor's encouragement and praise convinced me that I could be an historian, while his good nature and humor made leaving Buffalo difficult, indeed. At Chapel Hill, I had the tremendous fortune to work under some of the best people in the field. Konrad Jarausch believed in me from the beginning – among his countless contributions, that was the one I value the most. Gerhard Weinberg helped me to continually look at the issues in new and different ways. Others who helped in my development as a scholar and in the development of this project include Geoff Eley, Christopher Browning, Donald Reid, Jay Smith, Peter Coclanis, and Marion Gray. While in Germany, Peter Steinbach, Bernd Sösemann, and Uwe Puschner made me feel welcome so far from home. For help in a variety of ways I want to thank the history departments at the University of North Carolina, Chapel Hill and the University of Louisiana, Lafayette. The staffs at the archives and libraries I visited – the Federal Archives at Berlin-Lichterfelde and Koblenz, the Otto-von-Bismarck Stiftung in Friedrichsruh, the Geheimes Staatsarchiv Preussischer Kulturbesitz, the Landesarchiv Berlin, the Stadtsbibliothek Berlin, the Microfilm Archive at the Free University Berlin, and Davis Library at UNC Chapel Hill – were all critical for the success of this project, and I thank them. My thanks also to the German Academic Exchange Service (DAAD), whose generous grant allowed me to conduct my research in Germany. I am also grateful to Diethelm Prowe and the anonymous readers at the *German Studies Review* for publishing an article based on this project. I also want to thank the people at Berg Publishers – Kathleen May, Kathryn Earle, Ian Critchley and the readers – for taking a chance on this project and for all their help and enthusiasm along the way. In the end, friends and family are vital. Steve Pfaff was there at Chapel Hill from the beginning, and if he has since moved on, his influence on my work has remained substantial. Barry Jackisch helped make my stay in Berlin one of the most enjoyable times of my life. His mastery of the German Right has helped tremendously on this project and has never failed to astound me. Also Matthew Titolo, Patrick Huber, Joseph Gerteis, and Gray Whaley all have made my experience in academia a much more enjoyable one. Above all, I want to thank my family – for help in so many ways, for support, for faith in my ability, for love. Nothing I write here can adequately express what you've meant to me. Norman, Selma, Steve, Kathy, Eliana, and Joshua: this book I dedicate to you.

Introduction

The example of a great man can effect more changes in the world than all the social legislation. But beware, if the example be misunderstood! Then it may happen that a new type of man may arise, who sees in severity and repression, not the sad transition to humane conditions, but the aim of life itself. Weak and pacifistic by nature, he strives to appear a man of iron because, in his conception, Bismarck was such a man. Invoking without justification one higher than himself he becomes noisy and dangerous.

Heinrich Mann, *Der Untertan*[1]

In a Berlin pub around the turn of the century a group of devoted Bismarck followers met every Wednesday evening to reminisce about the recently deceased Reich Chancellor. At one of these meetings, Maximilian Harden – baptized Jew and publisher of the journal *Zukunft* – sat with a contemptuous look upon his face, listening as each sought to outdo the other with anecdotes of their common hero. Finally he leaped to his feet and yelled, "You with your Bismarck! What was so special about him? I first made him great." After a moment of awkward silence, the man sitting across from him, a Pan-German named Wilhelm Kollmann, rose to his feet, grabbed a wine bottle and yelled, "you damn Jew!" as he slammed the bottle on Harden's head, nearly fracturing his skull. In relating this story, Kollmann reassured his listener that Harden was fine. He had just given him a 'lesson'. Kollman felt himself fully justified: "Such a fellow wanted to lay his hands on Bismarck."[2]

This story helps illustrate a fascinating historical phenomenon – the critical role of Bismarck in German political culture from the late nineteenth century through the first half of the twentieth. Here we have a group of solid middle-class Germans meeting to discuss Bismarck. But this was not a homogenous group. While Harden was certainly a strong German nationalist and concerned himself intensely with issues of national power and prestige, he was no Pan-German, and men such as Kollmann had any number of issues that divided them from the baptized Jewish journalist. And yet Bismarck brought them together – but not completely. Despite their shared admiration for the Iron Chancellor, and their shared hopes for German greatness that were embodied in the symbol of Bismarck, they fought over him. Max Harden challenged the claims of those around him to be the true disciples of Bismarck and the rightful executors of his will by himself claiming to have 'made' Bismarck into the towering figure to whom they all bowed down. But his challenge was violently dismissed by another from that circle who refused to accept Harden's attempt to define this national symbol and in response proceeded to nearly shatter the man's skull. The emotions exhibited here go beyond a case of mere barroom bravado – they reflect on a small scale the very real struggles going on over the meaning of the nation and the contours of German political culture.

At the heart of these struggles stood Bismarck, or more accurately, a series of Bismarck images, each with their own meaning and their own lessons. Defining Bismarck in a very real sense meant defining the nation. To the victor went the opportunity to determine just what Germany would look like and what path it would follow. The violence with which Herr Kollmann reacted to Harden's asser-tion provides a small glimpse into one of those potential future Germanies: a Germany in which violence, based on Bismarckian precedent, is a perfectly viable and legitimate option for solving political disputes. And while all of Germany would feel the consequences of these battles, it was largely a fight among the German Right – mainly middle-class, but also aristocratic, Germans fighting over the symbol that, for them more than for other groups in German society, had the most resonance. But those fighting over Bismarck in the bar scene described above were not in power – their decisions did not make or break national policy – at least, not yet.

The fight for Bismarck would not remain for long on the level of the beer hall. These men were serious and they were not content to continue in the role of what Chancellor Bernhard von Bülow would derisively label as *Bierbankpolitiker*, or beer hall politicians. With a fervor that, as we shall see, could be described as reli-gious, Bismarckians would carry their icon into battle not only against other 'mis-guided' followers, but against a government increasingly seen to be out of touch with the 'spirit of Bismarck' and leading the nation in dangerous directions. If at the time of the Harden–Kollmann confrontation such efforts produced few tan-gible results, it would not be too much longer before these people would be moving from the margins of German politics to center stage. With a new brand of populist, radical nationalist politics espoused in Bismarck's name, they would break down the doors of *Honoratiorenpolitik*, or the politics of notables, that had barred them from national political roles. Leading new organizations with Bismarck as their founding inspiration, they would soon be brokering deals with political parties that had previously looked down upon them. Soon they would be pressuring the government with an effectiveness that made the chancellor's posi-tion an even more difficult one than before, with dangerous implications for German foreign policy. Eventually, Bismarckians would be in the government itself, having moved from the beer halls to the halls of power. The role that the Bismarck image and the cult that grew up around that image played in this process of developing and legitimizing a new style of right-wing politics is at the heart of this study.

From Bismarck to Hitler? The Nature of the Project

Few figures in history can match the scholarly attention devoted to modern Germany's founder and first chancellor, Otto von Bismarck. A look at the thousands of studies of him is clear testimony to that.[3] Otto Pflanze has noted that only two figures can claim to have inspired more historical investigation, both of whom have some connection to Bismarck: Napoleon, whose defeat at Waterloo in 1815 occurred the year Bismarck was born, and Hitler, whose Third Reich was meant to be a successor to Bismarck's creation, but in the end brought about its ultimate destruction.[4] And while the connection to Napoleon is more coincidence than anything else, the relationship between Bismarck and Hitler requires some discussion, both for the historiographical issues it raises as well as for the purposes of clarifying what this study is truly about. For while a great many Bismarck studies were produced before the world had ever heard of Adolf Hitler, much of the writing on the Iron Chancellor has involved an effort either to demonstrate or to disprove a link between the first chancellor of the Second Reich and the *Führer* of the Third. As it has with most areas of German history, the issue of Hitler's rise and success and the crimes committed in his name has settled over the field of Bismarck scholarship. In some sense, then, Bismarck scholars can be said to have been working in *Hitler's* shadow.

The question of the 'Bismarck to Hitler' connection occupied historians almost immediately following the fateful night of January 30, 1933, when the Nazi leader was named chancellor. Most of those early judgments recognized the connection and viewed it favorably. The defeat and devastation that followed the Second World War, however, led some to raise the question of continuity – just how much of the Third Reich could be seen to have already been developing in the Second? In *The German Catastrophe*, Friedrich Meinecke wrote that "the staggering course of World War I and still more of World War II makes it impossible to pass over in silence the query whether the germs of the later evil were not really implanted in Bismarck's work from the outset."[5] At first, the predominant response came from German nationalist historians such as Gerhard Ritter and Hans Rothfels, who answered in the negative.[6] In doing so, they sought to cleanse the German past of its Nazi stain by severing the Iron Chancellor from the *Führer*, depicting Bismarck as a man of morals and moderation – qualities completely absent from Hitler – and thus a truer product of German development. A new generation would take a new look and end up finding those connections between the Second and the Third Reich to which Meinecke alluded, and therefore between Bismarck and Hitler. In particular, the findings of Fritz Fischer and those who followed him with regard to the continuity in war aims from the First to the Second World Wars helped revive the debate.[7] The issue of continuity remains a critical element of German historical inquiry, and certainly this study will have something to say about it. But it will do so not through a direct comparison of the two men or even of the institutions of the Second and the Third Reich. This is a different kind of study.[8]

While it does deal in part with Bismarck's own impact on German political culture, overall this project takes a different approach in seeking to understand the particular path Germany followed during the first half of the twentieth century. In doing so, it asks not only what Bismarck did to Germany, but even more importantly *what Germans did to Bismarck* and what they did with the Bismarck they created to help shape a political culture in which someone like Hitler and a movement like National Socialism were not only possible, but considered viable candidates for power.[9] There is, however, much more to this story than simply the issue of Hitler, for the thirty-five years between Bismarck's death and the Nazi leader's appointment as chancellor were extraordinarily eventful years in their own right. And so the history of Bismarck's shadow should not be seen merely as a prelude to the Third Reich. Instead, it provides valuable insights into the development of several issues that are critical to a fuller understanding of German political culture, including a chronic leadership crisis, both real and perceived, and the transformation of the German Right, both in terms of its legitimacy and its radicalism, from the 1870s to the 1930s. The impact of these issues would be felt well before Hitler gained the chancellor's office.

The main issue this project seeks to address is a broad one, of which the rise and success of the Nazis is only one part, albeit an important one. At its heart it seeks to understand what Geoff Eley has described as the dramatic transformation, or metamorphosis, of the Right's character from the 1870s to the 1920s, particularly in terms of the drastic radicalization of its ideology and political style.[10] That the transformation did occur is beyond dispute – in the end, there did arise a German fascism. The question has been *how* it occurred. Hans-Ulrich Wehler and others in the Bielefeld School felt that they had found the answers in the failure of the bourgeoisie to unseat the Prussian feudal elite following unification. An anachronistic situation thus emerged whereby the old elites sought to cling to power through the use of a series of manipulative strategies including social imperialism and *Sammlungspolitik*, or the rallying together of the conservative elite forces in the empire.[11] In response to that interpretation, Eley and others looked to the tension between the ruling elites and more marginalized groups among the German middle classes and how those marginal groups, rather than being manipulated into nationalist stances, often were the ones leading the nationalist charge. In his own study of the German Right, and particularly the Navy League, Eley showed how the tensions brought about by the frustrated ambitions of middle-class Germans led them to develop a new populist style of politics – a politics of national opposition – that represented a radicalization of these groups and thus contributed to that more general transformation of the Right.[12] The question, though, is what mechanisms enabled these middle-class Germans to break the bounds of

Honoratiorenpolitik and stake out a new position within German political culture from which they could make their own play for political power and influence?

Here we need to look at the issue of political culture generally and then that of the German Right more specifically. Broadly defined, political culture can be seen as "the set of fundamental beliefs, values and attitudes that characterize the nature of the political system and regulate the political interactions among its members."[13] In effect, then, it involves the cultural parameters, or the framework, in which politics is played out. The cultural component of this definition is closely tied to the role of symbols in limiting and guiding political action. Symbols serve as outward expressions of those basic assumptions which guide people in their political activity by defining the borders within which politics may be practiced. They can limit the range of options open to political actors just as they can empower them to carry out a certain range of policies by bequeathing their legitimacy to that particular political persuasion. This is not to say that the structure of a nation's political culture is all powerful, leaving individuals in a straightjacket without the ability to affect their own destiny. Just as the features of a nation's political culture are not static, the properties of the symbols that make up that political culture also change over time. And they change as a result of a variety of factors, some of which are external – the result of calamities such as war, revolution, or natural disasters – and others which are the result of individual action. Thus the relationship between a nation's political culture and the individuals within it is one of give and take. The structure of a political culture acts upon individuals, making certain courses of action more likely than others, while at the same time individuals may act in certain ways, claiming and thereby shaping central political symbols or ideas, which result in a permanent alteration of that country's political culture.

While defining political culture has been described as trying to 'nail pudding to the wall', the challenges in using such a concept go beyond mere definition to the issue of setting boundaries.[14] For to speak about German 'political culture' can, in a sense, be deceiving, since it implies a uniformity which for the most part did not exist. In reality, Germany was a highly fragmented society, and the political culture reflected that condition.[15] From the Empire's founding in 1871, the nation was beset by regional, confessional, and class divisions which left their imprint on German politics for the next seventy-five years. Following the lead of recent scholarship in electoral studies, and in particular the work of Karl Rohe, it makes more sense to speak of a number of lager, or sub-cultures, which compete with each other for political influence.[16] Much is known about the Social Democratic and Catholic sub-cultures with their own organizations and self-contained worldviews.[17] The importance of such sub-categories within German political culture becomes particularly apparent when discussion turns to the early 1930s and attempts are made to explain the attraction or immunity to Nazism. But what about the other major sub-groups, the Protestant middle classes of white-collar workers and professionals, particularly the *Bildungsbürgertum*, as well as the conservative agrarian lager? These were the groups from which the Right drew its strength and where the overwhelming majority of Bismarckians were to be found. What role did the Bismarck image play for the people in these lager? Did the Bismarck Cult perform a similar integrating and insulating function to that of Marxism and Catholicism for the other major lager?

This leads us to one of the key themes of this book – the phenomenon of political religion, which I intend to show played a substantial role in helping those on the right to formulate and express political ideals and goals.[18] Out of the tension with the established political elites, as well as with a government increasingly unresponsive to those fearing a dangerous departure from Bismarckian precedent, there emerged a new form and style of political practice centered around a former political leader now raised to the level of political god.[19] Numerous groups and individuals channeled Bismarck's oppositional potential into new forms of expression that clearly combined the political with the religious in ways that could potentially galvanize an otherwise disparate movement. With new forms of monumental expression, speeches in the form of sermons delivered by a new priestly caste of German academics, and a world-view that combined a gospel-like story of good and evil, fall and redemption, and a promised land of national community and world power, the Bismarck Cult dug deep furrows, decade after decade, into the ground of German political culture.

It is also one of the assertions of this work that a full understanding of the dynamics of the Right's transformation is impossible without an analysis that takes those decades upon decades into account – that is to say, it must take a longer term view than anything that has been attempted previously.[20] This is as true for understanding Germany's crisis of leadership as it is for understanding the rise and success of Nazism. One cannot fully explain the development and acceptance of the political religion of National Socialism without a full picture of the political culture in which it took root – a political culture shaped for decades by the political religion of the Bismarck Cult.[21] This study can trace continuities and note important transformative moments that could not receive such treatment in shorter works. The remarkable duration and lasting intensity of the Right's fascination with Bismarck essentially requires such an approach.

The Development of an Obsession: Bismarck and the German People

"The present condition of our parliamentary life is a legacy of Prince Bismarck's long domination and of the nation's attitude toward him since the last decade of his chancellorship. This attitude has no parallel in the reaction of any other great people toward a statesman of such stature. Nowhere else in the world has even the most unrestrained adulation of a politician made a proud nation sacrifice its substantive convictions so completely."[22] Max Weber made these observations towards the end of the First World War in a series of articles outlining the problems of German political life of the past several decades. The focus of his wrath was the unique position of Bismarck in German political culture. The obsession he pointed to had already helped drive the nation into the war they were about to lose. It would cause even more problems in the years ahead as Germans sought to establish democracy on the ruins of the Bismarckian Empire. The relationship that Weber was describing between Bismarck and the German people is a rather fascinating phenomenon of modern history – the idolization, or more accurately the deification, of recently deceased political leaders. There have certainly been a number of cases of political leaders becoming idolized after their death. Napoleon, Lincoln, and Lenin are among the first to spring to mind.[23] For the Germans, their fascination with Bismarck proved extraordinarily intense and long-lasting, with consequences for both the nation itself and the wider world that would turn out to be regrettable.

Over the course of his many decades in office, Bismarck received a remarkable number of honors and awards.[24] During the wars of unification he rose to the level of prince. He became colonel general of the cavalry with the rank of field marshal though he had only one year of army service behind him. The Kaiser, in fact, awarded him every medal available along with at least one that had to be created just for Bismarck. From the public he received an equally remarkable number of awards and honors. Universities granted him honorary degrees, while dozens of cities made him honorary citizen. Paintings of Bismarck became a cottage industry and images of him could be found all over the country. His seventieth birthday and the twenty-fifth anniversary of his appointment as minister-president became national celebrations. During his years in office Bismarck did little to cultivate this unparalleled popularity. He rarely, if ever, spoke to public gatherings outside of parliament, preferring instead to exert influence through the print media. This silence, and even embarrassment, in the face of public acclaim, however, were not to last.[25]

With his unceremonious dismissal in March 1890, a major change took place that resulted in the expansion of Bismarck's legendary status still further, while at the same time it provided headaches for those in Berlin trying to fill his shoes. Bismarck now began to speak out. His estate at Friedrichsruh became the site of numerous pilgrimages by admirers of all kinds. Between March 1890 and 1895 he received and spoke to about 150 different groups of anywhere from dozens to thousands of people. Whatever the particular purpose of the visit, political issues often found their way into Bismarck's speeches. And whatever their relation to his actual policies while in office, he now tailored his message for the purposes of shaping a new image – in particular, a patriotic image. Exposure to the 'new' Bismarck was not limited to those in attendance, as newspaper reporters brought his words to a much wider public.[26] Bismarck's eightieth birthday gave an idea of the extent of Bismarck devotion in Germany. Between March and June he received more than fifty delegations of visitors, one of the largest being a group of over four thousand university students. Around 10,000 telegrams and 450,000 postcards arrived as well. And the celebrations were not limited to Friedrichsruh. In Berlin, as well as in many other cities and towns across the Reich, Germans celebrated Bismarck's birthday as a major national holiday.[27]

With his death in 1898, the pace of Bismarck's sacralization increased to the point where we can now speak of a new political religion: a Bismarck Cult. His followers transformed the anniversaries of his birth and death, as well as the *Sonnenwende* (summer solstice), into nationalist high-holidays. For those who could not make the most significant act of devotion – the pilgrimage to Friedrichsruh – local celebrations across the country provided the opportunity to participate. As the Cult developed, so too did a whole repertoire of ritual practices. Whether they were at his grave or in their hometown on the high-holidays, Bismarckians would attend ceremonies during which speeches were delivered in major halls, at Bismarck monuments, or at the newest expression of Bismarck worship – Bismarck fire-towers, which were planned and constructed at an amazing rate.[28] In both their numbers and their financing, these expressions of a new style of politics testified to the populist, spontaneous nature of Bismarck idolatry. Practically year in and year out newspapers of even mild nationalist persuasion published some form of tribute article on one or more of these key dates. And the language used at these ceremonies and in these articles mixed the political with imagery and emotion normally reserved for religious affairs. Over the years he was transformed from the flesh-and-blood chancellor to the hero; the heaven-sent liberator and savior; the leader who brought his people out of the pre-national wilderness to the promised land of national unity only to be sacrificed by an uncaring monarch and a jaded public. Talk grew of the time when there would arise a new Bismarck who would lead his people out of the division and disgrace of post-war Germany to a new promised land of unity in the long-sought-after 'national community'. In the meantime, Bismarck served as a model – a model of Germanness, of the 'correct' national politics. The 'spirit of Bismarck' would guide the Germans through this wilderness until they had once again raised themselves to the level of national consciousness where they would be deserving of a new leader.

This small glimpse into the various forms of Bismarck obsession suggests the question: Why Bismarck, and why Germany? Why did Germans elevate an aging, physically deteriorating, often grumpy politician, viewed by many at the time of his dismissal to be out of touch with the times, to the level of demi-god? And why did this occur in Germany? In the late nineteenth and early twentieth century Germany was the most modern, advanced industrial country in Europe. Why did it embrace a phenomenon that turned its back so dramatically on the modern world, a phenomenon of such seemingly irrational character? These are questions that must be investigated before we delve into the actual analysis of the Bismarck legacy. But, broadly put, the Bismarck phenomenon reflects a serious crisis of German political culture.

Defining the Nation: Bismarck and German National Identity

German unification occurred in the midst of the age of nationalism and the impact of that ideology on the new nation and the particular shape it took helped determine the course of German and European history for the next seventy-five years. While most European nationalisms contained strong elements of the irrational, German nationalism had a number of additional factors that gave it its particular characteristics. Unified only in 1871, the Second Reich lacked the long, sustained history enjoyed by countries such as Britain and France. In this age in which nationalism was quickly becoming the dominant ideology for unifying peoples and granting legitimacy to national governments, Germany needed to fashion its own identity as a legitimate nation-state equal in stature with the more established powers. Its belated arrival on the national scene led, in many respects, to a more boisterous form of nationalism – as cover for a perceived inadequacy of national credentials.[29] The particular means by which Bismarck unified the country – through three successful wars – also helped color the way many Germans viewed their nation. In addition, Germany underwent modernization at an extremely rapid and often disquieting pace. Such dramatic change led many to seek a haven in which their problems and uncertainties would be solved. That haven was the German national community, and its particular features were forged in the public discourse of the post-unification period.

Myths and symbols played a critical role in the forging of this national identity, serving to unify the people and giving them a sense of shared values and a common past.[30] The meaning given to those myths and symbols therefore played a critical role in determining the nation's characteristics – what it meant to be German, and what kind of role Germany should play in the world. It is obvious, then, that the right to define the national symbols is of immense value, since that right enables a group to imprint their own world-view upon the nation's political culture.[31] The struggles fought out in the German public sphere over this right were marked by an intensity which reflected the combatants' awareness of the benefits of victory and the price of defeat.

The spread of nationalism and the development of national identity through such battles depended upon a development which was well under way by the second half of the nineteenth century and was dramatically changing the face of European society – the expansion of the print media.[32] In the case of Germany, Volker Berghahn points out that "the culture of the *Kaiserreich* was a culture of the written and spoken word."[33] It is true that new media were being developed at this time, and that film and radio would play an increasing role during Weimar, but still "the press remained the most important medium through which people informed themselves about their locality or the wider environment and through which ideas and opinions were spread."[34] It was this central component of the public sphere which served as the battlefield for control of the national symbols, the right to define them, and thus the ability to give direction to the nation.

During the first half of the century there were few greater prizes in this struggle to define the nation than the first chancellor, Otto von Bismarck. His pivotal role in the wars of unification and his status as the founder of the Empire guaranteed him heroic stature. His next twenty years as leader of the nation and fulcrum of European politics served to solidify his historical position. The only question then was: what would the symbol Bismarck look like? While in office, the positions he took and the policies he enacted served to shape the growing legend. Though no longer in office after 1890, his stature remained a potent force, and its use in support of, or against, the government would have vital repercussions on the course of German politics at the outset of the Wilhelmine period. With his death in 1898, the situation changed once again. No longer able to play an active role in shaping his own legend, Bismarck now passed completely into the public domain. Clearly a name with tremendous symbolic power, the battle was now joined by all those who sought to claim this national hero for their own cause, define it based on their own political outlook, and thereby acquire the legitimacy for their program that such a symbol bestows. The victors in this struggle would thereby gain a powerful weapon for their arsenal, which they could then use to help drive German politics in their desired direction. It was a struggle within the Right itself, between the Right and the government, and between Bismarckians and anti-Bismarckians. Looking at the big picture, how did this struggle help define the nation in the years to come? More specifically, how did the tensions between the various parties to the conflict help shape the culture of German right-wing politics in the decades after his death?

Charismatic Authority and the Crisis of Leadership

"It is my fate always to stand in the shadow of the great man."[35] When Leo von Caprivi, Bismarck's successor, made this statement in June 1892, he was acknowledging the existence of a serious flaw in Germany's political structure that would haunt it until its demise in the Second World War. Emerging even during Bismarck's tenure, a crisis of leadership, both real and perceived, became a central feature of German political culture. A sense of frustration developed with the men who followed Bismarck as chancellor. The absence of anyone even approaching his political abilities combined with the government's actual, or imagined, inability to solve Germany's problems added to such concerns. As the process of national self-definition continued, the development of the symbol Bismarck combined with the fears of those in the Protestant bourgeois and conservative agrarian lager to give shape to another crucial feature of German political culture – the role of the charismatic leader. The wish to solve the problems facing them steadily contributed to the desire among many Germans for a savior – a charismatic leader who would end the crisis of leadership, as well as the dislocation and uncertainties of the modern world.

To gain an understanding of charismatic leadership, we must turn to the sociology of Max Weber. In its most basic sense, Weber defined charismatic leaders as "the bearers of specific gifts of body and mind that were considered 'supernatural' (in the sense that not everybody could have access to them)."[36] Such leaders shun any rationalized, regular source of income and are not bound by traditional rules, values, or systems of authority. In fact the charismatic leader is by nature a revolutionary figure. He is not elected by any traditional or rational system of selection but achieves his position through his belief in his own gift of grace (charisma) and his sense of mission. "The bearer of charisma enjoys loyalty and authority by virtue of a mission believed to be embodied in him; this mission has not necessarily and has not always been revolutionary, but in its most charismatic forms it has inverted all value hierarchies and overthrown custom, law and tradition."[37]

It is true that, while in office, Bismarck did not fulfill all of the criteria of the charismatic leader – his constitutional subordination to the monarch would be just one example. And in fact, by the end of his career, any charismatic features that he did have had all but left him. One of the most popular catchphrases circulating in the last year of his chancellorship, "nothing succeeds anymore," indicates the fragile nature of charismatic authority and the means by which it is lost. In addition to the belief the leader must have in his own gift of grace, the followers must also be convinced of his extraordinary abilities, and when the leader can no longer prove his powers, his charismatic hold on the people is lost. His mission ends "and hope expects and searches for a new bearer."[38] In the case of Bismarck and the aftermath of his dismissal, however, something remarkable happened. Instead of fading into the pages of history, the Iron Chancellor soon took on new life, beginning in the years of his retirement, but then taking off with even more strength following his death. Gradually, Bismarck became 're-charismatized' as more and more of the attributes of the true charismatic leader were applied to him. He had become the "new bearer" for whom the German people were searching.

To help explain this phenomenon we must understand the situations in which charismatic authority comes about. Weber wrote that "[c]harismatic rulership . . .

always results from unusual, especially political or economic situations, or from extraordinary psychic, particularly religious states, or from both together. It arises from collective excitement produced by extraordinary events and from surrender to heroism of any kind."[39] Seeking a more specific application of the concept of charisma, M. Rainer Lepsius developed the notion of the 'latent charismatic situation'.[40] It is only when the two criteria of the latent charismatic situation are met that a charismatic leader may arise. First, there must be a tendency to impute charisma – the culture must be such that there exists a belief that supernatural abilities can directly influence human fate and that these powers can be represented in human beings. Both German and European nationalism contained elements of myth and other quasi-religious features. As we move forward, a look at the particularities of the Bismarck Cult will help shed light on the potential for a 'latent charismatic situation' in the case of modern Germany. The second criterion for the existence of a latent charismatic situation is the perception and experience of a crisis. "The awareness of the incapacity to overcome the crisis delegitimizes the existing political institutions."[41] The consciousness of this inability leads to the expectation that a great leader will arise to change the situation. The key to remember here is the necessity for both of these criteria to be present. What role did the Bismarck image play in the crisis of German leadership? Could Bismarck have served as a charismatic leader for the nation in the years following his death and what did that mean for German politics over that time? What role did he play for the German Right? Was the image of this charismatic leader and the cult that built up around him one of the main unifying elements of an otherwise hopelessly fractured Right? And finally, could the legacy of Bismarck be seen to have played a role in transforming a latent charismatic situation into a manifest charismatic situation, thus contributing to the rise and success of Germany's most infamous charismatic leader, Adolf Hitler?

The Role of Bismarck in German Political Culture: Method and Structure of the Project

A study of the Bismarck image in German history runs the serious risk of growing beyond manageable proportions. The pervasiveness of the Iron Chancellor was such that he touched on almost all areas of life in Germany, from politics to literature, to the arts and to a whole cottage industry of Bismarck commercialization. Rather than provide a close analysis of those popular cultural elements of the Bismarck phenomenon, this project seeks to analyze the big picture of German politics as a whole in what should be a much more compelling study. German history, however, over the period of time covered by this project was remarkably eventful, to say the least. Limitations are thus critical. Rather than minutely tracing the details of the changes in Bismarck's image over this time, I will seek to bring out broad trends and tendencies with regard to his place in German political culture and, in particular, the relationship between the Bismarck Cult, the crisis of German leadership, and the transformation of the Right from the late nineteenth century to the middle of the twentieth.

This project involves the analysis of a phenomenon that unfolded in, and took its particular shape as a result of, the transformed public sphere of the late nineteenth and early twentieth century. The primary arena for this public sphere was the newspaper press. Newspapers representing various political shadings as well as regions therefore serve as the major source base.[42] These have been augmented by published speeches held at the countless Bismarck ceremonies held on his birthday, the anniversary of his death, or the *Sonnenwende*, as well as speeches at other national celebrations such as the 'Day of the Founding of the Reich' (*Reichsgründungstag*) or Sedan Day. In addition, election materials as well as the minutes of Reichstag debates have proven to be profitable sources. Using these materials, I have looked at the features attached to the symbol Bismarck. What kind of imagery did various groups and individuals use to describe him? Where was he made to fit along the spectrum of German right-wing politics? Finally, I looked for the concrete political issues of the day where Bismarck was used to advance the position of a particular party or individual. How did Bismarck fit into German political battles? The language used to describe him, whether of a more purely rational-political nature or some form of quasi-religious discourse, helped shed light on particular characteristics of German political culture over this period. The rather long time span that this project covers will provide a good sense of change over time with regard to the Iron Chancellor's various incarnations, as well as their position within the changing fabric of German political culture. The result should be a broadly based account of the role Bismarck played in German political discourse over a period of more than five decades.

The structure of the project is based on a chronological account of the development and usage of the Bismarck image. The first section of the book deals with the initial rise and early impact of the legend. The first chapter covers its emergence, development, and transformation from state-supporting symbol to icon of the national opposition thanks to the circumstances of his dismissal and the actions and inactions of the regime in dealing with what was becoming an alternative pole of national allegiance. The second chapter opens with the rise and development of the Bismarck Cult as a new political religion. In particular it traces the emergence of the rituals, monuments, and rhetoric that gave the movement its particular force and allowed it to legitimize the new populist brand of radical national opposition that had been developing since the 1890s. The third chapter examines a critical turning point in the development of the image and its role in German political culture. The crisis decade from 1914 to 1923 saw Germany experience a devastating war, a shocking defeat, a revolution, and a violent five-year civil war. Thus emerged the first 'latent charismatic situation' and the process of transforming Bismarck into a 'charismatic placeholder' with the characteristics that would make his image such a dangerous force in the political arena of the 1920s and 1930s. The last phase of the book deals with the consequences of this transformation and the impact of the new radical Bismarck on German political culture, first during the 'years of stability' when there appeared an opportunity – some breathing room – as a moderate and a radical Bismarck fought for dominance and thus for the success or failure of the republic. The fifth and final chapter examines the role that the Bismarck image played in Hitler's accession to power in 1933 and its subsequent usage through the remaining years of the Third Reich.

Over the decades that this study examines, the various elements that made up the German Right went from beer hall altercations to national power-political battles in which the fate of the nation hung in the balance. During those same years the political culture of the Right was dramatically transformed, from a traditional state-supporting ideology to a populist, radical nationalist movement that positioned itself in complete opposition to the state. Clearly tied to these changes on the right was the rise and development of a new political religion – a Bismarck Cult – in which most of the Right participated. This book seeks to demonstrate that the transformation of the German Right cannot properly be understood apart from an awareness of the critical role played by the Bismarck Cult in German political culture. In doing so, it hopes to provide further understanding of those crucial changes in the German Right that were to have such devastating consequences not only for Germany but for the rest of Europe and, indeed, the world during the first half of the twentieth century.

Notes

1. Heinrich Mann, *Man of Straw* (New York: Penguin, 1984), 169.
2. This story is related by Heinrich Class in his memoirs, *Wider den Strom. Vom Erben und Wachsen der nationalen Opposition im alten Reich* (Leipzig: Verlag von K. F. Koehler, 1932), 228–229.
3. One bibliography lists over six thousand entries. Karl Erich Born, ed., *Bismarck-Bibliographie. Quellen und Literatur zur Geschichte Bismarcks und seiner Zeit* (Cologne: Grote, 1966).
4. Otto Pflanze, *Bismarck and the Development of Modern Germany*, I, *The Period of Unification, 1815–1871* (Princeton: Princeton University Press, 1990), xvii.
5. Friedrich Meinecke, *The German Catastrophe: Reflections and Recollections*, trans. Sidney B. Fay (Boston: Beacon Press, 1963), 13.
6. See, for example, Hans Rothfels, "Problems of a Bismarck Biography." *The Review of Politics* 9(3) July 1947; Gerhard Ritter, "Europa und die Deutsche

Frage: Betrachtungen über die geschichtliche Eigenart des deutschen Staatsdenkens," in Theodore S. Hamerow, ed., *Otto von Bismarck and Imperial Germany: A Historical Assessment* (Massachusetts: D.C. Heath and Company, 1994).

7. Fritz Fischer, *War of Illusions: German Policies from 1911 to 1914*, translated by Marian Jackson (New York: W. W. Norton & Company, 1975); Volker Berghahn, *Germany and the Approach of War in 1914* (New York: St. Martin's Press, 1973).

8. It is also not a study of Bismarck historiography, either before or after the Second World War. Such historiographical discussions are plentiful, either in the many solid Bismarck biographies, or in more specific works. Lothar Gall, ed., *Das Bismarck-Problem in der Geschichtsschreibung nach 1945* (Cologne: Kiepenhauer & Witsch, 1971); George O. Kent, *Bismarck and His Times* (Carbondale: Southern Illinois University Press, 1978); Karina Urbach, "Between Saviour and Villain: 100 Years of Bismarck Biographies," *The Historical Journal* 41(4) (Dec. 1998): 1141–1160.

9. In the sense that it deals more with the *image* of a political figure rather than the figure himself, this project resembles in certain respects the work of Ian Kershaw: Ian Kershaw, *The 'Hitler Myth': Image and Reality in the Third Reich* (Oxford: Clarendon Press, 1987); also Lothar Machtan's collection of essays on aspects of the 'Bismarck myth', though they do not deal with the political-cultural ramifications as extensively as this project, nor is their focus the transformation of the German Right: Lothar Machtan, "Bismarck-Kult und deutscher National-Mythos 1890 bis 1940," in Lothar Machtan, ed., *Bismarck und der deutsche National-Mythos* (Bremen: Temmen, 1994).

10. Geoff Eley, "The German Right, 1860–1945: How It Changed," in Eley, *From Unification to Nazism: Reinterpreting the German Past* (Boston: Allen & Unwin, 1980).

11. Hans-Ulrich Wehler, *The German Empire, 1871–1918*, trans. Kim Traynor (New York: Berg, 1985).

12. Geoff Eley, *Reshaping the German Right: Radical Nationalism and Political Change after Bismarck* (Ann Arbor: University of Michigan Press, 1980).

13. Glenda Patrick quoted in Dirk Berg-Schlosser and Ralf Rytlewski, "Political Culture in Germany: A Paradigmatic Case," in Berg-Schlosser and Rytlewski, eds., *Political Culture in Germany* (New York: St. Martin's Press, 1993), 6.

14. Kurt Sontheimer, *Deutschlands politische Kultur* (Munich: Serie Piper, 1990), 10.

15. See Detlev Lehnert and Klaus Megerle, "Problems of Identity and Consensus in a Fragmented Society: The Weimar Republic," in Berg-Schlosser and Rytlewski, eds., *Political Culture in Germany*.

16. Karl Rohe, "German Elections and Party Systems in Historical and Regional

Perspective: An Introduction," in Karl Rohe , ed., *Elections, Parties and Political Traditions. Social Foundations of German Parties and Party Systems, 1867–1987* (New York: Berg, 1990); Karl Rohe, *Wahlen und Wählertraditionen in Deutschland. Kulturelle Grundlagen deutscher Parteien und Parteiensysteme im 19. und 20. Jahrhundert* (Frankfurt am Main: Suhrkamp Verlag, 1992). The terms 'lager' and 'sub-culture' will be used here interchangeably.

17. Vernon Lidtke, *The Alternative Culture: Socialist Labor in Imperial Germany* (New York: Oxford University Press, 1985); Ronald J. Ross, *Beleaguered Tower: The Dilemma of Political Catholicism in Wilhelmine Germany* (Notre Dame: Notre Dame University Press, 1976).

18. On political or civil religion, see Robert N. Bellah and Phillip E. Hammond, *Varieties of Civil Religion* (San Francisco: Harper & Row Publishers, 1980); David I. Kertzer, *Ritual, Politics, and Power* (New Haven: Yale University Press, 1988); Michael Ley and Julius H. Schoeps, eds., *Der Nationalsozialismus als politische Religion* (Bodenheim: Philo Verlagsgesellschaft mbH, 1997).

19. On the sacralization of political figures, see Emile Durkheim, *The Elementary Forms of Religious Life*, trans. Karen Fields (New York: The Free Press, 1995), 215.

20. Geoff Eley's exploratory essay "The German Right, 1860–1945: How It Changed" is one such effort.

21. Kershaw addresses this in *The 'Hitler Myth'*, 4–5.

22. Max Weber, *Economy and Society: An Outline of Interpretive Sociology*, Vol. III, eds. Guenther Roth and Claus Wittich (New York: Bedminster Press, 1968), 1385.

23. Robert Gildea, *The Past in French History* (New Haven: Yale University Press, 1994); Merrill Peterson, *Lincoln in American Memory* (New York: Oxford University Press, 1994); Nina Tumarkin, *Lenin Lives! The Lenin Cult in Soviet Russia* (Cambridge, Mass: Harvard University Press, 1983).

24. Much of the following information relies on Otto Pflanze, *Bismarck and the Development of Modern Germany*, II, *The Period of Consolidation, 1871–1880* (Princeton: Princeton University Press, 1992), 32–33; and III, *The Period of Fortification, 1880–1898* (Princeton: Princeton University Press, 1992), 409–410.

25. Pflanze, *Bismarck*, II, 32.

26. Pflanze, *Bismarck*, III, 410.

27. Ibid., 409–411.

28. For an analysis of local political debates surrounding the construction of Bismarck fire-towers, see Michael McGuire, "Bismarck in Walhalla: The cult of Bismarck and the politics of national identity in Imperial Germany,

1890–1915," (Ph.D. Dissertation, University of Pennsylvania, 1993).

29. Norbert Elias, "On the State Monopoly of Physical Violence and Its Transgression," in Norbert Elias, *The Germans: Power Struggles and the Development of Habitus in the Nineteenth and Twentieth Centuries* (New York: Columbia University Press, 1996), 178–179.

30. See George Mosse, *The Nationalization of the Masses: Political Symbolism and Mass Movements in Germany from the Napoleonic Wars through the Third Reich* (New York: Howard Fertig, 1975).

31. See Roger Chickering, *We Men Who Feel Most German: A Cultural Study of the Pan-German Leaugue, 1886–1914* (Boston: George Allen & Unwin, 1984), 15–18.

32. For the importance of the capitalist print media for the rise and spread of nationalism, see Benedict Anderson, *Imagined Communities: Reflections on the Origin and Spread of Nationalism* (London: Verso, 1991); see also Jürgen Habermas, *The Structural Transformation of the Public Sphere: An Inquiry into a Category of Bourgeois Society*, trans. Thomas Burger with the assistance of Frederick Lawrence (Cambridge, Mass: MIT Press, 1989).

33. Volker Berghahn, *Imperial Germany, 1871–1914: Economy, Society, Culture, and Politics* (Providence: Berghahn Books, 1994), 185–186. Berghahn notes that in 1912 there were over 4,000 journals and newspapers, some published several times per day, with an estimated total of five to six billion copies per year.

34. Ibid.

35. Leo von Caprivi, quoted in J. Alden Nichols, *Germany after Bismarck: The Caprivi Era, 1890–1894* (New York: W. W. Norton & Company, 1958), frontispiece.

36. Weber, *Economy and Society*, 1112.

37. Ibid., 1117.

38. Ibid., 1114.

39. Ibid., 1121.

40. Mario Rainer Lepsius, "Charismatic Leadership: Max Weber's Model and Its Applicability to the Rule of Hitler," in Carl F. Graumann and Serge Moscovici, eds., *Changing Conceptions of Leadership* (New York: Springer-Verlag, 1986), 56–57.

41. Ibid., 57.

42. For the value of newspapers in the study of political culture, and in the case of Weimar in particular, see Lehnert and Megerle, "Problems of Identity and Consensus in a Fragmented Society: The Weimar Republic," in Berg-Schlosser and Rytlewski, eds., *Political Culture in Germany*, 56.

–1–

The Living Legend, 1866–1898

Napoleon was considered a genius until he fell; then he was called a fool. Bismarck will follow in his wake.

Karl Marx, Interview in *Chicago Tribune*, 1879[1]

Late in the evening of June 15, 1866, Otto von Bismarck, Minister-President of Prussia, spoke with the British Ambassador, Lord Loftus, about the momentous events about to take place. He told him of the Prussian attack just under way which marked the opening of the Seven Weeks War. "If we are beaten," he said, "I shall not return here. I shall fall in the last charge. One can but die once; and if beaten, it is better to die."[2] Had that happened – had Bismarck died before the end of the Austro-Prussian War – few if any at the time would have missed him. Of course he did not die. Instead, within a matter of days he would become Germany's greatest living legend, inspiring a cult of leadership that would grow in intensity for nearly the next century. How did it happen? How are legends created in the modern world?

Bismarck rose to legendary status, as most such figures do, through the performance of deeds that are considered remarkable in some way. Such actions invest the individual with charisma. According to Max Weber, the individual is then "set apart from ordinary men and treated as endowed with supernatural, superhuman, or at least specifically exceptional powers or qualities."[3] Not accessible to everyone, these attributes are considered to be "of divine origin or as exemplary, and on the basis of them the individual concerned is treated as a leader."[4] In his analysis of charisma, Weber made sure to stress the importance of the group responding to the individual, to the importance of their perception of those extraordinary qualities rather than just to the actual presence of such abilities. In this sense, Emile Durkheim's work on religion can be seen to support the application of Weber's notions of charisma in the political realm since Durkheim pointed out the potential for even the most mundane objects to be elevated to the level of the sacred. "Now as in the past," he wrote, "we see that society never stops creating new sacred things. If society should happen to become infatuated with a man, believing it has found in him its deepest aspirations as well as the means of fulfilling them, then that man will be put in a class by himself and virtually deified. Opinion will confer on him a grandeur that is similar in every way to the grandeur that protects the gods."[5] Bismarck's diplomatic and military triumphs in the 1860s and 1870s were remarkable enough. The fact that they fulfilled what German nationalists considered to be the age-old dream of German unification added to the force of the legend and made him one of Germany's greatest national symbols.

Bismarck's twenty years as chancellor reinforced that status, while his relationship to the state also proved critical. His achievements during these years were remarkable, if not quite so dramatic. He wove a complicated web of alliances and alignments that tied all of Europe in some way to the Empire. He maintained the peace while overseeing Germany's transformation into a leading industrial power. His connection to the state for so long meant that this powerful new entity helped buttress the legend. This element of state sanction to the Bismarck legend is directly related to Germany's status as a 'new nation' and the importance of legitimizing symbols.[6] In trying to establish its own legitimacy, the Empire had a natural choice in Bismarck. The development of rituals around him began early and helped forge German national identity. Clearly then, at this point, Bismarck was a state-supporting symbol, representing a statist nationalism.

This coupling of Bismarck and the state would begin to disintegrate when Kaiser Wilhelm II dismissed him in March 1890. When Bismarck left for Friedrichsruh, he took with him the charisma with which he had been invested for years as well as his status as primary national icon. Wilhelm's disregard of him in the years that followed and his failed efforts to establish his own charismatic qualifications provided time for the Bismarck image to float away from the domain of the state. As it did, its charisma was increasingly free to be co-opted by others with alternative national visions. Bismarck's dismissal and the failure to institutionalize his charisma thus opened a space in Germany's political landscape for a right-wing national opposition to take root. As nationalists began claiming Bismarck as their inspiration, they gradually acquired the legitimacy that his name provided. In the struggle between the government and the national opposition to define the nation, having the force of Bismarck behind them gave radical nationalists a significant weapon. These two groups would spend the remaining years of the empire fighting for control of this critical national icon. This chapter will first trace the emergence of the legend and its development during his years in office. It will then look at the role of the legend within German politics during these years, focusing on the development of the German Right. The turning point marked by Bismarck's dismissal and its effect on the legend will be taken up in the third section, while the last part will discuss its impact on right-wing politics – in particular, in creating the conditions necessary for the emergence of a right-wing national opposition.

Establishment of the Legend: Bismarck as Founder and Protector of the Reich

Prussia's stunning victory over Austria at the battle of Königgrätz in 1866 had a remarkable effect upon many Liberals who had so recently opposed Bismarck.[7] Admirers began reinterpreting his actions in light of the current situation, playing down his violations of the constitution as acts intended to fulfill the greater good of national unification. The Liberal Gustav Mevissen described his feelings while watching the victorious troops march through the Brandenburg Gate. "I cannot shake off the impression of this hour," he wrote. "I am no devotee of Mars; I feel more attached to the goddess of beauty and the mother of graces than to the powerful god of war, but the trophies of war exercise a magic charm upon the child of peace. One's view is involuntarily chained and one's spirit goes along with the boundless rows of men who acclaim the god of the moment – success."[8]

Mevissen's confession points to one of the legend's central elements. As people would remember it and retell it, Prussia's seemingly insoluble political crisis was solved through a mighty act of will by one remarkable individual. And not only was the Prussian constitutional crisis solved, but the impasse that had prevented German unification had also been solved by that same man – the savior of Germany. That element of the power of individual genius and will received an added boost thanks to the war against France (1870–1871), in which diplomatic prowess was once again followed by stunning military action. As the force of the legend grew, this understanding of German history and Bismarck's place within it would contribute to similar hopes when new, seemingly insoluble crises arose to challenge the nation.

An additional element of the Bismarck legend that would also play an important role in the development of right-wing political culture was the particular method with which the savior delivered his people from crisis – military force. The importance of violence and the martial character of the Bismarck image should not be underestimated. After three remarkably successful wars, memories of unification – indelibly tied to the architect of that unity – brought with them memories of violence and military power, all in a positive sense. Norbert Elias has noted that the lessons of German unification contributed to the conclusion that "war and violence were also good and splendid as political instruments. Not the whole, but certainly very important sections of the German middle class developed this strain of thinking into the kernel of their ideology."[9] Bismarck himself, in fact, reinforced this connection through his preference for wearing military uniforms in public. Those who followed him in office during the Empire were to find such dress indispensable.

In the midst of his success, veneration of Bismarck began to take tangible form when the city of Worms granted him honorary citizenship on December 11,

1870.[10] The cult would gain periodic boosts in subsequent years. The celebration of his sixtieth birthday in 1875, for example, marked a clear rise in stature for Bismarck. At this point, during his struggle against the Catholics, the *Kulturkampf* theme was a central topic at most gatherings and with the building of Bismarck monuments, which also began at this time.[11] The predominantly Catholic city of Cologne became the first Prussian city in the west to grant him honorary citizenship, thanks, no doubt, to the fact that the Liberals dominated local politics there. The main speaker at the celebration accused the Catholics of conspiring with France and went on to say that their hatred for Bismarck was proof that he "embodies the spiritual force, the higher aspirations of the empire."[12]

The rhetoric at these celebrations points to a critical aspect of the Bismarck Cult at this time – its role in the process of national integration. The Second Reich, a new nation in the age of nationalism, desperately needed to sink its roots into the ground of national legitimacy. Bismarck, as the mighty genius who forged the nation in the cauldron of war, stood as a perfect candidate for national icon. Supporting Bismarck meant supporting the nation and celebrating Bismarck brought people together and gave them a sense of belonging to a larger community of Germans. In doing so, it helped foster the dream of the *Volksgemeinschaft*, or national community, a common theme in Bismarckian rhetoric. What was also clear at this point was the *way* in which Bismarck united Germans: bringing some together through the exclusion of others. With the *Kulturkampf* as a central element of the 1875 celebrations, it was made quite clear just who was, and who was not, a member of the nation. If, at this point, the Catholics were the enemy, at other times it would be democrats, Poles, and even conservatives. In a similar fashion then to the issues of success and violence, the friend/foe dichotomy so central to the Chancellor's political style would stamp itself deeply into the thinking, and thus the political culture, of the Right well into the next century.

Bismarck's continuance in office buttressed the legend, while his repeated displays of diplomatic prowess served to refresh his charismatic qualities. From 1871 he began to weave a remarkable web of relationships between Germany and the other European powers. By 1879 he had revolutionized diplomacy with the signing of an alliance with Austria. Over the following decade Bismarck added country after country to an elaborate system of alliances and alignments until nearly every major European state was tied in some way to the Reich. Such displays strengthened his charismatic position, which Germans acknowledged during his seventieth birthday celebrations.

Germans marked April 1, 1885, in the grandest fashion yet. Wilhelm visited Bismarck and presented him with the latest version of Anton von Werner's painting "The Proclamation of the Empire at Versailles." Numerous cities granted him honorary citizenship, universities granted him honorary degrees and student groups sent eulogies. Overall, he received 3,738 letters, 2,644 telegrams, and 175 addresses, as well as 560 gifts, including the 'Bismarck Fund', consisting of 2,379,144 Marks donated by Germans across the country and meant for a charity of his choice.[13]

At the celebrations it was becoming clear that, fourteen years into the Reich's existence, Bismarck's transformation from Prussian Junker to German was continuing apace. In Dresden he was described as "a Germanic hero in mind and body, the most powerful embodiment of German essence since centuries past and for centuries to come."[14] He was "not only a patriotic Prussian, but also a proud, patriotic German."[15] While foreigners would never deny that he is a great man, they could never fully comprehend him. "Only a German can completely understand him, since he is every inch a German."[16]

The afterglow of the celebrations had barely worn off when Bismarck stirred up popular passions once again following a Reichstag speech in 1888, when he declared: "We Germans fear God and nothing else in the world! And it is precisely the fear of God that leads us to love peace and to nurture it." In quoting only the first half, Germans found a phrase to attach to him almost as popular as his earlier 'blood and iron' declaration and equally as ominous. His trip back to the chancellery following the speech was difficult as crowds of cheering people filled the streets.[17] The speech also evoked praise from the princely houses as telegrams poured into the Wilhelmstrasse. The Grand Duke of Baden praised his "brave expression as a great action which promised prosperity, which still in the distant future will serve as a lode-star for the nation," while Heinrich IX Prince of Reuss wished to congratulate "the greatest statesman of all centuries."[18]

Such displays may have been growing less frequent, but they still served to demonstrate the power of the Bismarck legend as an element of German state-supporting nationalism. He remained a primary national symbol – founder and protector of the Empire – and the legitimacy he lent the regime, particularly after Wilhelm I's death, was still considerable. How did Bismarck's twenty-year presence at the center of politics affect the development of the German Right?

The Chancellor as Legend: Bismarck in Political Practice

The end of the Austro-Prussian war of 1866 brought an end to the constitutional conflict. It also helped bring about the existence of two liberal parties. The moderates formed the National Liberal Party, siding with Bismarck in foreign policy while hoping to guide him in a liberal direction domestically. It was a party that stressed the national over the liberal cause, and saw in German unification a greater goal than stubbornly holding out for victory in the Prussian constitutional struggle. They would provide Bismarck steady support for the remainder of his career. The left-liberals formed the Progressive Party, which was dominated by Prussians and held firm to the principles of the constitutional conflict. They remained Bismarck's dedicated opponents, operating under the stigma of *Reichsfeinde*, or 'enemies of the Reich'.

The Chancellor's promotion of liberal causes during the Reich's early years contributed to the National Liberals' enthusiastic support – and they, in turn, contributed to the growth of the Bismarck legend. This can be seen, for example, in the *Kulturkampf*, which the Chancellor began in 1872. For Liberals, the *Kulturkampf* was the further implementation of their program of rationalizing government and society by lessening the influence of 'superstitious' Catholicism. Measures such as civil marriage, ending of state support for religious education, and expulsion of the Jesuits were applauded by liberals everywhere. They made their support clear in numerous public pronouncements. For example, the city of Chemnitz granted Bismarck honorary citizenship in March 1872, noting his "manly engagement in the struggle against the dark plans of Roman greed for power" as renewed proof that he was a "tireless leader in the struggle for Germany's unity and greatness."[19]

For the Conservatives, 1866 also marked a turning point. While they alone welcomed Bismarck's arrival in 1862 as the man to save Prussia from liberal parliamentarization, they now began to harbor serious doubts.[20] Bismarck's decision to annex German states, dethrone princes, and confiscate their property struck at the heart of traditional conservative sensibilities. In one blow, he attacked both the divine right of princes and the sanctity of property. If this was too much for some, others did not have long to wait for his next questionable move.

Following the success at Königgrätz, attention turned to solving the constitutional conflict. When word leaked that Bismarck intended to offer his liberal opponents an olive branch in the form of an Indemnity Bill, asking forgiveness for his constitutional transgressions, Conservatives were outraged. After all, here was the man called in to save the monarchy and defeat the liberal challenge to its prerogatives now asking forgiveness from those who would undercut the King's powers? Having vindicated his strategy with a devastating military victory, many felt he should have completed his triumph by revising or even suspending the constitution. Many Conservatives, therefore, were dismayed, bitter, and angry. This led to a break between Bismarck and many of his one-time allies that would continue for more than a decade.[21]

Not all Conservatives chose opposition, however. Those who formed the Free Conservative Party, or *Reichspartei*, were more flexible and accepted Bismarck's methods as necessary for national unification. Led by Wilhelm von Kardorff, they stood by Bismarck more firmly than any other group and thus came to be known as the 'Bismarck Party, *sans phrase*'. They were among the first and most dedicated contributors to the development of the Bismarck legend.[22]

If the *Kulturkampf* helped build the Bismarck legend among Liberals, it marked one of several sources of conflict between Conservatives and the Chancellor that followed the break of 1866–67. While not necessarily friends of the Catholics, German Conservatives saw themselves as upholders of the traditional forces in society, which included religion. They realized that secularization of the state meant the end of support for not only the Catholic Church, but also the Protestant Church. Following this and other struggles, Bismarck began to refer to his ultra-conservative opponents as *Reichsfeinde* – a dramatic indication of the degree of opposition this represented.

Already bitter, the conflict between these one-time allies intensified. While some Conservatives saw that the path to influence and power led through Bismarck and thus sought a reconciliation, their path was blocked by those who continued to see him as their bitter enemy. A series of articles in the conservative *Kreuzzeitung* in early 1876 sought to drag Bismarck through the mud of financial scandal by linking his name to Liberal ministers, speculators, and Jews. He responded in February 1876 with a blistering attack in the Reichstag, accusing anyone who subscribed to the paper as being indirect participants in the slander. The Conservatives' response was further defiance – a growing list of *Deklaranten* who openly sided with the *Kreuzzeitung* against the Chancellor. As a result, Bismarck broke with many of his oldest friends.[23]

In the end, cooler heads prevailed and those who had sought a reconciliation won out in the founding of the German Conservative Party (DKP) in July 1876. The victors pushed aside the *Deklaranten* and helped the party take its position alongside the Free Conservatives as an ally of Bismarck. The continuing presence of oppositional forces, however, meant that an anti-Bismarck position remained. At the time of the DKP's founding, Kleist-Retzow, one of Bismarck's bitterest enemies, warned the new party that if it "does not wish to be untrue to its principles, it cannot swim with the government; rather, it must be an arrow in the flesh, an awakening of the conscience."[34] This mixture of pro- and anti-Bismarck forces resulted in an initially ambivalent relationship between Conservatives and Chancellor.

Within a few years the relationship between Bismarck, the Conservatives, and the Liberals shifted significantly. The *Kulturkampf* marked the high point of Bismarck's collaboration with the Liberals. It soon became apparent that the alliance would not last much longer. The Depression of 1873 led to calls for an end to liberal laissez-faire policies and a shift to protectionism. Bismarck, too, felt the need for a change and began maneuvering for a shift rightward. Following two assassination attempts on the Kaiser in 1878, Bismarck took the opportunity not only to crush Social Democracy, but more importantly to split the National Liberals. If the exceptional aspects of the *Kulturkampf* legislation did not lead many Liberal deputies to worry about compromising their principles, Bismarck's new Socialist Laws certainly did. After they rejected the first version of the bill, Bismarck used the second assassination attempt to turn the issue into a referendum on the 'national' qualifications of the National Liberals, thus ending their special relationship with the Chancellor. Bismarck was now clearly in the protectionist camp. The National Liberals then split – the right wing grudgingly accepting Bismarck's new position, while the left seceded by 1880. Such a shift by the Chancellor left many Liberals bewildered, and while some made the adjustment rather easily, it took others much longer to reconcile themselves and resume their previous role as Bismarckians.

Meanwhile, the shift to protectionism meant a new alliance of Conservatives and Free Conservatives. While the latter had played the role of Bismarckian party since 1866, for the former such a role was new. Still, under the leadership of Count Helldorff-Bedra, the party made the transition rather quickly, if not always smoothly. Helldorff was determined to align the party with Bismarck. The benefits to the Conservatives must not be underestimated. With an antiquated party structure, Bismarck's financial assistance allowed for the publication of party propaganda. On numerous occasions, individual party members came to the Chancellor for assistance, including numerous *Deklaranten* seeking reconciliation. In return, Bismarck got the DKP to de-emphasize the ideological differences between themselves and the two other parties of his right-wing coalition, the Free Conservatives and National Liberals, who came to terms with the Chancellor in 1884.[25]

This early manifestation of right-wing unity was by no means homogenous. United in their desire to hold back the growing threat from Social Democracy, they differed on a range of other issues. With Bismarck's public backing, though, all three benefited at the polls. At the same time, with the support now of all three right-wing parties, the Bismarck image received an even greater boost, as demonstrated during the 1885 birthday celebrations. And just as the Right's support fed the Bismarck image, the image helped promote the dream of right-wing unity.

Under the banner of the nation's founder the two Conservative parties and the National Liberals spoke about that elusive dream of a unified Right. In the excitement of the 1885 celebrations they set aside their differences and spoke of the 'above party' nature of the festivities. This was clear in Barmen, where a National Liberal accepted the invitation to speak at a Free Conservative Bismarck gathering since he could not refuse his participation in a 'national celebration'.[26] A speaker stressed this in Düsseldorf, where he described the day's celebration as "patriotic . . . a pure patriotic-national, and not by any chance a political party celebration! Because the man for whom it is meant stands high above the parties as the first servant of Kaiser and Reich, as the spiritual creator and champion of the united fatherland, as a pillar of its power and glory!"[27] New organizations also formed specifically for the purpose of spreading the Bismarckian gospel. The *Bismarck-Verein, Verein für nationale Politik* in Marburg recognized the 'petty party-spirit' that dominated Germany, whether it was the Liberals' fierce opposition that Bismarck needed to overcome in order to unify the nation, or the Conservatives' resistance following unification.[28]

The rhetoric of Bismarckians at this point provides a critical insight into the dynamics of German nationalism during the Reich's first two decades. Bismarck was becoming the dominant national icon, and with his position as Chancellor that meant that German nationalism was clearly a statist-nationalism. This posed some serious restrictions on the varieties and expression of nationalist sentiment. The impressive scope of the Bismarck image as patriotic symbol squeezed out nearly every other option for a German nationalism on the right. These limitations can be seen in the new patriotic organizations that were forming in the late 1870s and 1880s and the care with which they sought to establish their position.

These new organizations arose due to changes in society and politics during the Reich's formative years, which led to new conceptions of the nation and who comprised it. The rise of ethnic nationalism meant that there now existed a potentially serious counter to the statist-nationalism espoused by Bismarck and the government. The Chancellor had little interest in a politics of ethnic affinities.[29] Others did, however, and they founded a host of patriotic organizations during the 1880s, including the German School Association, German Language Association, and Colonial Society. The contrast between their definition of the nation and Bismarck's was clear, though they were careful to keep their criticism muted. Challenging Bismarck's patriotism was beyond the powers of most Germans (aside from the Social Democrats). Still, this challenge to the government as traditional guardian of the national symbols and thus the meaning of the nation was highly significant. A public announcement for a congress that was being called to unify the patriotic societies in 1886 declared that "[t]he responsibilities we face in this area are not political; governments need not concern themselves with carrying them out. They are instead general national responsibilities, and the people have to demonstrate themselves, in carrying them out, how much moral power resides in the people."[30] The idea that the people, not the government, possessed the power and the right to give meaning to the nation meant that an early form of populist, or volkisch, politics was present in the years before Bismarck's dismissal.[31] Here was a group seeking to establish a German nationalism, the legitimacy of which they based not on Bismarck, but rather on the people. In his own study of American populism, Michael Kazin notes that while populism speaks to the superiority of the 'people' over the government and their privileges and rights to define the nation and govern themselves, such movements tend to wind up seeking out a dominant leader-figure.[32] In the American case they found three: Jefferson, Jackson, and Lincoln. In the German case, the irony lies in the fact that after this early attempt at a form of oppositional nationalism – trying to step outside Bismarck's shadow – soon after he left office they would seek shelter under that very same shadow, choosing Bismarck as their ideal leader. This was no doubt aided by his volte-face on many issues during his retirement. At this point, however, the tension would build during his remaining years in office as he succeeded in keeping the lid on such populist energies.

Within the Conservative Party as well populist opposition was brewing by the late 1880s. Those around Baron Wilhelm von Hammerstein-Schwartow, for example, who made up the *Kreuzzeitung* group, had opposed Bismarck since the *Kulturkampf*, thus taking up where the *Deklaranten* and ultra-conservatives had left off. And beyond that, they found added cause for opposition in Bismarck's renewed alliance with the National Liberals in 1884 and more formally in the Kartell of 1887. The compromising of Conservative principles, which Bismarck allowed and which the party leadership under Helldorff supported, proved intolerable for this group. For the remainder of his chancellorship, they represented Bismarck's most vocal opposition on the right.

The *Kreuzzeitung* group was riding the crest of the rising populist wave within German politics generally and within the DKP specifically that was seeking to reform the party to allow for a position independent of the government, a more decentralized structure, and more participation from below. Helmut von Gerlach summed up the group's goals when he wrote about wanting "a party based on the trust of the people, who themselves made policy rather than having policy made by using them."[33] This new populist Conservative party that he envisioned, a Conservative *Volkspartei*, would be "Christian, monarchist, agrarian, militarist and social, but above all, independent, no Bismarckian party."[34] They saw the danger of remaining within the Kartell – further compromise of Conservative principles in favor of the liberalism of the NLP, and an overreliance on Bismarck which prevented the development of a modern, effective party capable of taking advantage of the growing political market of the late 1880s. Here again was an attempt to escape Bismarck's shadow and establish an independent national legitimacy. And while the vehemence of the group's opposition far outstripped that of the patriotic societies, it too would eventually find itself seeking the comfort of Bismarck's protection in the 1890s. For now, however, his shadow left little room for an independent right-wing nationalism and therefore the group would remain a minority, albeit a vocal one. And though they continued to work for Bismarck's downfall, they were forced to do so within the limits imposed by the power of the national icon still in office. They found hope, however, in the increasing age of both Kaiser and Chancellor.

The death of Wilhelm I in 1888 marked the first possibility for change. A younger generation was rising, symbolized by Kaiser Wilhelm II, leading many to see in Bismarck the symbol of an older, more conservative politics that was out of touch with the times. Though the relationship between the young Kaiser and his nearly seventy-five year old Chancellor was remarkably positive at first, their differences eventually grew unbridgeable.[35] It was then that Bismarck handed in his resignation. On March 20, 1890, Wilhelm accepted it, thereby ending one of the greatest political careers in European history. The Kaiser published his letter of acceptance in the official *Reichsanzeiger*, thus providing Germans with his own version of the break, while suppressing Bismarck's letter. This helped determine the general reaction to his departure. According to Wilhelm, it was a determined Chancellor who, against the repeated pleas of his imperial master to stay, demanded to be released from his offices. While those papers closest to him immediately leaked the Chancellor's own version, such anonymous reports could not stand up to the officially sanctioned story, and thus the press typically placed the blame with Bismarck. As Otto Pflanze points out, "Wilhelm II won handily the first round in the contest for public opinion."[36] As it turned out, it would be his last victory in the struggle with Bismarck. The dismissal released the constraints on a legendary figure that, as yet, had realized only a small fraction of his potential power.

The Chancellor Unbound: The Bismarck Legend in the Wake of the Dismissal

In 1888 a Free Conservative newspaper expressed confidence that: "The German people know what the Iron Chancellor sacrifices for it, when it demands of his patriotism that, until his last breath, he dedicate himself to the service of the fatherland."[37] Had that happened, had Bismarck actually died in office, the future of Germany might have been very different. The charisma that he embodied as leading national symbol would have transferred to the state and become institutionalized, supplying the Empire with the tremendous legitimacy that he himself once possessed. For a young Kaiser ascending the throne of a young nation, this would have been the best outcome. Even a quiet retirement would have made possible the eventual transfer of his charisma back to the state.

Of course neither scenario occurred, and Bismarck's dismissal would have dramatic consequences. When he left Berlin he took with him the charisma he had acquired over the past quarter-century. The symbol Bismarck, invested with all that charisma and national legitimacy, was now free to take on new meanings and new purposes once it was no longer constrained by the needs of the statist-nationalism it had previously served. This freedom would increase as Wilhelm paid little public attention to him, trying instead to be 'his own Bismarck'. The process of freeing Bismarck and, in a sense, 'refounding' the legend would begin shortly after his dismissal as various individuals proved willing to assist.

Critical to this process of reshaping Bismarck was the newspaper press, and considering the importance of newspapers in the print-dominated culture of Wilhelmine Germany, the former chancellor's allies in the press were some of the most important figures in his camp. Heinrich Hofmann, political editor of the *Hamburger Nachrichten*, served as Bismarck's mouthpiece. He provided Hofmann with notes, information, and drafts for articles that would often be reprinted throughout Germany and Europe.[38] The *Hamburger Nachrichten* enabled

Bismarck to vent his frustration with the government, while also helping refashion his image.

Maximilian Harden provided Bismarck with another channel though which he could voice his opinions. Bismarck provided Max Harden with the symbol which he could use in his own personal crusade against the Kaiser and his men. While the immediate impact of their alliance was to give the regime fits, even greater was Harden's long-term effect on the Iron Chancellor's image and legend. Harden helped transform Bismarck into a Nietzschean superman. By the turn of the century he was the most perceptive political observer in the Empire, and it was in large part through Bismarck that he gained his legitimacy.[39]

Harden became a supporter of Bismarck shortly after the Chancellor's departure. An early opponent of the Kaiser, he found in the recently deposed Bismarck the kind of 'misunderstood genius' that he respected. With the Chancellor now out of office, Harden could support him in any way he saw fit. He did so publicly in an article in July 1890 entitled "Phrasien," which depicted Bismarck as a giant among pygmies, a genius in a land that hates genius, a superman wandering amidst common rabble. While signaling the beginning of Harden's support for the former chancellor, it also marked the style he would use to describe his hero – a highly literary style that owed much to Harden's admiration for Nietzsche. Over the next several years, he continued to write flattering articles under the pseudonym 'Apostata'. He described the former chancellor as an "individual of completely fantastic magnificence and abundance, he is – Bismarck."[40] The Prince soon became aware of his admirer, though he did not know who he was. Once Bismarck found out the true identity of Apostata, he arranged a meeting at Freidrichsruh in February 1892. The meeting went well, and it marked the beginning of a relationship that continued until his death. The relationship has been described in various ways by different people depending on their opinion of both Harden and Bismarck, but it seems that it was one of mutual respect in which Harden admired the great man, though he often differed with him on particular issues, and in which Bismarck found an outlet for his views through an astute writer and observer. Whereas Hofmann at the *Hamburger Nachrichten* acted more as Bismarck's mouthpiece, Harden served as an ally to promote Bismarck on another level – a higher cultural, intellectual, and political plane.[41]

One of the most important figures in the Bismarck camp was Diederich Hahn. A man whom Eugen Richter described as possessing "demonic eloquence," one scholar has seen in him a forerunner of Adolf Hitler in terms of political style, and in his virulent anti-Semitism – the popular stump-speaker, the drummer who stirred up the masses for great national causes.[42] Certainly in his background as a middle-class figure from Lower Saxony, who worked his way up through university studies and the acquisition of the all-critical title 'Doktor', he personified the 'new men' who sought to break down the doors of *Honoratiorenpolitik* and, in doing so, helped give rise to the modern, popular politics of the 1890s. Through his activities, he would also help fuse the Bismarck image to that new brand of politics.

Hahn's devotion to Bismarck began early, during his student days. He played a leading role in the student movement, helping found the radical nationalist *Verein deutscher Studenten* in 1881. During one particularly revealing episode in 1882, he visited the train station in Berlin to see the Chancellor off as he left for his estate. Arriving just as the train was pulling out, Hahn leapt from the platform and caught hold of a bar just above Bismarck's window. The Chancellor opened the window and chatted with the man swinging back and forth in front of him. When he told the young devotee to come visit him some time, Hahn felt it to be a "vindication of his entire life and political activities."[43] Between 1886 and 1890 he visited the Chancellor frequently. He also founded the Berlin Bismarck Kommers, a banquet held annually on the Iron Chancellor's birthday, during which Hahn would often make the after-dinner speech.[44]

Having already devoted himself to Bismarck, Hahn experienced March 20, 1890 as a shocking and utterly disquieting turn of events.[45] The dismissal of Germany's first chancellor marked a dramatic turning point in his life. Working at the time for the Deutsche Bank, his speaking tours for the firm increasingly became tributes to Bismarck and denunciations of the government. He was now firmly rooted in the politics of 'national opposition' – a stance that would soon lead him to a prominent role in one of the most important oppositional organizations in the empire, the Agrarian League.[46] It would be some time, however, before men like Hahn were to make their full impact felt in German politics. Bismarck, however, proved more than capable of unnerving the regime all by himself.

When the former chancellor traveled to Vienna in 1892 to attend his son Herbert's wedding, the government immediately feared the implications if Bismarck were to turn his trip into a popular political speaking tour. Caprivi wrote to the Ambassador in Vienna that there was no reconciliation between Berlin and Friedrichsruh, and ordered him not to attend the wedding. He was to inform Kaiser Franz Josef of these orders, which meant that Bismarck was to be treated as a private citizen and thus was not to be granted an audience with the Austrian Emperor. Known as the "Uriah letter," the order was subsequently sent to all the major German courts in order to further isolate Bismarck and undercut his possible plans.[47]

The contrast between the government's attitude and that of the people towards Bismarck was striking. His journey through Germany to Vienna and back was a remarkable success. The public displays of devotion could not be attributed to a reaction against the official boycott attempts since the existence of the "Uriah letter" was not made known until the end of Bismarck's stay in Vienna. While in the Austrian capital he continually stressed his long-time friendship for that country but tried to avoid the appearance of endorsing the ultra-nationalist, anti-Semitic extremists who came to pay homage.[48] Such scenes were repeated throughout the trip. Although in Munich the royal family stayed away, the city government welcomed him with an official ceremony. Outside his room each night crowds filled the streets, including sixteen hundred torch-bearing students, while bands played, speeches were delivered, and patriotic songs sung. With the "Uriah letter" now known of, crowds defied official sanction even more brazenly as police barricades at the train stations could not prevent the people from waving him along on his trip home.[49]

Bismarck did not have to travel, however, to sense his growing popularity. Since his retirement, one of the most popular forms of expressing dedication to him was the pilgrimage to his estate, either at Varzin or Friedrichsruh. During his eight years in retirement, hundreds of groups came to pay their respects and hear him speak.[50] These *Huldigungsfahrten*, or journeys of homage, as they were known, were significant in several ways. They enabled Bismarck to develop his image for posterity. He therefore spoke often of his patriotic German spirit that guided his plans for unification from the beginning. He explained the motivations behind particular policies, promoting the successful ones, refashioning the failures. He also expounded on important current issues, typically doing so at the government's expense.[51] They therefore became a rallying point for all who were dissatisfied with the current leadership.

The eightieth birthday celebrations of 1895 marked the high point of the *Huldigungsfahrten*, and thus of Bismarck idolization during his lifetime. Thousands converged on Friedrichsruh to wish him well. The rectors of Germany's universities and technical schools came, as did official delegations from towns and cities bearing honorary citizenships, German princes and foreign dignitaries, and Chancellor Hohenlohe. Following the previous year's reconciliation, Wilhelm also appeared and dined with Bismarck.[52]

That this was a truly popular event can be seen first of all in the overwhelming number of greetings and congratulations sent by people throughout Germany. All told, Bismarck received several thousand packages, almost 10,000 telegrams, and 450,000 postcards, letters, and publications. It can also been seen in the extent to which the birthday celebrations reached into all parts of the Empire. At least sixty-four German cities held ceremonies where schools were closed and the streets were filled with flags and other decorations. Some fifteen more took place in Austria and more than two dozen around the world.[53]

The speeches at the ceremonies reflected Bismarck's increasing stature. He was the "creator of German unity, to whom we owe our whole national existence, he was the bravest fighter for Germany's greatness and perfection, the mighty founder of the new German Reich."[54] Diederich Hahn's Berlin Bismarck Kommers called him a "providential figure, a tool, as God himself chose."[55] It was only natural that, when they thought of Bismarck, it was the "mighty figure that floated before us, in the uniform of the cuirassier, which he always preferred to wear instead of the coat of the diplomat."[56] In Bonn, where the doors of the hall had to be shut well before the ceremony began because it was already over capacity, Bismarck was described as the man who "as the tool of divine providence" led the German people "out of night into light, out of weakness into strength, out of division to unity."[57] He was "the greatest man among the living, the hero in the Sachsenwald," "the greatest statesman of the century."[58]

Like past celebrations, the 1895 festivities featured calls to get beyond party differences and unite for the greater good of the nation. Here one can see the connection between Bismarckianism and the newly emerging populism. Some speakers stressed the diverse nature of the audience (true or not). It was "not the celebration of a class, not the celebration of a Party, but rather a people's celebration."[59] In Berlin the speaker for the Bismarck Kommers declared, "We stand with him, and we will hold to him for all time, and as the best inheritance we leave our children the warning of the great man: not the party, and not the majority, is the fatherland!"[60] Bismarck was becoming the people's icon for a politics of confrontation with a government seen to be diverging from the national mission established by its founder.

The events of 1895 marked a high point for Bismarck adulation during his lifetime. Over the next several years, visits declined as his health deteriorated. Groups still came to pay homage and to take back a little more of the national legitimacy that his status bestowed. They also continued to celebrate his birthdays and invoke his name in pursuit of their own particular brand of nationalist politics. For those who followed Bismarck, that brand of nationalist politics took on an increasingly oppositional tone. As the legend grew, freed from the fetters of the state, its increasing size and power helped open a space on the right where such a politics of national opposition could take root and develop. The consequences were ominous and would be felt for decades.

Reestablishing the Right: Bismarck in Retirement and the Politics of National Opposition

As a turning point in German political history, March 20, 1890 has few rivals. It marked the beginning of the crisis of leadership, both real and perceived, that would haunt Germany for the next half century. Through the growth of his legend and the direct result of his own actions, Bismarck left behind few if any capable successors. Certainly any country would have been hard-pressed to find someone who could immediately step in and measure up to the man who had dominated German and European politics for nearly three decades. But having been such an integral part of the Reich's foundation, many came to expect such a larger-than-life figure as the ideal leader. Such expectations would loom over his successors for decades.

In addition to marking the start of Germany's crisis of leadership, Bismarck's dismissal provided an enormous push towards a shift in political style and practice on the right that would have profound effects. Already during the latter years of his chancellorship, politics in general was undergoing a transformation towards increased popular participation and 'new men' seeking a hearing for their national visions that diverged from Bismarck's. While in office, he kept the lid on such oppositional pressures. His dismissal changed all that. It opened the possibility of a popularly based right-wing politics in which Bismarck provided legitimacy to a political course that openly opposed the government.

German nationalism, which had been the government's nearly unchallengeable preserve so long as Bismarck occupied the chancellor's office, became a truly contested area after March 1890. The nation's very meaning became the ultimate prize of the political battlefield. With his dismissal, the unity of government and national symbols was broken, and the most powerful symbol was no longer in Berlin, but Friedrichsruh. Supporting Bismarck meant supporting the nation, and thus there developed a source of national legitimacy separate from, and in opposition to, the traditional authority of the Kaiser and his government. The Iron Chancellor, once the very personification of statist-nationalism, now became the icon for all those on the fringes of politics looking for a way to break down the doors of *Honoratiorenpolitik*. With not a little irony, Bismarck was becoming the symbol of a populist brand of politics that originally sought legitimacy in opposition to him, but which now, together, would challenge German governments for decades.[61] Almost immediately upon his retirement, he set the process in motion, giving birth to the politics of 'national opposition'.

Back in Friedrichsruh, Bismarck sat isolated from the political world he had once dominated. Feelings of depression, bitterness and resentment churned within him as the desire to return to the fray grew increasingly irresistible. The determination not to leave the new leadership in Berlin unmolested led to the rise of what came to be known as the 'Bismarck Fronde'. Almost from the start there appeared people willing and eager to join him in an assault on Berlin, and this group would grow in size as the government embarked on paths the Fronde interpreted as dangerous to the national interest. During his eight years in retirement, the opposition would look to Friedrichsruh for advice and inspiration and Bismarck proved more than willing to put his immense symbolic power to use.[62]

In June 1890 Bismarck announced his determination to speak out against the government. In an article in the *Hamburger Nachrichten*, he compared himself to Metternich. Just like the deposed Austrian leader, Bismarck also had the right to criticize. Such criticism, however, was not meant to cause the government problems. It was, he insisted, a patriotic duty.[63] The article's implications were immense and marked a significant transformation in Bismarck's thinking and a radically new departure. He had, after all, made his living attacking anyone who criticized the government as an enemy of the nation. Now he was doing that very same thing. He set a powerful example that others would soon follow.

Almost immediately upon returning to his estate, Bismarck began to consider running for the Reichstag.[64] The object of scorn during his chancellorship, the Reichstag now figured in his thinking as a critical counterweight to the 'absolutistic' tendencies of the crown and general lack of leadership characteristic of Caprivi's New Course. Utilizing contacts with some influential friends, Diederich Hahn offered Bismarck the mandate of Neuhaus-Hadeln in Hanover.[65] He accepted, and in February 1891 stood as a National Liberal candidate. Hahn continued to play a critical role since Bismarck essentially accepted the candidacy on the condition that he did not actually need to appear in parliament. His unwillingness to exert himself meant that Hahn became the campaign's driving force, getting the former chancellor to sign statements that he, in fact, had written, and then passing them off as Bismarck's own words. Hahn not only played this behind-the-scenes role, but he also stood front and center as Bismarck's refusal to make campaign speeches meant that Hahn performed this function as well. In fact, Hahn took care of most of the campaign's requirements.[66] In the end Bismarck was able to gain only 43 per cent of the vote in an election in which only 55 per cent of the electorate turned out. He won the runoff only when another candidate withdrew after the first round – a rather inauspicious beginning to his new position as leader of the opposition. As it turns out, Bismarck never did make an appearance and Hahn ended up serving as his agent to the constituency. If, in the end, Bismarck's foray into the politics of national opposition did not have such an immediate impact, perhaps he could at least have taken solace in the fact that the mere possibility of his appearance in the Reichstag kept governmental officials in a constant state of unease.[67] Even Wilhelm felt the need to clarify the situation after Bismarck's victory, declaring in Düsseldorf, that "there is only one ruler in this Empire and I am he. I will tolerate no one else."[68]

As had been the case during his chancellorship, Bismarck was still not the man to lead a popular movement or party. His performance in the Reichstag elections was just one indication that the people seemed to prefer the *symbol* Bismarck to the man himself, and were much less interested in his actual return to office. This difference – between the man and the symbol – would prove critical, however, as the 1890s wore on and new, radical nationalist organizations were forming which would carry his name forward in their struggles with the government. Under their custodianship, Bismarck's image, much more than the man himself, would become a truly powerful, dangerous force in the political arena.

With the hope that reigned at the outset of the New Course quickly evaporating, and the confidence once invested in the young Kaiser also drying up, new organizations were forming that expressed this discontent and sought to channel it to a wide audience through new methods of political agitation. Forming out of the situation that was already developing during Bismarck's last years in office, groups like the Pan-German League and the Society for the Eastern Marches marked the emergence of a new kind of politics, related to but separate from that of the traditional political parties, and usually at odds with the government. These organizations took up the spirit of Bismarck's 'national opposition' in their battles with the regime and never failed to remind people that they derived their legitimacy from Friedrichsruh. Along with other 'radical nationalist' groups they were to play a significant role in the development of the Bismarck legend. As some of the most vocal claimants to his legacy, they were to have a sizable influence over the nature and uses of the legend.

Founded by some of the same individuals from the 1886 attempt at nationalist unity, the Pan-German League emerged in 1891.[69] It was formed primarily by those 'new men' who stood outside the traditional bounds of the politics of notables. Like Diederich Hahn, they generally emerged out of the National Liberal lager, with most coming of age after unification.[70] They tended to be frustrated by the limits imposed by *Honoratiorenpolitik*, finding little room for themselves in the upper echelons of the party apparatus.[71] One such figure was Heinrich Class.

Born in 1868 to a middle-class family in Hesse, Class's formative years were spent in the period after unification, during Bismarck's twenty years as chancellor. He was trained as a lawyer in Berlin, where he imbibed Treitschke's anti-Semitic nationalism.[72] Like Diederich Hahn, Class not only espoused a virulent anti-Semitism, but also found in Bismarck the ultimate symbol which gave meaning to his politics. For Class, too, March 20, 1890 was a transformative experience. News of the dismissal struck him "like lightning." "So the 20th of March was for me the day on which I went over consciously to *national opposition*, which in this particular sense did not yet exist at the time."[73]

Under the influence of men like Class and Alfred Hugenberg, frustrated with the politics of notables, the Pan-German League sought to establish itself 'above parties'. It sought legitimacy as the truest interpreter of the national symbols, as the ones who knew best the meaning of the nation. With Bismarck divorced from the government, such a path of direct challenge to official nationalism suddenly became viable. The League thus grounded its claim to be the truest interpreters of the nation in an unequivocal devotion to Bismarck.

Though the Pan-Germans at first were somewhat cool to the former chancellor, seeing in him the representative of an old, tired generation in contrast to their own dynamism, they were soon claiming him as their reason for existence. As they grew increasingly disappointed with the nation's course, they moved closer to Bismarck. They made their ties to him explicit throughout their newsletter and in countless speeches at birthday celebrations and other nationalist gatherings.

Bismarck was "ours" – "something we in particular in the General German League may say, we who go the ways that he has showed us and to which we for all time have stood true, in joy and sorrow."[74] They also made their goals inseparable from his.

If the goals of the General German League comprise the stimulation of patriotic consciousness and the fighting of all directions that are set against the national development, furthermore the bringing together of all German elements on the whole planet and finally the promotion of an energetic interest politics in Europe and overseas, so do we only follow the great thoughts which have determined and led the politics of Prince Bismarck.[75]

Despite the firmness with which they based their assertions, it is certainly doubtful whether Bismarck as Chancellor would have advocated all of their policies. Here we see a phenomenon which would grow more widespread after his death. The difference between Bismarck the Chancellor and Bismarck the Pan-German was a result of both the League's desires and the refashioning of his image that he himself was performing during his retirement. Many of his post-retirement utterances clearly contradicted positions he had taken as Chancellor, and thus with a little selective memory followers could fashion the proper mix of policies that would make him theirs. Still, this process of Pan-Germanizing Bismarck could not go too far too soon. He was still around and could easily douse their enthusiasm with a stiff rebuke – something he was not averse to doing. Still, he did appear to feel enough of a common interest with the League to become an honorary member in 1895.[76]

The distinction of being the most radical and *völkisch* nationalist movement went to a smaller organization: the Deutschbund.[77] A devout anti-Semite and Bismarck enthusiast named Friedrich Lange founded the group to "take upon itself the stewardship of the continuing work on the national idea as Bismarck's legacy."[78] Lange made the bond between the Deutschbund and the Iron Chancellor explicit when he founded it on Bismarck's birthday in 1894. While its direct impact on the public might have been minimal, its overall effect should be seen as much larger and more sinister than one might suspect. Lange kept membership deliberately low to maintain the purity and extreme nature of its beliefs. Though its membership peaked at 1,534 before 1914, it played a significant role in German politics, nevertheless, through the infiltration and dissemination of its extreme ideas to other groups, including the Pan-German League.[79] Many Deutschbund members were also leading figures in the League, including Heinrich Class, who founded a branch of the Bund in Mainz and then brought it into the League. This infiltration of personnel and ideas helped in transforming the Pan-Germans into an extreme *völkisch* organization. The spread of ideas was also facilitated through the press. Originally writing at the *Tägliche Rundschau*, Lange founded his own paper, the *Deutsche Zeitung*, which was soon financed and then purchased by the

Pan-Germans. Through the *Deutsche Zeitung*, participation in Bismarck ceremonies, and the influence of Bund members on other nationalist organizations, the
Deutschbund's impact as Bismarckian organization of the most radical degree
would be felt throughout the remaining years of the Empire and into Weimar.

Having as their primary organizing principle the 'national' issue, both the Pan-
German League and the Deutschbund symbolized one of the most prominent goals
of German right-wing politics – nationalist unity. Both the 1886 episode and the
founding of the Pan-German League marked efforts to get beyond party differences and the limited goals of more specialized organizations like the School and
Colonial Leagues. The dynamic political situation unleashed in part by Bismarck's
dismissal led to renewed attempts at achieving the dream of nationalist unity. The
perceived crisis of leadership resulting from his absence proved one of the key elements in the push for a unified right-wing party. One of the manifestos for the
founding of such a 'National Party' decried the Caprivi government's "weakness
and lack of clarity" in all areas of policy.[80] In all such cases, Bismarck served as
the inspiration and the symbol that would bring unity to the Right.

For some on the Right, the attempt to found a 'National Party' centered on the
Pan-German League and its transformation into a true political party. The leading
figures in this drive to turn the League into a 'National Party' around 1892 were
united by their "unreserved acceptance of Bismarck's political ideas about authoritarian government and about a monarchy that would not threaten the status-
quo."[81] Within the League itself, it was some of the younger generation around the
organization's first leader, von der Heydt, who, as Dirk Stegmann points out, "considered themselves to be Bismarck's legitimate heirs," who advocated the founding
of a strong popular party to support a strong national government.[82] Opinion
within the League was divided, however, and although men like Kardorff of the
Free Conservatives and Lange of the Deutschbund favored such a transformation,
others like Alfred Hugenberg wished to maintain the League's 'above party' character. Later efforts foundered as well, including an attempt in 1893. Again, the
contrast between Caprivi's New Course and the superior policies of Bismarck,
whom the leaders "styled as a national hero and as a symbolic figure for the new
party," took center stage."[83]

More limited efforts on the right took the form of a proposed 'Economic Party'.
Bismarck himself had advocated such a party, and his statements were used by
Emil Kirdorff and others in early 1891 in a drive to make it a reality. Pilgrimages
to Friedrichsruh by Kirdorff and the advocates of an 'Economic Party' also served
to give the plan added weight. Like the 'National Party', this also failed to mate-
rialize. Bismarck inspired another attempt in 1893. He had been calling through
his newspaper network for the establishment of a corporatist system, and within it
an "alliance of all productive forces," harkening back to his Kartell politics of the
late 1880s.[84]

The presence of the Conservative von der Heydt and the Free Conservative Kardorff among those seeking a reformation of the party structure on the right indicates the impact that Bismarck's dismissal had not only on National Liberals, but on Conservatives as well. While the Conservative Party took a pro-government position following Bismarck's fall, disillusionment soon set in over Caprivi's New Course. Even old-time Bismarck foes like Wilhelm Freiherr von Hammerstein soon found themselves on the side of their former nemesis. His one-time oppositional stance gained new life and new intensity thanks to the changed circumstances after March 1890. Bismarck's dismissal and his own outspoken opposition to the government legitimized the same strategy for men like Hammerstein, who, it turns out, was actually indirectly working with Friedrichsruh against the Caprivi regime.[85] Thus a radical anti-government politics – an anti-government Conservatism – emerged with greater force than existed during the Reich's first twenty years.

The government was acutely aware of the danger such anti-governmental Conservatism posed. In May 1891 Holstein wrote to the Kaiser's best friend, Philipp Eulenburg, about his concern over the fate of Helldorff, the moderate DKP leader and Caprivi supporter who, at the time, was being attacked by the Hammerstein/Stöcker wing of the party. "Helldorff is being pursued with the most extreme bitterness by the followers of Bismarck," he wrote, "because of his relation to the Kaiser. The Kaiser, *if* he wants to have support, *must* advance his friends and push back his opponents."[86] Such concerns were heightened following the Hammerstein/Stöcker wing's victory at the Conservative Party's Tivoli congress in 1892, which introduced more demagogic, anti-Semitic features into the party program. Such a victory, it was feared, would benefit Bismarck and other Frondeurs. This was, after all, at the height of discussions in the press about the possible founding of a new Bismarckian 'National Party'.[87]

The fact that a Bismarckian party never materialized did not make the government's fears any less real. "Fear of Bismarck," wrote Chancellor Hohenlohe in 1894, "is the reigning epidemic in Berlin . . . It's disgusting."[88] Nor should it lead one to downplay Bismarck's significance as a political force in the 1890s. That he failed to bring about right-wing unity at this point is true. This was beyond anyone's powers. But the failure here should be seen more in terms of the limitations imposed by a living and physically declining Bismarck. Very few (including probably the old man himself) wanted him back in office. As far as leading a parliamentary party was concerned, he was simply not the man for the job. He never was a party man. His performance as Reichstag deputy made this clear, and his vision of a return to the politics of Wilhelm I, as Wolfgang Stribrny has pointed out, was not the most inspiring of political programs. In fact, his own opposition seemed to be inspired more out of sheer personal animosity to the leadership in Berlin – opposition for opposition's sake – than any genuinely positive platform.

With the decline of his own energies, the chances of a Bismarckian party declined as well. But the force that his *name* and *image* lent to the hopes and desires of those who dreamt of nationalist unity would prove an ominous foretaste of what was to come when he would finally be laid to rest.

The dynamic and fractured nature of the Conservative movement was made even clearer by a new organization born in the spirit of national opposition. The Agrarian League (*Bund der Landwirte*, BdL) was formed out of the tension between the party's traditional politics of notables and the cauldron of growing populist pressures developing throughout the Right.[89] If the immediate issue was opposition to Caprivi's tariff policies, the longer term cause was the growing pressure from below by the likes of anti-Semites in the west and smaller farmers with few ties to East Elbian junkers. Here was an organization that clearly fitted the new style of post-Bismarck politics. In stark contrast to traditional conservatism, the BdL advocated a strikingly modern, *völkisch* ideology that contained within it a virulent racial anti-Semitism and the attempt to tap new sources of support among the population. Thus, its significance lay in the combination of its aggressively nationalistic politics, demagogic style, and anti-Semitic overtones with its large membership base.[90]

Like the Pan-German League, the BdL was, as Hans-Jürgen Puhle noted, " 'bismarckian' in a very dogmatic sense."[91] He served as hero, the model against which all other politicians were judged. The relationship between the BdL and its idol, however, was apparently more strained than that between Bismarck and other radical groups. He most likely appreciated the trouble that the League sought to cause the regime, but he never wholeheartedly supported it. His contacts with the League were brief and limited. Still, despite the tension, the League used his name to strengthen its authority in the struggle against Berlin.[92]

Perhaps the League's greatest asset in its efforts to combine modern agitational practices, racism, and dedicated Bismarckianism was Diederich Hahn, who became director of the BdL in Hanover and was one of the League's three leading figures. Hahn, as we have already seen, was one of the 'new men' of German politics seeking to break through the barriers imposed by the politics of notables. In fact, it was through direct opposition to the tactics of *Honoratiorenpolitik* that Hahn himself entered the political arena when he had to battle the hand-picked candidate of the National Liberal Party (for which he was also running) in his quest to take over Bismarck's Reichstag seat in 1893. He sat as a 'guest' of the National Liberals until his increasing radicalism led the party to expel him in 1894. He then sat with the Conservatives.[93] Through his work during Bismarck's time as deputy, Hahn grew increasingly aware of the plight of Germany's farmers, and that, combined with his intense anti-Caprivi position, helped transform a solid, well-educated burgher into an agrarian populist. Upon entering the League, he brought to it a remarkable speaking ability. Hahn's demagogic style was also deeply colored by a vicious anti-Semitism. With his impressive speaking ability, his anti-Semitism, and his Bismarck image, Hahn represented the new style of populist politics perhaps better than anyone else at this time. The advantage he brought the Agrarian League in its struggles against the government and the Conservative Party was immeasurable. With his help, the League took a position, along with the Pan-Germans, as one of the most important and powerful groups within the growing national opposition.

If the relationship between the Agrarian League and Bismarck was a strained one, the same could not be said of the other major radical nationalist group to form during this period. The Society for the Eastern Marches (*Ostmarkenverein*), also known as the Hakatisten, took special pride in its relationship to the former leader. Just as the Agrarian League had formed largely in opposition to Caprivi, so too did the Eastern Marches Society come together to combat the new Chancellor in response to what they perceived to be the selling out of German interests in the east in favor of the Poles. While the 'New Course' did include some concessions to Prussia's Polish population, they were at best half-hearted and in the end served only to inflame German nationalist passions while failing to satisfy Polish demands. True to form, Bismarck pounced on this opportunity to attack his successor, claiming that these concessions endangered vital German national interests. Seeing in Bismarck the ultimate source of legitimacy, three large landowners from Posen, Ferdinand von Hansemann, Hermann Kennemann, and Heinrich von Tiedemann, sought to enlist him in their radical nationalist campaign.[94] His poor health delayed any action until late summer 1894 when two massive pilgrimages were made to his estate at Varzin. It was out of these events that the Eastern Marches Society was founded later that year.[95]

Here, it would seem, was a group with perhaps the strongest claim to be carrying the Bismarckian torch. Unlike the Agrarian League, the Hakatisten could, with more confidence, argue that he was "a zealous member of the Eastern Marches Association to the end of his life."[96] The Polish question had always been important for Bismarck and it remained so into his retirement. Still, it is important to note that there were differences here as well between the Iron Chancellor and the *Ostmarkenverein*. The hostility felt by many Hakatisten towards the Poles was based largely on race. While Bismarck was certainly hostile to Caprivi's Polish policies and rarely had a kind word for the Poles, his animosity stemmed more from reasons of state than racial prejudice. The Hakatisten were aware of this and regularly sought to play down what they considered to be Bismarck's 'outdated' notions. Nevertheless, their relationship remained close. Ferdinand von Hansemann kept him informed during the establishment of the organization and Bismarck responded with a letter of approval and encouragement. Bismarck received the three leaders numerous times, and, after his death, "it was the H-K-T society which stood foremost in the Eastern Marches in making a cult of his memory."[97]

The political landscape had changed dramatically since Bismarck's arrival in 1862. The weight he lent to a state-supporting nationalism provided a relatively stable base on which to establish the legitimacy of government policies. And over the years the cult of his leadership continued to grow. Still, during his last decade in office a rising force was seeking to undermine Bismarck's position as custodian of German nationalism, and to establish an independent national legitimacy. It was a testament both to the weakness of the populist movement at the time and the immense power the Iron Chancellor wielded as the embodiment of the nation that he was able to resist such pressures. With his dismissal, he turned around and took advantage of those new conditions that had once threatened him. He now used them for his own purposes, helping guide them against the regime, a course towards which they themselves were increasingly inclined as they perceived a growing crisis of leadership. This joining of forces points to one of the ways in which March 1890 marked a critical turning point. It meant the abandonment of the earlier populist effort to escape Bismarck's shadow and establish an independent national legitimacy. Instead, the national opposition was to be based upon the symbolic power of the Iron Chancellor himself. If it posed a slight danger during Bismarck's tenure, the weight he provided the movement made it a potentially regime-threatening force after March 1890. Times had certainly changed, but not completely. The physical presence of the old man served as a limitation, both in terms of the heights to which the legend could rise, and the uses to which it could be put. It would take Bismarck's death in 1898 to see the legend raised to the next level, and, with it, the Right's politics of national opposition would take the next step on its path of progressive radicalization.

Notes

1. Karl Marx and Friedrich Engels, *Collected Works*, vol. 24 (New York: International Publishers, 1989), 578.
2. Story related in Pflanze, *Bismarck*, I, 305.
3. Max Weber, *On Charisma and Institution Building: Selected Papers*, ed. S. N. Eisenstadt (Chicago: University of Chicago Press, 1968), 48.
4. Ibid.
5. Durkheim, *Elementary Forms*, 215.
6. Lynn Hunt, *Politics, Culture, and Class in the French Revolution* (Berkeley: University of California Press, 1984); Mona Ozouf, *Festivals and the French Revolution*, trans. Alan Sheridan (Cambridge, Mass: Harvard University Press, 1988).
7. Liberal criticism was extensive up until the victory over Austria. Erich Eyck, *Bismarck and the German Empire* (New York: W. W. Norton & Co., 1950), 58.
8. Mevissen quoted in Pflanze, *Bismarck*, I, 331.

9. Elias, "On the State Monopoly of Physical Violence and Its Transgression," 180–181; see also James M. Diehl, *Paramilitary Politics in Weimar Germany* (Bloomington: Indiana University Press, 1977), 13; Michael Geyer, "The Stigma of Violence, Nationalism, and War in Twentieth-Century Germany," *German Studies Review*, Winter (1992): 75–110.

10. McGuire, "Bismarck in Walhalla," 4; numerous cities followed in rapid succession. See also Deutsches Historisches Museum, *Bismarck – Preussen, Deutschland und Europa* (Berlin: Nicolaische Verlagsbuchhandlung, 1990), 366.

11. *Bismarck – Preussen, Deutschland und Europa*, 405.

12. Quoted in McGuire, "Bismarck in Walhalla," 6.

13. Pflanze, *Bismarck*, III, 185.

14. Ibid., 18; see also M. Evers, *Rede auf den Fürsten Bismarck. Gehalten bei der vaterländischen Feier zu Ehren des 70. Geburtstages des Fürsten Reichskanzlers zu Düsseldorf am 31. März 1885* (Düsseldorf: L. Voß & Co., 1885), 16.

15. Prof. Dr. Otto Kaemmel, *Festrede zur Feier des siebzigjährigen Geburtstages Fürst Bismarcks gehalten im Saale des Gewerbehauses zu Dresden am 31. März 1885* (Dresden: Carl Höckner, 1885), 7–8.

16. Ibid., 17.

17. Pflanze, *Bismarck*, III, 272.

18. Bundesarchiv Lichterfelde (hereafter cited as BAL) R43I/2825 Reichskanzlei, Personalakten betreffend des Reichskanzlers Fürsten von Bismarck, Band 4, Juni 1887 bis Januar 1889, #79, #82, #91.

19. Quoted in McGuire, "Bismarck in Walhalla," 5.

20. For their initial support, see *Kreuzzeitung*, September 26, 1862.

21. Pflanze, *Bismarck*, I, 331–334.

22. See Siegfried von Kardorff, *Wilhelm von Kardorff: Ein nationaler Parlamentarier im Zeitalter Bismarcks und Wilhelms II. 1828–1907* (Berlin: E. S. Mittler & Sohn Verlag, 1936).

23. James N. Retallack, *Notables of the Right: The Conservative Party and Political Mobilization in Germany, 1876–1918* (Boston: Unwin Hyman, 1988), 14–15; see also Pflanze, *Bismarck*, II, 58.

24. Kleist-Retzow quoted in Retallack, *Notables*, 19.

25. Ibid., 30–32.

26. Dr. Karl Theodor Reinhold, *Fürst Bismarck als Reformator des deutschen Geistes. Eine Festrede*, Second Edition (Barmen: D. B. Wiemann Verlag, 1887), 9.

27. Evers, *Rede auf den Fürsten Bismarck*, 7–8.

28. Bismarck-Verein, *Mittheilungen des "Bismarck-Vereins" Verein für nationale Politik* (Marburg: N. G. Elwert'sche Verlagsbuchhandlung, 1885), 32–33.

29. Chickering, *We Men*, 26–27.
30. Quoted in ibid., 45.
31. Ibid., 45–46.
32. Michael Kazin, *The Populist Persuasion: An American History* (Ithaca: Cornell University Press, 1995), 17–25.
33. Gerlach quoted in Retallack, *Notables*, 45.
34. Ibid.
35. Christopher Clark, *Kaiser Wilhelm II* (London: Longman, 2000), 36.
36. Pflanze, *Bismarck*, III, 376; Wilhelm Mommsen, *Bismarcks Sturz und die Parteien* (Stuttgart: Deutsche Verlags-Anstalt, 1924), 140–141.
37. BAL, R43I/2825, #125: *Deutsches Wochenblatt*, April 11, 1888.
38. Pflanze, *Bismarck*, III, 384–385.
39. Harry Young, *Maximilian Harden, Censor Germaniae: The Critic in Opposition from Bismarck to the Rise of Nazism* (The Hague: Martinus Nijhoff, 1959); B. Uwe Weller, *Maximilian Harden und die "Zukunft"* (Bremen: Schünemann Universitätsverlag, 1970).
40. Apostata, April 20, 1891, "Genosse Schmalfeld," in Maximilian Harden, ed. Ruth Greuner, *Maximilian Harden: Kaiser-Panorama; literarische und politische Publizistik* (Berlin: Buchverlag der Morgen, 1983), 70.
41. Young, *Maximilian Harden*, 36–53; see also Pflanze, *Bismarck*, III, 386.
42. See George Vascik, "Agrarian Conservatism in Wilhelmine Germany: Diederich Hahn and the Agrarian League," in Larry Eugene Jones and James Retallack, *Between Reform, Reaction, and Resistance: Studies in the History of German Conservatism from 1789 to 1945* (Providence: Berg, 1993), 229–260.
43. Ibid., 234–235.
44. Ibid., 232.
45. George Vascik compared the effect of this psychic blow with the effect of the German defeat in the First World War on the mindset of a young Adolf Hitler. Ibid., 237–238.
46. Ibid.
47. Pflanze, *Bismarck*, III, 395–398. For more of Wilhelm's frustration with the popular displays of support for Bismarck, see Lamar Cecil, *Wilhelm II: Prince and Emperor, 1859–1900* (Chapel Hill: UNC Press, 1989), 221–222.
48. Ibid., 396–397.
49. Ibid., 397–398.
50. Manfred Hank, *Kanzler ohne Amt: Fürst Bismarck nach seiner Entlassung 1890–1898* (Munich: Tuduv-Verlagsgesellschaft, 1977), 687–696.
51. See, for example, Ted M. Kaminski, "Bismarck and the Polish Question: The 'Huldigungsfahrten' to Varzin in 1894," *Canadian Journal of History* XXII (August 1988): 235–250.

52. Pflanze, *Bismarck*, III, 410–411.
53. Ibid.; Hank, *Kanzler ohne Amt*, 584–591.
54. Paul R. Lehnard, *Festrede zum 80. Geburtstage Sr. Durchlaucht des Fürsten Bismarck* (Mülhausen: G. Danner Verlag, 1895), 1.
55. Prof. Theodor Schiemann, *Fürst Bismarck. Festrede zu seinem achtzigsten Geburtstage. Gesprochen auf dem Commers des Bismarckausschusses zu Berlin* (Berlin: Wilhelm Hertz Verlag, 1895), 3.
56. Ibid., 7, 14.
57. Speech by Dr. Wilhelm Kahl in Bonn, in *Neue Bonner Zeitung, Die Bismarckfeier in Bonn 1895* (Bonn: Emil Strauß Verlag, 1895), 4.
58. Speech by Geheimrat Dr. Brassert in Bonn, in ibid., 21.
59. Professor Dr. Loeschke in Bonn, in ibid., 6.
60. Schiemann, *Fürst Bismarck*, 15.
61. For German populism in the 1890s, see Eley, *Reshaping*, 184–205.
62. Hank, *Kanzler ohne Amt*; Wolfgang Stribrny, *Bismarck und die deutsche Politik nach seiner Entlassung (1890–1898)* (Paderborn: Ferdinand Schöningh, 1977).
63. Stribrny, *Bismarck und die deutsche Politik*, 32.
64. For Bismarck's candidacy, see ibid., 73–100.
65. Vascik, "Agrarian Conservatism," 238–239.
66. Ibid., 239–240.
67. Hank, *Kanzler ohne Amt*, 258–270; Pflanze, *Bismarck*, III, 382–384; For a sense of the apprehension, see the letters from Friedrich von Holstein to Philipp zu Eulenburg on March 14 and April 18, 1891, in Philipp Eulenburg *Philipp Eulenburgs politische Korrespondenz, Band I, Von der Reichsgründung bis zum Neuen Kurs 1866–1891* ed. John C. G. Röhl (Boppard am Rhein: Haraldt Boldt Verlag, 1976), 647–648, 667.
68. Wilhelm II quoted in Cecil, *Wilhelm II*, 219.
69. See Chickering's *We Men*; for the role of the Bismarck image in the League, see Ludwig Freisel, "Das Bismarckbild der Alldeutschen: Bismarck im Bewußtsein und in der Politik des Alldeutschen Verbandes von 1890 bis 1933; ein Beitrag zum Bismarckverständnis des deutschen Nationalismus" (Ph.D. Dissertation, Würzburg, 1964).
70. Chickering, *We Men*, 50.
71. Geoff Eley documents this frustration in *Reshaping*.
72. Ibid., 214.
73. Class, *Wider den Strom*, 22.
74. *Alldeutsche Blätter* (hereafter cited as ADB), April 1, 1894.
75. Ibid.
76. ADB, April 1, 1895.
77. Dieter Fricke, "Der 'Deutschbund'," in Uwe Puschner, Walter Schmitz and

Justus H. Ulbricht, eds., *Handbuch zur "Völkischen Bewegung" 1871–1918* (Munich: K. G. Saur, 1996), 328–340; Dieter Fricke, "Deutschbund" in Dieter Fricke, ed., *Lexikon zur Parteiengeschichte*, I, 517–525.

78. Friedrich Lange, *Reines Deutschtum: Grundzüge einer nationalen Weltanschauung*, fifth edition (Berlin: Verlag von Alexander Duncker, 1904), 349.

79. Fricke, "Deutschbund," 517.

80. Dirk Stegmann, "Between Economic Interests and Radical Nationalism: Attempts to Found a New Right-Wing Party in Imperial Germany, 1887–1894," in Jones and Retallack, *Between Reform, Reaction, and Resistance*, 176.

81. Ibid., 172.

82. Ibid., 173.

83. Ibid., 181.

84. Ibid., 179.

85. Retallack, *Notables*, 81.

86. Holstein quoted in James Retallack, "Conservatives contra Chancellor: Official Responses to the Spectre of Conservative Demagoguery from Bismarck to Bülow," *Canadian Journal of History* XX (August 1985): 211.

87. Ibid., 212.

88. Hohenlohe quoted in Cecil, *Wilhelm II*, 220.

89. Geoff Eley, "Anti-Semitism, Agrarian Mobilization, and the Conservative Party: Radicalism and Containment in the Founding of the Agrarian League, 1890–1893," in Jones and Retallack, *Between Reform, Reaction, and Resistance*, 187–228.

90. For the Agrarian League, see Hans-Jürgen Puhle, *Agrarische Interessenpolitik und preußischer Konservatismus im wilhelminischen Reich (1893–1914). Ein Beitrag zur Analyse des Nationalismus in Deutschland am Beispiel des Bundes der Landwirte und der Deutsch-Konservativen Partei* (Hannover: Verlag für Literatur und Zeitgeschehen, 1966); Retallack, *Notables*; Dieter Fricke and Edgar Hartwig, "Bund der Landwirte (BdL) 1893–1920," in Dieter Fricke, ed., *Lexicon zur Parteiengeschichte: Die bürgerlichen und kleinbürgerlichen Parteien und Verbände in Deutschland (1789–1945)*, vol. I (Cologne: Pahl-Rugenstein Verlag, 1983): 241–270; Dirk Stegmann, *Die Erben Bismarcks: Parteien und Verbände in der Spätphase des Wilhelminischen Deutschlands. Sammlungspolitik 1897–1918* (Cologne: Kiepenheuer & Witsch, 1970).

91. Puhle, *Agrarische Interessenpolitik*, 87.

92. Ibid., 87–88.

93. Vascik, "Agrarian Conservatism," 243–244.

94. It was from the initials of the founders' family names that the organization

also became known as the H-K-T Society, or the Hakatisten.

95. Richard Wonser Tims, *Germanizing Prussian Poland: The H-K-T Society and the Struggle for the Eastern Marches in the German Empire, 1894–1919* (New York: Columbia University Press, 1941); Kaminski, "Bismarck and the Polish Question"; Edgar Hartwig, "Deutscher Ostmarkenverein (DOV) 1894–1934," in Dieter Fricke, ed., *Lexikon zur Parteiengeschichte*, II, 225–244.

96. Ludwig Raschdau, quoted in Tims, *Germanizing Prussian Poland*, 45.

97. Ibid., 45.

–2–

"Forward in the Spirit of Bismarck!"
1898–1914

O heavens! die two months ago, and not forgotten yet? Then there's hope a great man's memory may outlive his life half a year.

Shakespeare, *Hamlet*[1]

Late in the night of July 30, 1898, Otto von Bismarck died quietly in his bed at his estate in Friedrichsruh. As family members consoled themselves, a young man was setting up his photographic equipment just outside the window of the room where the former chancellor lay. In less than ten minutes he had his prize and had disappeared into the night. The man who escaped was a photographer named Willy Wilcke. Having supplied the public with Bismarck photographs since the early 1890s, Wilcke realized the great business opportunity that awaited him if he could actually photograph him on his death bed. Working through an insider at the estate, he seized the moment, and the picture he escaped with was soon being advertised for sale in a number of newspapers. What it showed was an old man withered with age and battered by disease. A white cloth wrapped around his head from under his jaw punctuated the body's frailty. It certainly was not the image most Germans had of the Iron Chancellor, and thanks to his son, who fought successfully to have the negatives confiscated, it was an image most Germans would not see for decades. Spared the reality of the mortal Bismarck – the weak, frail, decaying old man portrayed in the photograph – the nation embarked upon a process that would see the Iron Chancellor become the center of a political religion that would help shape the culture of German politics for decades. If life made him a hero, death made him a myth.[2]

The Wilhelmine era was a dynamic period in German history. Industrialization increased dramatically, bringing prosperity to many, while also giving rise to serious concerns. Alongside an existing streak of confidence there developed a growing sense of pessimism, particularly among the middle classes. This pessimism found one of its main targets in the area of politics. The real or perceived failings of Germany's leaders came under increasing attack as many saw their position threatened by a growing Social Democratic movement. In addition to this internal threat, people watched with mounting concern as Germany's world position seemed to deteriorate from the heights of previous decades. More and more people came to see the genius in Bismarck and the tragic mistake of his dismissal. As they moved further from 1890, and his death in 1898, such perceptions intensified. The desire for a 'return' of Bismarck, or salvation through faith and action in the 'spirit of Bismarck', grew as part of a new political religion – a Bismarck Cult.

Related to this, the intensification of the crisis of leadership helped feed another important development in the Right's political culture – a process of progressive radicalization. Following the turn of the century, the national opposition would travel further right from the National Liberal camp towards the Conservatives. With a diplomatic debacle in 1906 and two major scandals in 1907 and 1908, German politics can be said to have entered a period of sustained crisis. Not by coincidence, the Bismarck Cult took a dramatic step forward during this period, as the Right grew increasingly desperate for a way out. In the last years of peace, Pan-Germans and Conservatives were pressing for increasingly aggressive policies, including a brand of *Weltpolitik* that far outstripped the regime's own already ambitious program. In addition, the populist, *völkisch* style of politics that had developed after Bismarck's fall would begin to come into its own. Under the leadership of Heinrich Class, the Pan-Germans espoused a radical anti-democratic, anti-Semitic program at home while pressing for Germany's rightful 'place in the sun' abroad. The Right's populism reflected a growing confidence that showed itself in ever more numerous confrontations with the government over possession of the national symbols. What role did Bismarck play in facilitating this radicalization of the German Right?

In the last years of peace the national opposition and the government fought their battles over the meaning and direction of the nation in the expanding public sphere, represented largely by the newspaper press and the spectacles conducted in the shadow of an ever increasing number of national monuments. Throughout this struggle, Bismarck played a prominent role as the two sides fought for control of his legacy.[3] It was a contest in which the Right called into question the government's leadership ability and its national credentials against the standard of the first chancellor. At the same time, Berlin sought the power of Bismarck as a moderating influence to justify its own policies. The rise of the Bismarck Cult as political religion and its confrontations with the government, therefore, can help shed valuable light on the dynamics of the German public sphere at the outset of the twentieth century. This chapter will follow the Cult's development from 1898, its influence on the Right's culture and practice of politics, and thus its role in the very public struggles to define and guide the nation through the last critical years before the war.

Death, Deification, and the Development of the Bismarck Cult

In 1913 the Berlin Bismarck Committee issued a summons: "Every year thousands of German men assemble to strengthen their faith in the future of the fatherland by remembering Bismarck. The German Reich faces great tasks. Surrounded by enemies, we must preserve what Bismarck fought to attain. At such a time Bismarck should be the focus of our thoughts! In view of his mighty deeds and remembering him in unswerving love and loyalty, we want to celebrate the day on which Bismarck was born to the German people."[4] The language clearly betrays the new function the Iron Chancellor was to serve in the new century, as the center of a new political religion – a Cult of Bismarck.[5] Already during his retirement, the national community that his followers were defining had an increasingly anti-governmental potential. The Cult itself, and the dynamics of its development, cannot be understood apart from the tension that existed between middle-class nationalists and the government. The radical nationalist community saw the regime's efforts to control such a vital national symbol as a threat to its own political world-view. This tension showed itself immediately following Bismarck's death.

Having already experienced the headaches caused by a living Bismarck, Wilhelm II sought to undercut the potential power of an immortal, deified Bismarck and end the conflict over the national symbols by claiming the very body of the former chancellor. Upon news of his death, Wilhelm began planning for Bismarck's burial in Berlin Cathedral, next to his own Hohenzollern ancestors. Knowing that he would become a primary destination for nationalist pilgrimages, Wilhelm hoped to make it impossible to honor him without simultaneously paying homage to the house of Hohenzollern. Herbert Bismarck, however, rejected Wilhelm's offer in favor of the deceased's wish to be buried at Friedrichsruh with his wife. His testament also dictated that his epitaph should read: "A loyal German servant of Kaiser Wilhelm I."[6] Unfortunately for the Emperor, Bismarck's politics of national opposition would continue after his death.

Wilhelm's next effort at co-opting Bismarck's symbolic power only days later met with equally meager results. On August 4, 1898, the government held a memorial service in the Kaiser Wilhelm Memorial Church. The guest list included the highest-ranking figures in the government, military, and diplomatic corps. Organ music softly accompanied the chorus in the singing of songs and psalms before court-pastor D. Faber addressed the audience.[7] He praised Bismarck, "the mighty man in his natural power, with his iron will, his path-breaking thoughts," who offered his king the best that "an *Untertan* may offer."[8] In addition to this model of dedicated service to his king, Bismarck also served as an inspiration for current and future generations. His name would remain "a magic power for every German, on which the youth will inspire itself, the strong inflame itself, the weak take courage, and the spirit of the people will steel and refresh itself."[9] It was a quiet, dignified service, which, thanks to Bismarck's testament, lacked the central object of devotion – the body itself. It also lacked the Bismarck family, for while Wilhelm had reserved the imperial box for them, none came and so the empty box represented yet another striking rebuke from Friedrichsruh.

Three days later, on August 7, 1898, the Berliner Bismarck-Ausschuß held its own service. In doing so, it challenged the 'official' nature of the imperial event while going beyond the accepted format for such events as prescribed by imperial tradition.[10] This challenge to the government over ritual practice and thus the ability to define Bismarck continued the trend from the early 1890s of a populist nationalism claiming legitimacy against the regime. In contrast to the official ceremony, the one held at the Kroll Opera House was a more impressive event, both to the eyes and ears. As with the imperial ceremony, laurels, palms, and flowers bedecked the scene. Huge black curtains hung down from either side of the stage. On the left they read: "1815. Schönhausen. Hail to the house and its star. Praise the Lord," while on the right: "1898. Friedrichsruh. You took him from us, Lord, we bow ourselves." Approximately one thousand mourners from Berlin's middle and upper-middle classes entered the hall to the sound of Beethoven's Eroica symphony, at the end of which the curtains opened to reveal the stage bathed in reddish light. In the background stood the castle of the gods in Walhalla, while in the center was a pedestal with a massive bust of Bismarck, on either side of which stood a golden candelabra. To the right was the pulpit, draped in black and gold, where Ernst von Wildenbruch, a dramatist of some renown in turn-of-the-century Germany, delivered a poem that would be repeated often at future ceremonies. "Do not let the Bismarck in you die!" he intoned in his poem, in which Bismarck the man played a lesser role than Bismarck the inspiration.

> Bismarck was dead, is no longer dead.
> In your soul, which lifts itself,
> He rises before you, comes again and lives.
> Comes and is here,
> Omnipresent and near,
> Germany, your Bismarck, he lives![11]

Following Wildenbruch to the stage was Professor Wilhelm Kahl, whose presence in such a prominent role helped set the Kroll affair apart from the imperial ceremony. While the official event had a pastor deliver the eulogy, the Berlin Bismarckians set their own stamp on Bismarck ritual that would characterize it for the next half century. In the civic religion emerging around Bismarck, academics were to play the role of high-priests. And considering the culture of Germany's academics at the time, the confluence of Bismarckian and academic culture seemed to reveal a natural fit. As Fritz Ringer observed in his study of the 'German

Mandarins', academics increasingly stressed 'ideals', or the 'spirit of politics' over the fundamentals. The desire to escape from 'interest politics' "helped to lead many educated Germans into the pseudoidealistic world of anti-Semitism and aggressive nationalism."[12] Nationalism became central to both groups that Ringer distinguished within the academic community – the 'modernists' and the 'orthodox'. They were, according to him, "totally and quite uncritically committed" to it.[13] "They missed no opportunity to preach German greatness, always with the hope that patriotic sentiment would 'overcome' the petty egotism of the parties. Here was a field of concern in which the mandarin intellectual could still play the role of the spiritual leader, directing the attention of Germans away from their material demands, demonstrating the ideal priority of the 'whole' over the short-range interests of its members. It was too tempting a prospect."[14] One can therefore see the significance of the Cult for both of these groups. For the academics, the rise of the Cult provided a powerful conduit through which they could channel their 'mandarin nationalism' to the wider nationalist public. For the Bismarckians, the support of the academics, considering their status and position within the *Bildungsbürgertum*, gave the Cult an added dimension. It gave it an intellectual legitimacy which provided a powerful counterweight to the power and authority that the government could bring to bear in the struggle with the national opposition.

The Bismarck that Kahl focused upon was less the man himself than the model, the inspiration, or "the conscience of the German people!"[15] This was not to say that in every situation they should ask what Bismarck would have done. Their freedom of decision was critical. But with Bismarck as the people's conscience, they would remain on the path that he had laid out for them. His particular political opinions were not so critical. Rather, his importance lay in "the greatness of his political character, the pure heights of his love of Fatherland, the moral force of his entire patriotic conduct."[16] Bismarck's eternal being would protect and inspire Germans for years to come.

If things are going badly in the Empire, if the waves of passion rise and even the best wish to doubt the future, then we will come to you, then we will open the pages of your life and create new energy and new joy over the grandeur of the Reich. If enemies dare to lay a hand on your legacy, the tocsins will sound, then the troops of your German sons, who wish to fight and die for the fatherland, will draw by your coffin, for all times faithfully ready, for the splendor of the Reich.[17]

Thus Kahl assured Bismarck that his followers would "set foot upon and protect the German ground in which you sleep as a national sanctuary."[18] Nevertheless, he assured his audience that they were not there to deify men. It was no false religion they were practicing, but rather the striving after the "highest models of patriotic virtue, to rise up to the highest performances of human power and human intellect, with which to fortify, to fire themselves, and to steel their holy resolutions."[19]

In a sense, Kahl was correct, but not completely. This was not a traditional religious ceremony. While it used some of the outer forms of religious ritual, it altered their meaning and application, while still seeking to produce the same results, that is to establish a connection to something higher, something outside of themselves: the national community of all Germans, at the core of which they saw themselves, the community of Bismarckians. What took place at Kroll, then, was much more clearly the manifestation of a middle-class German-national civic religion.[20] What they deified was less the departed chancellor than the image of the German nation to which they aspired. It was a nation modeled on themselves, on middle-class values, which they projected on to Bismarck or took from him as their own. They were thus celebrating themselves as the true national community. In sanctifying those symbols which united them and represented their highest values, they thereby raised themselves and their values to the highest level.

In staging their own ceremony with such a powerful emotional appeal and disregard of imperial protocol, these Bismarckians were clearly distinguishing themselves from the government and thereby challenging its claim to proprietorship over the national symbols. They were continuing to claim the right to define the nation. Bismarck provided them with this opportunity more than any other icon in large part because of the oppositional potential he had already shown and his position beyond the reach of official nationalism. The government still needed to establish its national legitimacy. Part of this challenge involved the attempt to reclaim Bismarck and thus end the dispute over the national symbols. At the same time, however, and particularly for Wilhelm II, it also involved the development of the government's own repertoire of nationalist symbolism and ritual.

Wilhelm II hoped to become a truly popular leader, a *Volkskaiser*, who could unite the nation and lead it to a bright future. At the time of his coronation, and even after Bismarck's dismissal, he embodied the hopes of many who saw in the young ruler a welcome breath of fresh air after years of stagnant rule by the aging Chancellor. If Wilhelm sought to take advantage of such hopes, he soon lost his chance as he attempted to establish the regime's legitimacy with a national vision that failed to take into account the Kaiserreich's newly developing political culture. At a time in which the people – from the Social Democratic Left to the radical nationalist Right – were pressing for a voice in national politics, Wilhelm projected a national vision that looked back to dynastic loyalty and a medieval, corporatist society. Ritual under Wilhelm was also proving less and less effective. Wilhelm I had done little to encourage the promotion of his birthday as a 'national' celebration of the German Kaiser since he had little enthusiasm for the title.[21] His grandson, however, thought differently. He saw Kaiserdom as a "symbol of the nation and of the imperial monarchy by the grace of god," and himself playing the role of "representative of the nation."[22]

If some in Berlin sought to hold on to Bismarck as a national symbol, Wilhelm usually ignored him in public.[23] Instead, he posited a cult of Hohenzollern, which involved the promotion of his grandfather. Not only did these efforts founder, but they tended to evoke hostility among middle-class nationalists. Certainly Wilhelm I remained quite popular, but people typically saw him more as a genial, fatherly figure, while founding and protecting the Empire they credited to Bismarck. Their resistance to the Kaiser's efforts peaked in 1897 when Wilhelm attended the dedication of his grandfather's statue at the Kyffhauser monument. There he spoke of how "Wilhelm the Great" founded the Reich with help from Bismarck and Moltke, whom he described as "lackeys and pygmies."[24] Count Anton Monts wrote about the increasing resentment towards the Kaiser and the secret suspicions among many that he was insane.[25] "Perhaps the masses will still yell at him during the manoeuvers," he wrote, "but the hearts of the patriotic middle-classes are now surely lost to him forever."[26] This is not to say that Germans turned their backs on Kaiserdom. As Elisabeth Fehrenbach noted, "[c]riticism of the Kaiser was based on the example of the past, on the Bismarckian myth of the 'Iron Chancellor,' but this acknowledged in its turn the cry for a 'politician in the grand manner.'"[27] In 1906, for example, the German National Commercial Employees Union wrote: "The political reformer Bismarck followed the religious reformer Luther, and the national reformer, 'the Kaiser of the future,' must follow them, for only then is the German people the most glorious of all."[28] The leadership ideal that Bismarck had imprinted so deeply into German political culture remained. Criticism from the Bismarck press was not directed at the personal nature of rule by a leader, but rather at the problematic execution of that role by the current holder of the position. For growing numbers of Germans, "Kaiserdom stood in the shadow cast by the Chancellor myth and the Bismarck legend."[29]

At this point, imperial ritual failed to establish itself and win over middle-class nationalists, in part because of Wilhelm's personal example, but also because of the very basis of the two possible poles of German nationalism – the official and the Bismarckian. Going back to the early nineteenth century, German nationalist festivals and ritual were oppositional, directed usually against the dynasties as obstacles to national unity. As George Mosse notes, "this opposition infused the national liturgy with an élan stressing popular participation against the political establishment."[30] With the achievement of national unity, national festivals were now within the purview of the establishment and, over time, were increasingly staged and seen as such by the bourgeois national community.[31] The Bismarck Cult and its rituals offered a return to that original 'élan' of German national celebrations by virtue of its oppositional component. This oppositional element gave the Bismarck movement a dynamic and an appeal that official imperial ritual increasingly lacked. A member of the radical nationalist German National Commercial Employees Union pointed to the decline of imperial ritual when, in writing about a Bismarck ceremony in 1912, he noted the contrast between the two. "An enthusiasm dominates here," he wrote, "like I had only in the most distant memories of our Sedan festivals in school."[32] Here was a movement that increasingly based its authority on the people's right to define the nation. And it was 'the people' who took the initiative in celebrating its political god.

Perhaps no area better demonstrated the contrast between governmental and Bismarckian nationalism than monument building. Germans had been building Bismarck monuments for years. Death, however, accelerated the process of separating the Bismarck symbol from the man himself. The result was a new, unique style of monument. In December 1898 a group of student organizations, including the radical nationalist *Verein deutscher Studenten*, met to develop this new type of monument. The result was the Bismarck fire-pillar, first designed by Wilhelm Kreis. In their declaration they described their inspiration. "As the old Saxons and Normans once erected over the bodies of fallen warriors plain, undecorated rock columns topped by fiery beacons, we want to construct massive granite beacons in honor of Bismarck on all the heights of our homeland from which one can look out over our glorious German landscape."[33] With the fires visible throughout the land, Bismarck would be celebrated "like no German before him" as a constant witness to the nation's virtues – "devout love of fatherland, German loyalty to the death."[34] These new-style monuments brought into focus the central fact of the Bismarck Cult – the object of devotion was much less the man than the symbol. He was the embodiment of German values and thus of the nation itself.[35] Those at the *Staatsbürger Zeitung* described the pillars as "[a]ltars of sacrifice for the German spirit . . . dedicated not only to his memory, but rather a visible sign that his spirit lives further among us so long as there exist German men."[36]

Along with the grave at Friedrichsruh, these monuments provided followers with holy sites. In 1903 the *Dresdner Nachrichten* described the effect that a visit – a "pilgrimage" – to these holy sites was to have on the devout. It was to be "like a national purification."

> German patriots feel new holy life rising up inside of them when, at the grave in Friedrichsruh, they hold holy dialogue with the spirit of their hero. Through the still loneliness of the forest it rustles like a revelation and on the consecrated site the devout national pilgrim receives a wealth of the richest impressions, which impart to him goal and direction for his whole life. There lies a mysterious, endlessly life giving power in such a national pilgrimage in spirit to the resting place of the greatest of all Germans.[37]

As with any holy sites, therefore, these Bismarckian locations served as sacred ground on which to honor the idol and from which followers could draw energy and inspiration, meaning and direction. Before the massive Bismarck monument in Hamburg, one speaker declared in 1912: "We thank you, Bismarck, that you gave us the foundation for national work and thought. We vow anew to maintain your ideas and your words as holy. We affirm this, as we direct our eyes towards you, the dead and yet ever living Bismarck and call: hail to you, you loyal one!"[38]

The new and unique characteristics of the Bismarck towers also provided followers with sites and symbols distinct from those of the government. They therefore served as perfect platforms for a nationalist politics seeking to distinguish itself from a government increasingly considered insufficiently nationalist.[39] Unlike many of the monuments built during the Empire, Bismarck towers were not sponsored by the government, but rather by independent initiative, making clear the movement's unofficial nature. Between 1898 and 1914 more than 700 monuments were planned, with more than 500 constructed.[40] The total cost of all the Bismarck monuments has been estimated at around 14 million Marks (equivalent to approximately 250 million DM in 1980). The sheer size of this undertaking, combined with the underlying political motivation, conveys a good sense of the Cult's potential populist, oppositional power.[41]

In addition to ceremonies and monuments, the calendar, too, provided opportunities to distinguish Bismarckians from official government nationalism. A number of dates quickly emerged on which they could celebrate their particular national vision on days distinct from the traditional Prusso-German holidays. Most important were the anniversaries of his birth (1 April) and death (31 July). In addition, thanks largely to the radical *Verein deutscher Studenten*, the summer solstice emerged as a day to honor Bismarck.[42] Here again was fresh ground on which to stake a claim to national legitimacy. The effect of such regular, ritual events was to create among Bismarckians an effervescence – to heighten their sense of community, of common belief and purpose, and thus revive their sense of mission.[43] In 1912 a member of the German-National Commercial Employees Union described how he was affected by one such ceremony: "My heart was carried away, and the waves of patriotic inspiration carried me high above the everyday as together we laid a wreath on the monument of the great master. Immediately in these first days I knew that here I had found what I needed and I came to know a new, high duty: the fostering of the national feeling."[44]

As the calendar developed, so too did a set of rituals. Typically they began with a procession to the monument. For ceremonies in Friedrichsruh they would make the short walk from the station to the mausoleum. In the case of nighttime ceremonies, columns of torch-bearing followers added an impressive dimension while harkening back to some timeless Germanic past. At most events the ritual involved laying wreaths, singing songs, reciting poems, delivering speeches, often, as with the Kroll ceremony, by German academics. But while the Cult itself gained intellectual legitimacy as a result, the purpose of these rituals did not lie in the intellectual realm.[45] As Alfred Hugenberg explained, those who attended Bismarck ceremonies were not there, as historians "in order to learn."[46] They wanted something different. "We want to approach him in spirit . . . In thought, we want to shake his weather-hardened hand and in consideration of his essence and work to try to fill ourselves with his spirit."[47]

While the rituals provided opportunities for Bismarckians to come together as a community, there existed other means of spreading the gospel, and to an even larger audience. Newspapers played a vital role in the growth and spread of the Cult. Following the Bismarckian calendar, newspapers covered the annual ceremonies, reprinting speeches while also printing their own stories and tribute articles. And just like those who pontificated from the shadows of the monuments, the press used a clearly religious vocabulary and style. The *Berliner Neueste Nachrichten*, for example, opened its eulogy with Christ's last words on the cross: "It is done [Es ist vollbracht]," while the *Hannoversche Post* expressed surprise that, with Bismarck's death, "signs and wonders did not occur, as in that hour where the son of God died on the cross."[48]

Between 1898 and 1914 the Bismarck Cult established an increasingly regular repertoire of rituals, symbols, monuments and holy sites, all given added weight thanks to the backing of Germany's intellectual elite. This is not to say, however, that the Cult had solidified into a firmly established and organized movement. In many ways it resembled the early stages of a new religious community.[49] For example, it lacked a firm central organization. The Bismarck-Bund, an organization founded to promote construction of Bismarck monuments, represented one effort at a national body. Something of a loose umbrella organization for local Bismarck societies, it never included much more than fifty of the more than three hundred that sprang up across the country.[50] Its effectiveness was thus limited. Without a powerful central organization, spreading the gospel was left to a number of nationalist organizations and political parties. As we have already seen, radical nationalist groups claimed him early on as their inspiration and thus played an important role in the initial phase of Bismarck veneration. With his death, their role in the growth and spread of the Cult grew. Most radical nationalist groups made sure to take part in the Cult. They expressed enthusiasm for the construction of Bismarck monuments and the national spirit that they represented, often holding their own Bismarck ceremonies in their shadows.[51]

With its lack of central organization, it should not be surprising that the Cult also lacked a single dogma. Still, there did emerge a general story line, a Bismarckian 'gospel', which could serve as a unifying force for otherwise diverse groups. Central to the story was the theme of fall and redemption. For centuries, according to Bismarckians, Germans were forced to wander through the wilderness of statelessness. While they cried out for a savior, none arrived. Eventually, Bismarck, the 'messiah', the 'savior'[52], the 'divine gift'[53], was sent to lead his people to the holy land of national unity. This messiah, however, was not initially recognized as such and was scorned and cursed by his people. As "a tool in the hands of God,"[54] though, he worked miracles in unifying the nation and quickly those who had previously doubted him now realized who he was – "the appointed leader sent by God to the German people."[55] Eventually, though, the savior was betrayed by a new Kaiser and by the people as well, who had grown soft and comfortable. Bismarck was sent away, cast off to his estate in the Sachsenwald. But he was not forgotten. In his absence, the "forces of darkness, which had to give way before the triumphant sun-like power of his spirit, appeared now to be able to begin their work of destruction unhindered."[56] With his death, talk of a return, a resurrection, was never far away, and as his followers perceived their country to be sinking further into crisis, that longing, that hope for a return, grew correspondingly stronger. Until then, followers would keep alive his spirit within themselves. They would spread the word, enlarging the community of Bismarckians until Germany was once again worthy of his return.[57] As a young community of believers, Bismarckians drew strength from their symbols and rituals, while opposition to the government, if not immediately comfortable, eventually helped galvanize them still further.

Crying in the Wilderness: The Early Cult in Political Practice and the Quest for Legitimacy

In the years immediately following the Iron Chancellor's death, both the radical nationalist opposition and the Bismarck Cult which inspired it were still fairly new phenomena. The Bismarck image itself had yet to be fully defined and thus stood available to a variety of potential suitors, including an imperial government seeking to establish its own legitimacy. The radical nationalists, certainly, had yet to fully establish their position on the national stage. They, too, sought legitimacy in order to be able to play their desired role as guardians of the national symbols and the national interest. At the time of Bismarck's passing, men like Heinrich Class and Diederich Hahn lacked the credentials to play such prominent roles in national politics. The Cult, though, had the potential to provide them with the legitimacy they needed. Participating in all aspects of the Cult, they sought to transfer Bismarck's charisma to their particular organization. As they did so, they could define the image, shaping it to fit their political vision, and in the process not only deny the government its authority, but also hammer away at it with the force of Germany's ultimate national icon. The government, they complained repeatedly, lacked clear goals and direction, hence its numerous failures and embarrassments on the world stage. The cult provided precisely what the regime lacked – goals and direction. With the spirit of Bismarck as their guide, these radical nationalists would succeed where the government failed. If they did not achieve their goals as soon as they had hoped, they still continued to press for a role in national decision-making based on their populist political vision. It is in these early years that we can see the role of the Cult in shaping the discourse they would use in their quest to move from the wilderness to the center of German politics.

Already for years before 1898, the organizations of the national opposition had sought to drape themselves in the Bismarckian mantle. They celebrated his birthday, sent him telegrams, traveled to his estate, all with the hope of adding weight to their political claims. That goal of legitimacy through Bismarck remained a priority after his death and the Cult served to provide it. Whether at monuments or in newspapers, right-wing Germans expressed their political vision in the language and through the narrative of the Cult. Looking back one year after his death, the Pan-Germans saw the rise of 'dark forces' unleashing their 'work of destruction' now that Bismarck's 'warning voice' had been silenced.[58] But participation in the Cult gave them the security and confidence to be able to deal with this situation. "For ever and ever we will save ourselves from the day's conflict, from the confused waves of opinions, like a quiet sanctuary in his thoughts and reminiscences, which he left to the whole German people as his greatest legacy."[59] It was within the comfort of that "quiet sanctuary" that they would "find composure in the distraction of everyday hassles, the immortal German essence will reveal itself to us there for ever and ever, and when goal and direction appear lost to us in the hustle and bustle of the present, there we will continually find again the bright pole-star of true Germandom, to which we have to set the path."[60] For the German people, Bismarck had become "a bright source of fire, from which the warmth of patriotic enthusiasm and the clarity of political thinking stream up to all who approach with hearts willing to receive."[61] He was particularly important for the Pan-Germans. They were, after all, amongst his most devoted disciples, who clearly claimed for themselves a leading role in the emerging Cult. As such, their task involved keeping his spirit alive within them and spreading it to prepare the country, making it worthy of such a leader once more. Just what that spirit meant to them cannot be said to have corresponded to the Right as a whole. But like most on the right, the League was confident in its own interpretation. "We work in his spirit," they wrote in 1899,

> when we call the entirety of Germandom to unification and warn it, in consideration of its world power position, to hold back everything divisive before the great feeling of common blood; when we let the national thoughts shine high over the petty goings-on of the parties; his spirit is with us when we declare war on spineless cosmopolitanism and set our German sense of self with quiet pride against all other peoples; when we demand German interest-politics, which knows absolutely no other guideline than the well-being of our people.[62]

The Pan-Germans, however, were not the only ones sworn to go 'forward in the spirit of Bismarck'. The Agrarian League, too, grieved over the loss of what it called "the greatest German of this century, if not of all times, the truest son of his passionately beloved fatherland."[63] He was, after all, the "spiritual father" of the organization.[64] "We who came together to fight for German work – we may in a completely special sense call him ours. He declared himself to us – that time, as he greeted the founding of the 'Bund der Landwirte' with unconcealed joy."[65] Still, Bismarck's death was also the opportunity to promote the national vision that he represented – the future German national community in which divisions of party, class, confession, or region played no role. Until the reality of that national community came to pass, they would work further in his spirit, inspired and guided by him.[66] The Hakatisten as well confirmed their devotion to Bismarck upon his passing. The Eastern Marches Society, they made clear, "was founded, as a result of his advice, above the parties, only on the ground of holy love of fatherland."[67] He was "a patron and a protector."[68] Out of this bond with Bismarck they found their task for the future.

If Bismarck's dismissal had allowed the development of a politics of national opposition, his death opened up further possibilities. For radical nationalists, most of whom had come of age politically after 1871, the new century promised a new stage in German development. And despite having passed from the scene, Bismarck still had a role to play. Whereas in the 1860s he had redeemed the fallen nation through the establishment of the *kleindeutsch* Second Empire, now, in the twentieth century, his spirit would redeem the fallen Reich of the epigones through the establishment of the German *world* empire. With his passing, Bismarckians were no longer bound by his approval or rejection of their plans. This was the age of *Weltpolitik*, and the cult would now inspire its followers to go 'beyond Bismarck' in the further establishment of German power and glory. 'Beyond Bismarck,' however, did not mean leaving him behind. It meant correctly interpreting his spirit and moving forward in the changed circumstances of a new era. Through the rituals of the Cult, they could be sure of their interpretations and feel confident in their position. "If today with our demands we go beyond what he achieved and attempted," declared the Pan-Germans, "then we deal justly in his spirit, since not byzantine inactive admiration, backwards directed world-fleeing observations of his greatness, but rather active work in his sense, creation, joyfully in the present, striding into the future, of the current work appropriate to our German life – he demands that of us."[69] It was a positive, forward-looking attitude that took pride in the changes Bismarck had produced in the German nation, and his followers now looked forward to their new mission. At a League meeting in Hamburg in August 1899, the Pan-Germans proclaimed: "It is the great work set for our people to be the upholder of civilization of all mankind, but no more in the sense in which the nation of poets and thinkers finds its complete satisfaction to enrich others through the treasures of its spirit, but rather in the powerful realism of Bismarck, that we also obtain our share of sunlight, of the domination of the world."[70]

Events occurring beyond Germany's borders soon gave Bismarckians the opportunity to act upon such grandiose ideas. Foreign policy had been the area in which Bernhard von Bülow had engendered such high hopes among the Right. Disillusionment with him in this realm, therefore, proceeded slowly but steadily. While many were willing to give him the benefit of the doubt, considering how he had to overcome the damage wrought by his predecessors, others were less forgiving. By the turn of the century, ethnicity came to play an increasingly important role in German national identity, particularly among the Pan-Germans. With this came the obligation of the Reich to protect fellow Germans and Germanic peoples anywhere on earth. Thus, when the government seemed to be leaving its ethnic brethren in southern Africa, the Boers, to their fate in their war against the British, many decried this violation of Bismarckian principles.

The anger resulted in a confrontation in the Reichstag between Bülow and Pan-German leader Ernst Hasse in 1900. Criticizing German policy since Bismarck's fall, Hasse attacked the government's national credentials. The Chancellor responded with a masterful counterattack, mixing backhanded praise with criticism of the League's irresponsible positions. Commenting that he found it interesting to see "how excitedly Herr Deputy Hasse splashed around in the blue waves of the unbounded sea of the politics of conjecture," Bülow stressed that he could not engage in such pleasures, but rather had to "remain on the *terra firma* of reality."[71] A policy of sentimentality, of racial affinity for the Boers, could not be the focal point of German foreign policy. "We only have to defend German interests in the world."[72] Responding to Hasse's boast that German opinion stood firmly behind the League on this, Bülow pointed to another Bismarckian principle – the need to take unpopular positions. Helping foreign peoples was a noble part of the German character, he noted, but in politics it is a mistake. In concluding his attack, he stressed that "[t]he politician is no judge of morals. He only has to defend the interests and rights of his own country. From the standpoint of pure moral philosophy I cannot carry out foreign policy – Bismarck had also not done that – and also not from the standpoint of the beer hall."[73]

This exchange made clear the challenge faced by the nascent national opposition hoping to escape the fringes of German politics. While some left the League as a result, those who remained and those who would join in the future were the more dedicated, hard-core nationalists – the true-believers for whom the government's nationalist credentials grew increasingly questionable. Despite this increase in intensity, though, the fact remained that they were still on the outside, and Bülow's rhetorical skills threatened to keep them there indefinitely. His condemnation of them as little more than beer hall politicians proved a stigma for radical nationalists for years to come.[74] Even more threatening was his challenge to their very right to define the Iron Chancellor. Just as a successful claim to Bismarck by the Right would serve to undermine the government's position as upholder of the national interests, Bülow's use of Bismarck against Germany's most devoted Bismarckians represented a similar danger to them. A 'governmental Bismarck' held the potential to defeat their claim to a populist legitimacy that based itself on the ultimate national icon.

The official challenge to radical nationalist claims of legitimacy through Bismarck continued the following year when Bülow himself took part in one of the central rituals of the Bismarck Cult. In June 1901 he spoke at the unveiling of what was originally meant to be the national Bismarck monument in Berlin. His intent was clear from the outset as he attacked those who considered it a patriotic duty to approve of everything the first chancellor said and did. "Only fools or fanatics will want to assert that Bismarck never made a mistake."[75] Nor did he set up maxims to be applied to each situation without consideration of the particular circumstances. Bismarck, he asserted, did not think highly of dogmas, but what he did teach was that "not personal fondness, not popular currents of the moment, nor gray theory, but rather always just the *salus publica* may be the guideline of a rational and morally justified policy."[76] In the face of the risk-filled policies the national opposition constantly advocated in the name of the first Chancellor, Bülow put forth his own vision of Bismarckian politics: moderation. "In politics it depends on precisely recognizing in each moment the limits of the achievable, to set the attainment of what can be attained for the benefit and advantage of the country above everything."[77]

The Chancellor's ability to tap into the Bismarckians' rhetorical style posed a potentially serious threat to an opposition still seeking a firm position in the political landscape. The nationalists' hero was just that – national. "No party," Bülow declared, "can lay claim to Prince Bismarck for itself alone, but all can and should, despite opposition in this or that question, drop the daggers before this departed one. He belongs to no coterie, he belongs to the whole nation; he is a national possession."[78] He was, in fact, the purest embodiment of the nation, "a German in the fullest sense of the word. He is only imaginable on German soil, only understandable for the Germans."[79] The intent here was clear, just as it had been in the Reichstag the previous year – the nationalization and the moderation of the Bismarck image. But this was not the Reichstag. It was a ceremony within the growing Bismarck Cult, a place for emotion, for spiritual connection. And Bülow could speak the language of the Cult. "So then," he declared, "may the name of the great man draw before our people as a pillar of fire in good and in difficult days. May his spirit be with us forever, with us and our flag flying."[80]

Once again Bülow had struck at the heart of the national opposition, appropriating its language, while explicitly denying its right to claim what it considered its most sacred national symbol. From the sidelines they lashed out with a populist counter-attack that placed the task of redirecting the national mission in the hands of the people. At a speech in Halle, Diederich Hahn complained that, despite

Bülow's words of praise and recognition of the great leader, he had not developed anything like a Bismarckian program. It was up to the people "to intercede so that Bismarck's policies will again be taken up in all areas against the current dealings of the government."[81] How different was the system now, compared to that of Bismarck, "who constantly steered the ship of state in a clear direction."[82] Now a completely different system dominated. The government lacked goals. "Clear recognition of plans is not to be found with the current government."[83] The answer lay with Bismarck and those who truly understood him, for they had a sense of direction, of goals. Bismarck provided it, whatever Bülow might think about systematizing him. If he could not recognize that truth, they had to make sure that others did. The nation's future depended on it. "It is up to us to defend Bismarck's legacy and to set all powers for the strengthening of Germany in all areas within the country as well as against the outside world . . . As there is a Goethe tradition in art, a Lutheran tradition for evangelical Christianity, so there also stands in politics a Bismarckian tradition, which we cannot allow anyone to take from us."[84] For their part, the Pan-Germans did not even mention the speech when discussing the statue's unveiling. They did not need to assert anew what Bismarck meant to the German people, and in particular what he meant to the League itself. Without him, they declared, "a pan-German project would be completely impossible." Because of that, they loved and honored him "not only as the creator of German unity and greatness, but rather," they continued, because "he is also for us a pathbreaker and *Führer*, the teacher and master of the work of the binding together of all of Germandom on the earth; not only the building of a utopian, pan-Germanic world empire, but rather for the spiritual unity of a powerful German consciousness."[85] In the end, they wrote, "Bismarck was German through and through, German his feelings, thoughts, and dealings."[86] The responses of the national opposition demonstrated a sense of faith in their new political religion that could withstand the harsh blows of official condemnation. They would need that faith, for at this point the true believers in the Cult remained on the fringes of German national politics. And their situation, it turns out, would get worse before it got better.

For the Right in general 1903 was a bad year. Gaining twenty-five seats, the Social Democrats pulled out a surprising victory in that year's Reichstag elections. For the Pan-Germans, it was particularly painful, as all League-affiliated candidates failed to win seats.[87] At such a low-point, the League's leaders considered it an opportune time to reflect on the recent past, on the path that had led to such a position. As an indication of their sense of desperation, they chose perhaps the League's most radical figure, Heinrich Class, to deliver the keynote address at the annual meeting.[88] As a retelling of recent German history through the narrative of the Bismarckian political religion, his speech clearly reflected the cult's influence and its importance in right-wing political culture.

The general outline of the story he told was of fall and redemption. The fall followed Bismarck's dismissal. In all this time the ultimate goal, the creation of the national community, had yet to be achieved. This was, in large part, "because one allows oneself to be governed by the Center and Social Democracy, instead of practicing, like Bismarck in 1863–1867, powerful German national politics, if necessary against majorities in the Reichstag and Landtag."[89] The result was that "the prestige of the imperial throne, of the dynasties and the monarchy has sunk, the German Reichstag has lost the respect of the people, and the office of Reich Chancellor has been robbed of its essential attributes."[90] This was not a regime that acted in Bismarckian fashion. In contrast to the decisive man of action who founded the Reich, those who succeeded him spoke a great deal, but their actions were few and, in the end, hollow. In particular, Class condemned the government's efforts to cultivate nationalist sentiment among the people and to tie that sentiment to the regime. "Showy spectacles and celebrations, parades and monument unveilings, as well as a press influence to a degree never before practiced, falsify the image of our public life, but do not obscure the judgment that we really have no government."[91] In explaining the leadership's failures, Class turned once again to a common complaint of the Right – the lack of goals. "Great goals are unknown; where they are spoken of, they are unclear."[92] It should not be any wonder, then, "if the worst spirit of pessimism has come over wide circles of our educated and national people, that they withdraw, hopeless and bitter, from public life."[93] This has been the result, according to Class, of all government policy since Bismarck's dismissal.

As a follower of the Cult, however, Class was not about to give up, for belief in Bismarck meant faith that the fall must be followed by redemption, and that redemption was to come through the people themselves. It was the populist vision inherent in the Cult that inspired Class and gave him hope. He took comfort in the memory of another period of fall and redemption, when the German people suffered through the humiliation and weakness of statelessness, but were eventually saved when the 'right men' were called. But until that happened, what could they themselves do, these people on the fringes of power, without any direct influence? "Fulfill our political manly duty," was Class' response. This would not be easy, he assured his audience. In doing so, he appeared to be taking upon himself and those around him the role of a young group of fervent believers who would suffer for their convictions. But they had to go forward, "without allowing ourselves to be influenced or scared by the mockery and scorn of opponents, by the considered rejection of those in the government, by the lack of understanding of the masses, to prepare the political rebirth of our people, in which we open their eyes to the national work of the future and the dangers of the present in which we seek to teach them political sense; in which we awaken in them pride and joy in their own nationhood, and help to victory a promising, national world-view."[94] They had, in other words, to take the national mission into their own hands. With a government either unwilling or unable to act in the best interest of the nation, the nation had to act in its place, and it was up to the Pan-Germans to mobilize the people. "We must free up the moral forces in our people for a national policy that puts the people above the state when both come into conflict."[95] Class warned that they would have to make the people realize "how absurd and unworthy it is to expect all salvation, all help from above; that in the life of a people it will be said: 'The people is everything' and that every national comrade is responsible before history and the grandchildren for what happens today and is left behind; we must raise this feeling of responsibility to a driving force of our national life.[96] In the absence of Bismarckian leadership, the people themselves must step up and carry the national mission forward. The motivation for such action was simple. "When we set to work, so will we raise the courage, in which we think about the man who created the German Reich for us, about Bismarck, whose work we want to defend, maintain, and lead further; who, in spirit, is our duke and will lead us to victory."[97]

Clearly Class had lived up to his radical image. With his speech he had made an extreme statement, what he himself called "the first step towards resolute and complete 'National Opposition'."[98] He had questioned the government's authority to act in the national interest. Through its failures, he questioned its very right to define the national interest. That right he claimed for himself and those around him. He could do so through the Cult of Bismarck and the faith, goals, and confidence it provided.

The League's leadership was pleased with Class' bold statement and it quickly published the speech as a pamphlet entitled "The Balance of the New Course," distributing 60,000 copies to both League members and parliamentary officials.[99] Class' speech would end up establishing the League's path for the next decade, though it did not yet immediately bring clarity and determination to the movement. The political position that he had charted was still fairly new and not everyone was comfortable with such determined opposition to the government and the official condemnation it drew. Concern showed itself within the League in heated debates among members in local chapters and in the continual decline in overall membership.[100] But those who remained were the true believers. And Class had made it clear that the work of awakening the spirit of Bismarck in the people was difficult. The populist legitimacy that he sought was still in the future. Redemption through Bismarck that he had preached at Plauen was years away. Events would show whose vision was true.

Nationalist disillusionment with the government's leadership continued to grow as Germany's world position appeared to fall ever further from the high point at which it stood in 1890. The failure of Bülow's Morocco policy marked another stage in this apparent decline. The Pan-Germans had been advocating for some time already the acquisition of territory in this North African kingdom before it fell completely under French control. When, in 1905, Bülow objected to French moves which seemed a prelude to annexation, he raised the hopes of many that finally they were seeing the Chancellor's own admiration of Bismarck translating into Bismarckian actions. The French Prime Minister's fall and the Kaiser's visit to Tangier led many to think that the German Reich was moving back to the bold power politics of its founder. When the crisis ended in Germany's humiliating public isolation at Algeciras, those hopes proved false, and the cynicism towards the government grew.

Heinrich Class pointed out the problems which the nation now faced. "We stand alone – and our diplomacy must begin from today forward where once Bismarck had begun."[101] The failure at Algeciras strengthened the awareness of a crisis of leadership. One found no evidence of success, either foreign or domestic, by the government. Was there any sign of a plan – a plan that would be followed calmly and patiently? "No, the reins drag on the ground – the government appears as only a bureaucratic authority for the everyday administrative work, not the leader of a people; it lacks the greatness of its conception – it lacks goals."[102] The problem, however, was bigger than just the government. It went beyond the "lack of desire and ability within the state leadership" to the "political lack of insight and the indifference in the people."[103] Germany lacked a national will. If, after the great accomplishments of the founding period, Germans focused on economic development and shied away from political self-education, the nation had nothing to worry about so long as "that man directed its destiny, who restored to it the national will. As he departed, the will was lacking – his absence led to where we stand today."[104] The people needed to raise themselves up to become political. Class knew "that a political genius is a gift that will not often be bestowed upon a people, and we are not so unjustified to make the complaint about the current men, that they are no geniuses; but we believe that the greatness that they themselves lack can be compensated for through the political conviction and the national will of the people that stands behind them."[105]

Yet again the populist dimension of right-wing politics came to the fore. Here was a direct challenge to the government's authority to be the true interpreters of the national will. Rather than from Berlin, that national will would come from the people themselves, or more accurately from those most in tune with the essence of the nation, whose self-set goal was "to awaken the national instinct, to strengthen the energy of the *völkisch* consciousness and its application – in a word, to create the national will."[106] Class had thrown down the gauntlet. The national leadership lacked the will and the ability once displayed by Bismarck. It was up to those attuned to his spirit to set the nation's agenda and steer it back on the paths laid out by their hero.

Once again, Bülow moved to counter such allegations of weakness and fend off the challenge to the government's right to define the national interest. And again,

Bismarck served as his weapon of choice. In November 1906 in the Reichstag Bülow responded to an interpellation by National Liberal leader Ernst Bassermann. The situation, he declared, was not so bleak as some feared. The problems lay with Bismarck, or more precisely, with the image of him that too many people had created and the harmful effects of his legacy on German politics. A thorough study of this "incomparable statesman," Bülow asserted, "will convince anyone that his greatness did not exist in the clinking of spurs, the wearing of cuirassiers' boots and not in the rattling of the saber, but rather in a sober assessment of men and of things. The dogmatization of Prince Bismarck has become not only a mania with us, but rather a calamity. We are suffering under the misunderstood Prince Bismarck."[107] The problem was, though, that times change and demand new means. Bismarck was a product of his times, and those who follow him cannot afford to fall into slavish imitation. Bülow therefore called for adjustment. "If developments demand that we go beyond Bismarckian goals, then we must do it, even if Prince Bismarck in his times and under seemingly similar circumstances judged things differently."[108]

Bülow had once more faced a challenge to the government's definition of the national interests. Once again, the Bismarck image had shown itself useful for the purpose. The Bismarck Cult was still young and unsure of itself. But the claim to Bismarck had been made. The Cult continued its development as a political religion that provided goals, inspiration, and a sense of history that would help shape the Right's understanding and practice of politics. Bismarckians would further develop their populist claim to national legitimacy, and, with the country on the verge of a lengthy crisis, they would soon find that their message of salvation through Bismarck had gained a great deal of resonance. Their time in the wilderness was nearly over.

The Legitimization of Right-Wing Populism and the Radicalization of the Right during the Wilhelmine Crisis Period

In 1908 the magazine *Jugend* placed on its cover the image of Bismarck in the guise of Wotan, as a wanderer in the night with walking-stick in hand and around whose shoulders fluttered two ravens. Accompanying such dark imagery, was the ominous text:

> Forebodings of storms I sense in the air,
> And danger for your best possessions.
> As an admonisher I rise from the grave,
> As a warner I come and as a protector![109]

It was the tenth anniversary of his death, and Germans came out in force to mark the occasion.[110] The fact that the anniversary fell during the height of a crisis period that would plague Wilhelmine Germany through its remaining years of peace translated into a dramatic increase in the Cult's intensity. Salvation through Bismarck now took on a more tangible meaning as diplomatic setbacks exposed what appeared to be German weakness for all to see, while internal scandal provided evidence of weakness at the highest levels of government. The degree of reaction varied, but fundamentally German nationalists were losing faith in the government. In such a situation, the Bismarckians' populist rhetoric grew increasingly extreme and found greater resonance than before within the Right. Certainly the ability of Bismarck was lacking in Berlin, but so too was his spirit. If the government would not or could not act in Germany's best interest, then the Bismarckians would. These men, who had been carrying the word through the wilderness, were now set to move center stage. The combination of the crisis situation and the image they carried before them provided a legitimacy they had previously lacked. Bismarckians continued their calls for change, but now people would have to listen.

The events of the First Moroccan Crisis disturbed German nationalists. The story of the nation's fall had gained a new chapter. From the height of Bismarck-designed greatness at the center of an elaborate system of alliances and alignments, the country now stood virtually alone, backed only by the Austro-Hungarian Empire. The debacle at Algeciras alone confirmed for many the existence of a leadership crisis. As it turned out, though, the events of 1905–06 marked only the start of a period of serious, sustained crisis that would shake the foundations of the Wilhelmine system. For it was the story *behind* Algeciras that led to much deeper concern among German nationalists regarding the abilities and the nationalist credentials of the leadership.

The dramatic reversal of fortune suffered at Algeciras cried out for explanation. In 1906 Max Harden sought to provide answers by revealing the existence of a homosexual cabal around the Kaiser.[111] The presence of homosexuals at court had long been suspected. Brought out in the open, however, at a time when the country's weakness had just been so glaringly exposed to the world, the existence of 'un-German' and 'un-manly' influence at the highest levels caused shock waves and seemed to provide some explanation for Germany's recent misfortune. This is especially significant when one considers the image of Bismarck as the ultimate embodiment of the German man. The trials of Harden for libel – the first of which opened on October 24, 1907 – and their extensive press coverage provided Germans with an opportunity to clash over issues of national identity and leadership. While the object, and degree, of criticism varied, faith in those running the country generally suffered a serious blow.

The crisis of leadership unleashed by the scandal resonated particularly strongly among Bismarckians, who just happened to be marking the tenth anniversary of their ideal leader's death. The desire for salvation gained added significance as the country's leaders proved themselves even more un-Bismarckian than anyone had previously imagined. *Jugend* was certainly not alone in resurrecting the Iron Chancellor. The *Münchener Neueste Nachrichten* sought to reassure its readers when it wrote: "Yes. Bismarck lives. His spirit watches over us. He outlasts time and space and ensures our nation's future."[112]

The country had not yet fully recovered from the Harden revelations when it faced a second crisis – the publication on October 28, 1908 of Wilhelm's interview with the British *Daily Telegraph*. In it, he discussed his warm feelings for England, which had led him to send battle-plans for its fight against the Boers. Wilhelm's indiscretions caused a general uproar throughout the country. Discussion raged over the Kaiser's 'personal regime' and its resulting difficulties, leading even to calls for constitutional limits on his role.[113] If most Germans found Wilhelm's latest indiscretion disturbing, for radical nationalists it was devastating. Here was Wilhelm proudly explaining how he had actively worked *against* one of the most important planks of the Pan-German program – the loyalty of all Germanic peoples! Clearly, something needed to be done, and at least one Bismarckian had an idea.

Only months before the Kaiser's latest offense, Heinrich Class had been named leader of the Pan-German League. Having already made a significant impact on the League, now, as leader, he would continue his efforts to awaken the people to the dangers posed by the government. The rise of this most radical of Bismarckians to the leadership of Germany's most important radical nationalist organization, coinciding with the outbreak of the crisis period, meant that the populist claim to the national symbols would be put forward with greater force than ever.

One of the first steps in this process came immediately after the *Daily Telegraph* affair, when Class spoke in Leipzig to a specially convened League meeting. His speech, "The Collapse of Imperial German Policy and Its Consequences," addressed the ramifications of the "black days" of October and set forth in the strongest terms yet the Right's populist claims as inspired by the Bismarck Cult. For Class, the problem was bigger than just the Kaiser. It went all the way back to that watershed moment of Bismarck's dismissal in 1890. He placed blame with both the Reichstag and the people around the Kaiser. But the problem also stemmed from Wilhelm, and the solution, at least in part, lay in his hands. A gap had opened between the Kaiser and the public, and just as it was the people who must work to close that gap, so too must the Kaiser exert himself towards the same goal.[114]

In the end, though, Class placed his greatest stress on the people and the need for them to perform their proper function. In large part this involved control over a Reichstag that itself needed to watch over the nation's leadership. The Pan-Germans were there to make sure that the people performed this function. Class took confidence in the fact that, as he saw it, the League had been correct all along. If they had been ridiculed before as *Bierbankpolitiker*, for example, they were now justified in "claiming to be the embodiment for the organization of public opinion at least for the educated middle strata of the *Bürgertum*, as far as the important areas of foreign policy, of overseas relations, and the solidarity between all Germans on earth, particularly in Europe, are concerned."[115] According to Class, the fact that the League had been continually correct meant that it could be trusted. "Therefore we may raise the call to the German *Bürgertum* to follow us, to join together to work to it, that in the Pan-German League the people possess an organ to bring its opinion to expression *vis à vis* the government and the Reichstag."[116] While Class' claim that the League was no longer a negligible force was not completely untrue, it was still an exaggeration. Financial difficulties around this very same time nearly led to the organization's demise. Very soon, though, those problems would be solved in such a way as to make the League forget its financial troubles for the rest of the pre-war period. This change would come about as part of a more general trend, which saw the Right coming increasingly together in the last few years of peace, and in the process becoming more of a force in imperial politics. If he had been crying in the wilderness back in 1903, Class' speech at Leipzig came on the verge of the League's breakthrough to legitimacy.

In July 1909 Wilhelm named Theobald von Bethmann Hollweg as Chancellor. While the nation itself was probably stronger and more prosperous than ever, its situation both internally and externally was somewhat precarious. Bülow's bombastic *Weltpolitik* had left Germany isolated and mistrusted, while internally the political system was grinding to a halt. Inheriting this situation was a man aware of his own limitations, who "with a heavy heart" accepted his new position, "compelled by his sense of duty."[117] He saw the need for domestic reform, and though not well acquainted with the intricacies of foreign policy, he devoted himself to that area with enthusiasm. The change in style became apparent immediately as he sought to pull back from Bülow's overblown approach to diplomacy and find another route to world power. Efforts to move in such a direction, however, failed to satisfy those on the right, momentarily pleased with the demise of their nemesis von Bülow. Their honeymoon with Bethmann would be short indeed. By 1910 the *Hamburger Nachrichten* was by no means alone when it observed that "Bismarck's gigantic shadow stands constantly behind the power holders of today, warning and threatening. On the lips of all German patriots, moreover, hangs the question: would it not have been otherwise and better for the German Reich, if one had let the old hero peacefully die in office, as he had wished?"[118]

The danger to which such pressure and expectations could lead became all too apparent during Germany's next attempt, in 1911, to gain its place in the sun. Just as in 1905, Morocco provided the backdrop for the Empire's latest colonial adventure. Alfred von Kiderlen-Wächter, Germany's new Foreign Secretary, called

Heinrich Class to his office to arrange for cooperation between the League and the Foreign Office on agitation, as he planned to reopen the issue following the arrival of a French military mission to Fez in early 1911. To the Pan-Germans it seemed that the government was returning to the Bismarckian path. Shortly thereafter, the Pan-German press began expressing confidence in the government. When the German gunboat *Panther* arrived at the Moroccan port of Agadir in July 1911, the German national public was ecstatic. Very soon, however, the mood shifted to impatience and then outrage, as it became clear that Kiderlen was seeking a compromise without acquisitions in Morocco. At a meeting of delegates of the *Centralverband Deutscher Industrieller* (Central Association of German Industrialists), the government's weakness and lack of will came under attack as one speaker rose to declare to lively applause that he did not want to debate whether it would have been better for Germany in the Moroccan question "if the imperial government had ... from the beginning more strongly stressed the German claims and had taken to itself somewhat more as a guide the old word of our great Chancellor that the great questions of our time are not solved through speeches and conferences but rather that here, only and alone, action is the main thing." The problem, he claimed, was that: "The feeling that the will to action in our foreign as in our domestic policy does not always assert itself at the right time, that a manly chord only seldom still sounds, has unfortunately spread to the widest circles of our population."[119]

It quickly became apparent to Kiderlen that his tactic of 'letting all the dogs bark' had backfired. If the League's initial agitation was helpful in making him seem moderate in the face of boisterous demands, once England entered the picture and the prospect of war became real, it immediately proved itself a serious liability in his attempts at a peaceful solution. In a conversation with naval officials, Kiderlen pointed out that "one could certainly not go to war over Morocco; we have absolutely no interests in Morocco; surely Bismarck would have said we want no window on the Mediterranean which one can smash on us."[120] Clearly, though, this moderate Bismarck did not correspond to the model of the radical nationalists. After reading an article which complained that Germany lacked Bismarck, Kiderlen noted in his diary that he agreed. The authority of a Bismarck was lacking. However, it was not lacking "in order to put through a daring policy, but rather to support the principles of moderation and caution firmly laid by him in the face of an increasingly reckless public opinion."[121]

In the end, the government suffered intense criticism as Bethmann attempted to defend his and Kiderlen's actions. The reaction to the Chancellor's explanations in the Reichstag was cold, if not hostile. Of particular interest was Conservative Party leader Ernst von Heydebrand. He followed the Chancellor at the podium and delivered a stinging rebuke of the government's actions. Bethmann's 'yielding' policy would not guarantee peace – "only our good German sword can do that."[122]

The speech clearly reflected a change of attitude among the party leadership. In taking a stand which, as James Retallack has noted, "rivaled what Pan-German agitators had been saying for years," Heydebrand acknowledged the legitimacy of the national opposition and its potential as a desirable and effective strategy. Clearly, the radical nationalist message was spreading to more of those who were inclined to the Bismarckian ideal, some of whom carried significant political weight. The implications for the regime were becoming increasingly clear. The liberal *Vossische Zeitung* provided an indication of where the government stood in the struggle to define the national symbols when it noted that even "the call [by Bethmann] to Bismarck's expressions against preventive war made no impression at all."[123]

The war scare that resulted from Kiderlen's Moroccan adventure brought home once again to Germans their utter isolation. Surrounded by enemies in the midst of large rearmament programs, radical nationalists turned their attention back to the continent and the likelihood of war in the near future. The call for increased expenditures on the army, neglected for so long in favor of the navy, went out from the Pan-Germans, and an organization that formed as a result of the League's direct inspiration and effort. Emerging as it did, from the womb of Germany's most important radical nationalist organization, the German Army League was imbued with a similar spirit of national opposition to the government and fanatical devotion to Bismarck.[124] Already schooled in the gospel and language of the Cult, the League made sure to participate in its central activities, as, for example, when Eduard von Liebert spoke at a birthday celebration sponsored by Diederich Hahn's *Berlin Bismarckkommers* in 1912. There he spoke of "how the generation of the epigones, out of which the right leader does not want to arise, calls for the savior from crisis according to the name Bismarck."[125] But history does not repeat itself. They must instead be satisfied with the reflection of Bismarck's star down upon them. "We must seek to permeate this splendor, to warm ourselves upon it and arouse our national feeling until finally the time comes when again genuine Bismarckian spirit guides the rudder."[126] Liebert ended his speech with an even more explicit appeal, declaring that "the call arises from the soul of our people: Bismarck, descend from Walhalla, or send us . . . the strong man, whom we need! Help your people, Bismarck, Bismarck, Bismarck!"[127]

It should come as no surprise, then, that in justifying their demands the Iron Chancellor played a prominent role. Advocates of military increases contrasted Bismarck's quick, decisive, and forceful efforts for a strengthening of the army with the seemingly slow and unsure moves by the current regime.[128] For the Army League, Bismarck's connection to the army and to military values was obvious.[129] This renewed emphasis on the needs of the army was part of a larger trend in nationalist opinion towards the growing possibility and necessity of preventive war. Towards the end of 1912 Friedrich von Bernhardi's *Germany and the Next War* explicitly called for Germans to be prepared for the inevitable necessity of war to achieve the nation's world political goals. Bethmann rejected Bernhardi's views when he wrote: "In no case has the honor and dignity of Germany been violated by another nation. Who desires war without such cause must do so for vital interests that cannot be reached without war," as the Iron Chancellor's goals had been in 1864, 1866, and 1870.[130] "Bismarck drastically condemned any prestige policy as un-German. He and we have seen where it leads with Napoleon III."[131]

Bethmann sought to confront the radical nationalist challenge with a moderate form of imperialism. It is important to remember, though, that the Chancellor and his liberal imperialist allies all shared the fundamental belief in Germany's natural right to expand, and in some cases their ideas sounded remarkably similar to those of their Pan-German opponents.[132] They differed mainly in degree and felt that the best way to expand was through cooperation, not confrontation, with Britain. The journalist Hans Plehn had spelled out such an approach in his 1913 pamphlet *German World Policy and No War*, but the reaction it received indicated the strength of the tide against which Bethmann had to fight. The *Deutsche Volkswirtschaftliche Correspondent*, representing heavy industry, "recalled the traditions of Bismarckian policy and demanded an 'offensive policy'," while National Liberal Ernst Bassermann condemned it as a "silly book of weary resignation."[133] The Pan-German journalist Franz Sontag attacked the concept of liberal imperialism as weakness, writing: "Now as before we believe in the liberating deed of a single man, in the victorious genius of that statesman who will once again lead his German people to such heights as when Otto the Unique's mighty genius raised it to a Great Power."[134] With his foreign policy under constant attack, Bethmann also found himself under increasing pressure thanks to another trend that made German nationalists shudder.

Increasing democratization in general, and the rising strength of the Social Democratic Party in particular, marked two of the most important political trends of the Wilhelmine Empire, and for German nationalists one of the nation's gravest dangers. Having served as one of Bismarck's most hated enemies, the Socialists continued to inspire fear and distrust among nationally minded Germans. This fear, as well as their exclusion from the national community, was perhaps one of the Iron Chancellor's most enduring legacies. In 1912 the Socialist danger rose to new heights as elections produced a dramatic victory for the SPD, in which it garnered nearly one-third of the vote and captured 110 seats, making it the largest party in parliament. The three parties of the Right, meanwhile, suffered dramatic losses. The German-national community was stunned. Fear and pessimism spread throughout its ranks, as did the conviction that decisive action was needed.

In large part, this sense of crisis found expression in attacks on the government for its weak and indecisive posture in confronting the Socialist threat. The spread of democracy at this time was a Western phenomenon, not limited to Germany. But for those imbued with the Bismarckian gospel, the current crisis was just further evidence of the nation's fall since 1890.[135] Democracy grew, the Conservatives declared, because "no new Bismarck knows how to control it."[136] Were the Iron Chancellor still in office, he would certainly take care of the situation. Reviving the spirit of Bismarck would thus solve one of the Empire's biggest problems. A Bismarckian strong man seemed the best hope. "When will the statesman come, who will once again place the bridle and the leash on the spreading democratic tendencies of the age?"[137]

If nobody knew just when that new leader would come, one man had a rather clear idea of just what he should do. In 1912, writing under the pseudonym Daniel Frymann, Heinrich Class published *Wenn ich der Kaiser wär'* [*If I were the Kaiser*] – the most extreme expression of right-wing populism in pre-war Germany. Intensifying the line of argument he had been following from Plauen through Leipzig, Class addressed what he saw as the needs of a nation in crisis. The problem was a government incapable of providing leadership. This was a time generally felt to be one of transition. In such times, "a strong leader is necessary, who forces the step towards recovery, to inner and outer consolidation, which will hinder the development towards ruin."[138] The entire country was dissatisfied with the political leadership – a result, he wrote, "that would be unthinkable without the worst mistakes of the government, and which alone already contains within it a horrible indictment, if one sets against it the enthusiasm that greeted the newly founded Reich or also just the mood that Bismarck's struggle for the Septenat in early 1887 called forth."[139] Class' criticism of the German leadership extended to foreign policy as he made his clearest and most forceful calls yet for expansion. He claimed that a transformation had taken place in German public opinion regarding the need for expansion. That misunderstood concept of German 'Saturiertheit' no longer held. "Development and necessity show that we have again become hungry, hungry for land, and therefore the tasks of German statecraft are set to go beyond Bismarck."[140] Class credited the start of this shift to the Pan-Germans – "this transformation was thought through and completed first and most decisively by the circles that had been Bismarck's truest followers – after his dismissal and after his death."[141] They had avoided the critical mistake made by the government, which had turned Bismarck's words – in this case, his concept of 'Saturiertheit' – into a school of thought and a basis for action. For his *true* followers, however, "the word of the master had never bound them; his spirit, his attitude, his will and his essence was and is what provides direction."[142] The product of more than two decades during which the Bismarck image shaped and guided his conception of politics, Class' *Kaiserbuch* marked the ultimate stage and most extreme expression of radical nationalist thought in the pre-war period.

These years also marked a period of crystallization for the Right as a whole – a moment in which right-wing unity seemed on the verge of realization. And as with

Class, the central element was Bismarck. If the various groups of the Right shared anything in common it was a devotion to the Iron Chancellor as an ideal against which to judge the national leadership and as a means by which to legitimize their politics. In March 1912 *Die Post* justified the Right's custodianship of the Bismarck symbol by pointing to the regime's failure to defend the national interests. That task was now left to the organizations of the national opposition. "Since the German people feel that Bismarck's primary tasks are no longer understood by the imperial government or are even fought against, it has, out of concern, joined together in great associations in order to protect and defend Bismarck's legacy."[143] Since 1908 Class and the Pan-Germans had been developing closer relations with other radical nationalist organizations, the National Liberal Party and the Free Conservatives. Meetings between Class and leading members of the Agrarian League, including Diederich Hahn and Conrad von Wangenheim, helped bridge the gap between their two organizations, while the Conservative Konstantin von Gebsattel helped bring the Pan-Germans and the German Conservative Party closer by 1913.[144]

The example most commonly cited in discussions of the Right and its potential in pre-war Germany is the so-called *Kartell der schaffenden Stände*, or Kartell of Productive Estates. The debate over its actual effectiveness and thus its overall significance has yet to be definitively settled.[145] The notion, for example, of the *Kartell* as a true manifestation of right-wing unity has been criticized in the historical scholarship, as no party of the Right officially belonged, nor did some of the most important radical nationalist groups. While this may be so, it is still quite useful in understanding the centrality of the Bismarck image and the fundamental tenets of the Bismarckian political religion to the political culture of the Wilhelmine Right. In this sense, the *Kartell* may be seen as one of the potential outcomes of Bismarckian political culture as it evolved after 1890. Both the groups directly involved in the *Kartell*'s founding meeting at Leipzig in August 1913 and those groups and individuals invited as guests shared a common devotion to the Iron Chancellor. The organization itself consisted of the Agrarian League, the Central Association of German Industrialists (CVDI), the Imperial German Mittelstand League, and the Union of Christian Peasants' Associations. Beyond that, however, Bismarckian Eduard von Liebert attended, as did representatives of the right wing of the National Liberal Party, Saxon Conservatives and National Liberals.[146] In addition, the recently established relationship between the Pan-Germans and the Agrarian League and Pan-German connections that ran deep into the leadership ranks of the CVDI meant that Germany's most important Bismarckian organization was never far from the thinking of the *Kartell*.[147]

The idea of the *Kartell* itself harkened back to Bismarck's own policies of 1879 and similar suggestions he floated while in retirement. As Geoff Eley noted: "Intimations of the past and Bismarckian allusions permeated the Leipzig proceedings."[148] Ferdinand Schweighoffer of the CVDI called upon Bismarck as the "greatest of all Germans," while a whole series of newspapers drew on the retired chancellor's contribution to the *Hamburger Nachrichten* in 1897 in favor of such an organization.[149] But there was a difference between this and earlier efforts at *Sammlung*; a difference which, rather than distancing this new entity from its Bismarckian roots, actually made it even more clearly a product of the Bismarck Cult. In pointing out the ambitious nature of its program, Roger Chickering noted, "not only did the Cartel envisage an aggressive foreign policy and the salutary effects of war as weapons in the fight against socialism, but it made no secret of its desire – in the name of patriotism – both to unseat the government of Bethmann Hollweg and to change the constitution in order to downgrade or eliminate the Reichstag."[150] This *Kartell* was to be a united force for *opposition*, not for support. It was clearly then a manifestation of the Right's continuing radicalization. It was, after all, at least in part, a product of the most radical elements of the Bismarck Cult, and as such constituted an important component of the increasingly vociferous national opposition. Left-wing National Liberal leader Ernst Bassermann saw the implications of at least the inspiration behind this new movement when he described its essential principles as "high-protection, water-tight tariffs, anti-Socialist laws, no suffrage reform in Prussia, at first an unobtrusive struggle against the national suffrage, struggle against all that is liberal, struggle against Bethmann-Delbrück, the yearning for the strong man."[151]

In the end, it seems, the question should not be whether or not the *Kartell* was a truly effective organization and thus represented true right-wing unity in Wilhelmine Germany. Throughout most of German history the Right was much too complicated a phenomenon to ever be united for long. Whether because of basic policy differences, personal animosities, or the irrational fears and delusions that arose from its paranoid style of politics, unity in any practical sense required conditions that simply did not prevail in pre-1914 Germany. The *Kartell*'s importance, and, more generally, that of the organizations of the national opposition, was the potential that had been opened for the future. Heinz Hagenlücke has noted their significance as having opened the door through which 'new men' could step on to the stage of German politics.[152] Now men like Heinrich Class and Diederich Hahn could play roles that had been all but closed to them before. Even in the decade and a half after Bismarck's dismissal, Class was still a fairly marginal figure in national politics. But with the onset of the crisis period, those years of devotion to the Cult and the cultivation of the Bismarck image had begun to bear fruit. He was now a major player – the middle-man, brokering the relations between his own organization and the political parties. The impact of the radical nationalist organizations and the *Kartell* went still beyond the details of such arrangements to a change in political style, which marked one of their most important contributions to German political culture. The populist-nationalist rhetoric that developed within the confines of the Bismarck Cult would eventually spread to all the parties of the Right. In the end, as Hagenlücke notes, they pointed to future possibilities.[153] If they did not achieve the Bismarckian dream of unity of all nationally minded Germans, they showed what might eventually be achieved, keeping that dream alive when, perhaps, more congenial circumstances would arise. For now, the importance of right-wing radicalization and the growing confidence of the national opposition lay in the rhetorical realm. That is not to say, however, that one could dismiss it as a harmless annoyance.

Whether it was from the *Kartell* or the individual groups of the national opposition, the last years of peace saw Bismarck continuing to generate pressure for Bethmann to take a decisive stand against Germany's enemies, both external and internal. Speaking before the Conservative Union and the Agrarian League in Trebnitz, DKP leader Ernst von Heydebrand combined the appeal for the maintenance of the "achievements of Bismarckian politics" domestically with the demand for a strong foreign policy.[154] The Hamburg banker Max von Schinckel told a group at the Bismarck celebration of the Hamburg Conservative Association that "when, sooner or later, the new hour of destiny strikes in which the German Empire must defend itself against domestic and foreign enemies no longer with words but rather with blood and iron, so may god at least give us again men who understand, as once Bismarck did, how to inflame the glowing spark to bright enthusiasm for Germany's power and greatness!"[155] For these men, Bethmann was clearly not such a man. In a 1913 memorandum by Gebsattel, the Pan-Germans, with the Crown Prince's support, argued for a coup that would end the years of national crisis. In sending the memorandum to the chancellor and the Kaiser, the Crown Prince enclosed a letter in which he called for a Chancellor who "fears neither death nor the devil and who takes drastic action even if it means stepping on other people's toes."[156] While Bethmann rejected Gebsattel's memorandum with a twenty-page reply in which he cited Bismarck to argue against preventive war, the Kaiser at least appeared to sympathize with certain aspects of the program. "What we lack," he wrote to his son, "are strong men with a passion to fight, and if they exist they have such serious shortcomings in other respects that they are useless for leading positions."[157]

It was against the backdrop of the pressure from the national opposition and the growing desire for a strong leader that Wilhelm continued his quest to gain national legitimacy for his own Hohenzollern dynasty. Clearly, this fight would not only be against the socialist Left, but perhaps even more so against middle-class Germans who had found a popular alternative in Bismarck.[158] The year 1913, in fact, marked the opening of a kind of "imperial offensive" for the purpose of legitimizing the monarchy before the German people.[159] Both the twenty-fifth anniversary of the Kaiser's reign and the one-hundredth anniversary of the Battle of Nations against Napoleon provided Wilhelm with the opportunity to make progress in an area that had long eluded him. In both cases, however, he proved unable to break out of his narrow vision of the nation. As before, he continued to express his nationalism in dynastic or corporative terms, relegating the people to the sidelines and the people's hero, Bismarck, to the shadows cast by Wilhelm's Hohenzollern ancestors.[160] In the end, "these celebrations reflected and indeed exacerbated the persistent dialectic between 'monarchy' and 'nation' in Wilhelmine Germany."[161]

It is in this tension, then, that one can see the attraction of the Bismarck Cult, a political religion that spoke the language and practiced the rituals of modern populist nationalism, that provided grand visions of expansion abroad and harmony at home through the establishment of the national community marching to the will of a great leader. What had begun as the expression of frustrated middle-class Germans previously shut out of the political process had evolved through persistent effort in the public sphere, and grown in intensity as a result of a substantial crisis. The cult now had the weight of legitimacy behind it. It challenged the Hohenzollern dynasty as a legitimate pole of allegiance, represented by figures now playing key roles in imperial politics. The Bismarck Cult had come a long way. But it was not finished. It had not yet achieved its goal. At the Berlin Bismarck ceremony in 1913 mentioned earlier in this chapter, Professor Ludwig Bernhardi spoke on the political culture of the Germans. "As we gather today to celebrate Bismarck, we do so in somber awareness that we still have much to expect from the dead Bismarck. We stand at the beginning of a time that should show how Bismarck will influence world history. Great men live twice! First, during their creative years on earth and, then again after death. And Bismarck, the dead Bismarck, has yet another great task to fulfill."[162] This political religion, intensified through the crisis period of Wilhelmine Germany, would reach new levels of intensity as a result of an even greater crisis that was about to engulf the nation. Bismarck did indeed have further tasks to fulfill. The outcome of a decade of war, revolution, and civil war would help determine just what those tasks would be, and how he would fulfill them.

Notes

1. William Shakespeare, *The Tragedy of Hamlet, Prince of Denmark* (Baltimore: Penguin, 1957), Act III, scene ii.
2. This story is told in Lothar Machtan, *Bismarcks Tod und Deutschlands Tränen. Reportage einer Tragödie* (Munich: Wilhelm Goldman Verlag, 1998), 70–74, 153–194.
3. See Rudy Koshar's discussion of 'framing strategies and devices' in *From Monuments to Traces: Artifacts of German Memory, 1870–1990* (Berkeley: University of California Press, 2000), 9–10.

4. Quoted in Pflanze, *Bismarck*, III, 451.

5. On political or civil religion, see Robert N. Bellah and Phillip E. Hammond, *Varieties of Civil Religion* (San Francisco: Harper & Row Publishers, 1980); David I. Kertzer, *Ritual, Politics, and Power* (New Haven: Yale University Press, 1988); Michael Ley and Julius H. Schoeps, eds., *Der National-sozialismus als politische Religion* (Bodenheim: Philo Verlagsgesellschaft mbH, 1997).

6. Pflanze, *Bismarck*, III, 428; McGuire, "Bismarck in Walhalla," 96–99.

7. Description from *National-Zeitung*, Nr. 447, August 4, 1898.

8. *National-Zeitung*, Nr. 448, August 4, 1898.

9. Ibid.

10. Descriptions from Machtan, *Bismarcks Tod*, 210–215.

11. Wildenbruch quoted in ibid., 212.

12. Fritz Ringer, *The Decline of the German Mandarins: The German Academic Community, 1890–1933* (Cambridge: Harvard University Press, 1969), 135.

13. Ibid., 139.

14. Ibid.

15. Wilhelm Kahl, *Bismarck lebt. Gedächtnisrede bei der allgemeinen Trauerfeier in Berlin am 7. August 1898* (Freiburg i. B.: Verlag von J. C. B. Mohr, 1898), 7.

16. Ibid., 8.

17. Ibid., 16.

18. Ibid., 15.

19. Ibid.

20. Durkheim made clear the similarity in goals, techniques, and results between traditional religious ceremony and that of a social/political gathering. Durkheim, *Elementary Forms*, 429.

21. Fritz Schellack, "Sedan- und Kaisergeburtstagsfeste," in Dieter Düding, Peter Friedemann, Paul Münch, eds., *Öffentliche Festkultur: Politische Feste in Deutschland von der Aufklärung bis zum Ersten Weltkrieg* (Hamburg: Rowohlt, 1988), 286–288.

22. Ibid.

23. At the centennial celebration of Wilhelm I's birth, Wilhelm II did not mention Bismarck once. Pflanze, *Bismarck*, III, 425. Interestingly, both Lamar Cecil and Christopher Clark note Bismarck's influence on the young Kaiser's politics. In terms of style, Clark sees Wilhelm as an example of Max Weber's prototype of those who respected the violence and brutality of Bismarck's methods. Clark, *Kaiser Wilhelm II*, 49–51; Cecil, *Wilhelm II*, 207–208.

24. John C. G. Röhl, "The emperor's new clothes: a character sketch of Kaiser Wilhelm II," in John C. G. Röhl and Nicolaus Sombart, eds., *Kaiser Wilhelm*

II: New Interpretations, the Corfu Papers (Cambridge: Cambridge University Press, 1982), 37.

25. Ibid.

26. Monts quoted in ibid.

27. Elisabeth Fehrenbach, "Images of Kaiserdom: German attitudes to Kaiser Wilhelm II," in Röhl and Sombart, eds., *Kaiser Wilhelm II: New Interpretations*, 282.

28. Quoted in Iris Hamel, *Völkischer Verband und nationale Gewerkschaft: Der Deutschnationale Handlungsgehilfen-Verband, 1893–1933* (Frankfurt: Europäische Verlagsanstalt, 1967), 84.

29. Fehrenbach, "Images of Kaiserdom," 283.

30. Mosse, *Nationalization*, 89–90.

31. Schellack, "Sedan- und Kaisergeburtstagsfeste," 286; Mosse, *Nationalization*, 90–93; Max Baeumer, "Imperial Germany as reflected in its mass festivals," in Volker Dürr, Kathy Harms, Peter Hayes, eds., *Imperial Germany* (Madison: University of Wisconsin Press, 1985), 66.

32. Wilhelm Hoppe quoted in Hamel, *Völkischer Verband*, 85.

33. Student declaration quoted in Pflanze, *Bismarck*, III, 448.

34. Ibid.

35. Thomas Nipperdey, "Nationalidee und Nationaldenkmal in Deutschland im 19. Jahrhundert," in Nipperdey, *Gesellschaft, Kultur, Theorie: Gesammelte Aufsätze zur neueren Geschichte* (Göttingen: Vandenhoeck & Ruprecht, 1976), 169.

36. BAL, Reichslandbund Pressearchiv (cited hereafter as RlbPa), R8034 II, 7087, #27: *Staatsbürger Zeitung*, Nr. 352, July 30, 1899. See also, *Bismarck-Bund*, Nr. 7/8, July/August 1909, 123–125; *Bismarck-Bund*, Nr. 9, September 1910, 133.

37. BAL, RlbPa, R8034 II, 7088, #83: *Dresdener Nachrichten*, Nr. 91, April 1, 1903; for other descriptions of Friedrichsruh as a holy site/place of pilgrimage, see *Allgemeine Zeitung*, Nr. 210, August 1, 1898; BAL, RlbPa, R8034 II, 7087, #22: *Staatsbürger Zeitung*, Nr. 350, July 29, 1899; BAL, RlbPa, R8034 II, 7089, #11: *Dresdener Nachrichten*, Nr. 240, August 30, 1903.

38. From ceremony of the German National Commercial Employees Union at the Hamburg monument, April 1, 1912. BAL, RlbPa, R8034 II, 7093, #39: *Hamburger Nachrichten*, Nr. 156, April 2, 1912.

39. Nipperdey, "Nationalidee und Nationaldenkmal," 170.

40. See Mosse, *Nationalization*, 36; Hans-Walter Hedinger, "Bismarck-Denkmäler und Bismarck Verehrung," in Ekkehard Mai und Stephan Waetzoldt, eds., *Kunstverwaltung, Bau- und Denkmal-Politik im Kaiserreich* (Berlin: Gebr. Mann Verlag, 1981), 281.

41. Ibid., 282.
42. McGuire, "Bismarck in Walhalla," 104–105.
43. Durkheim, *Elementary Forms*, 211–212.
44. Wilhelm Hoppe quoted in Hamel, *Völkischer Verband*, 85; see also BAL, RlbPa, R8034 II, 7093, #39: *Hamburger Nachrichten*, Nr. 156, April 2, 1912.
45. Ernst Cassirer wrote that the person participating in ritual "lives a life of emotion, not of thoughts." In David Kertzer, *Ritual, Politics, and Power*, 67.
46. Hugenberg at a Bismarck celebration in Posen, April 12, 1902, in Hugenberg, *Streiflichter aus Vergangenheit und Gegenwart*, 275.
47. Ibid.
48. These quotes were reported in *Germania*, Nr. 178, August 7, 1898, Drittes Blatt.
49. For an early, general discussion of the religious elements of the Bismarck Cult, see Hans-Walter Hedinger, "Der Bismarck-Kult. Ein Umriß," in Gunther Stephenson, ed., *Der Religionswandel unserer Zeit im Spiegel der Religionswissenschaft* (Darmstadt: Wissentschaftliche Buchgesellschaft, 1976), 201–215.
50. Hedinger, "Bismarck-Denkmäler und Bismarck Verehrung," 282.
51. ADB, March 22, 1902.
52. Kahl, 9.
53. Ibid.
54. BAL, RlbPa, R8034 II, 7085, #57: *Hamburgischer Correspondent*, Nr. 364, August 6, 1898, Abend-Ausgabe.
55. BAL, RlbPa, R8034 II, 7085, #10: *Staatsbürger Zeitung*, Sonder-Ausgabe, August 1, 1898.
56. ADB, July 30, 1899.
57. BAL, RlbPa, R8034 II, 7091, #20: *Der Reichsbote*, Nr. 61, July 29, 1908.
58. ADB, July 30, 1899.
59. Ibid.
60. Ibid.
61. Ibid.
62. Ibid.
63. BAL, RlbPa, R8034 II, 7085, #42: *Korrespondenz des Bundes der Landwirte*, Nr. 44, August 3, 1898.
64. Ibid.
65. BAL, RlbPa, R8034 II, 7085, #13: *Deutsche Tageszeitung*, Nr. 354, August 1, 1898.
66. *Korrespondenz des Bundes der Landwirte*, August 3, 1898.
67. BAL, Akten der Reichskanzlei, Bismarck, R43I/2828/168–169: *Die Ostmark: Monatsblatt des Vereins zur Förderung des Deutschtums in den Ostmark*, Nr. 8, August 1898.

68. Ibid.

69. Ibid.

70. BA Koblenz, NL 1024, Nachlass Bismarck, A73/792: *Hamburger Nachrichten*, Nr. 204, August 31, 1899.

71. *Stenographische Berichte über die Verhandlungen des deutschen Reichstags*, Vol. 169, December 12, 1900, 474.

72. Ibid.

73. Ibid., 475.

74. Class, *Wider den Strom*, 60.

75. Bülow's speech in the *Frankfurter Zeitung*, Nr. 166, June 17, 1901, Abend-Ausgabe.

76. Ibid.

77. Ibid.

78. Ibid.

79. Ibid.

80. Ibid.

81. Diederich Hahn as reported in the *Frankfurter Zeitung*, Nr. 168, June 19, 1901.

82. Ibid.

83. Ibid.

84. Ibid.

85. ADB, June 22, 1901.

86. Ibid.

87. Chickering, *We Men*, 214.

88. For his preparations, see Class, *Wider den Strom*, 91–96.

89. Heinrich Class, "Wandlungen in der Weltstellung des deutschen Reichs seit dem Jahre 1890," delivered at a League meeting in Plauen, September 11, 1903. In Alldentscher Verband, *Zwanzig Jahre alldeutscher Arbeit und Kämpfe* (Leipzig: Dieterich'sche Verlagsbuchhandlung, 1910), 187.

90. Ibid., 188.

91. Ibid.

92. Ibid.

93. Ibid.

94. Ibid., 188–189.

95. Ibid., 189.

96. Ibid.

97. Ibid.

98. Class, *Wider den Strom*, 93.

99. bid.; Chickering, *We Men*, 216.

100. Ibid., 216–217.

101. Heinrich Class, at Pan-German congress, Dresden, September 1–2, 1906, in *Zwanzig Jahre*, 284.

102. Ibid., 286.

103. Ibid.

104. Ibid., 287.

105. Ibid.

106. Ibid.

107. *Stenographische Berichte*, vol. 218, November 14, 1906, 3625.

108. Ibid.

109. *Jugend* quoted in Machtan, „Bismarck und der deutsche National-Mythos," fn. 34.

110. Ibid.

111. Bismarck was one of Harden's main sources for this information. Helmuth Rogge, *Holstein und Harden: Politisch-publizistisches Zusammenspiel zweier Außenseiter des Wilhelminischen Reichs* (Munich: C. H. Beck Verlag, 1959), 171.

112. *Münchener Neueste Nachrichten*, Nr. 352, July 30, 1908.

113. For the Harden–Eulenburg scandal, see Isabel Hull, *The Entourage of Kaiser Wilhelm II, 1888–1918* (Cambridge: Cambridge University Press, 1982), 109–145; for the *Daily Telegraph* affair, see Lerman, *The Chancellor as Courtier* (Cambridge: CUP, 1990), 221–227; Terence F. Cole, "The *Daily Telegraph* Affair and Its Aftermath: the Kaiser, Bülow and the Reichstag, 1908–1909," in John C. G. Röhl and Nicolaus Sombart, eds., *Kaiser Wilhelm II: New Interpretations* (Cambridge: Cambridge University Press, 1982), 249–268.

114. Heinrich Class, "Zusammenbruch der reichsdeutschen Politik und seine Folgen," in *Zwanzig Jahre alldeutscher Arbeit und Kämpfe*, 390–395.

115. Ibid., 396–397.

116. Ibid., 397.

117. Bethmann quoted in Konrad Jarausch, *The Enigmatic Chancellor: Bethmann Hollweg and the Hubris of Imperial Germany* (New Haven: Yale University Press, 1973), 66–68.

118. BAL, RlbPa, R8034 II, 7092, #32b: *Hamburger Nachrichten*, Nr. 133, March 20, 1910.

119. Schweighoffer in July 1911, quoted in Klaus Wernecke, *Der Wille zur Weltgeltung. Außenpolitik und Öffentlichkeit im Kaiserreich am Vorabend des Ersten Weltkrieges* (Düsseldorf: Droste Verlag, 1970), 111.

120. Johannes Lepsius, Albrecht Mendelsson Bartholdy, Friedrich Thimme, eds., *Die Große Politik der Europäischen Kabinette*, XXIX (Berlin: Deutsche Verlagsgesellschaft für Politik und Geschichte, 1922–1927), 318; conversation recorded by Admiral von Tirpitz in his diary.

121. Quoted in Ernst Jäckh, ed., *Kiderlen-Wächter. Der Staatsmann und Mensch, Briefwechsel und Nachlaß*, II (Stuttgart: Deutsche Verlags-Anstalt, 1924), 162.

122. Heydebrand in the Reichstag, November 9, 1911, quoted in Retallack, *Notables*, 209.

123. *Vossische Zeitung* quoted in Wernecke, *Der Wille zur Weltgeltung*, 115.

124. Founding member Karl Litzmann asserted: "We are all sworn devotees of Bismarck." Quoted in Marilyn Shevin Coetzee, *The German Army League: Popular Nationalism in Wilhelmine Germany* (New York: Oxford University Press, 1990), 87.

125. Eduard von Liebert, *Fürst Bismarck und die Armee. Vortrag beim Bismarckkommers in der Philharmonie am 30. März 1912* (Berlin: Ernst Siegfried Mittler und Sohn, 1912), 3.

126. Ibid.

127. Ibid., 15.

128. See, for example, BAL, RlbPa, R8034 II, 7093, #34–35: *Die Post*, Nr. 154, March 31, 1912; also BAL, RlbPa, R8034II, 7093, #30–31: *Berliner Neueste Nachrichten*, Nr. 168, April 1, 1912.

129. Liebert, *Fürst Bismarck und die Armee*, 4.

130. Bethmann quoted in Jarausch, *Enigmatic Chancellor*, 146.

131. Ibid.

132. Fritz Fischer, *War of Illusions: German Policies from 1911 to 1914*, translated by Marian Jackson (New York: W. W. Norton & Company, 1975), 263.

133. *Deutsche Volkswirtschaftliche Correspondent* and Bassermann quoted in Fischer, *War of Illusions*, 267. See also Jonathan Wright, *Gustav Stresemann: Weimar's Greatest Statesman* (New York: Oxford University Press, 2002), 56–57.

134. Sontag quoted in Jarausch, *Enigmatic Chancellor*, 144.

135. Gustav Buchholz, *Bismarck und wir: Betrachtungen an seinem 99. Geburtstage* (Leipzig: Dieterich'sche Verlagsbuchhandlung, 1914), 7.

136. *Kreuzzeitung*, Nr. 152, March 31, 1914, Abend-Ausgabe.

137. Gustav Buchholz, *Bismarck und wir*, 8.

138. Daniel Frymann (pseud. Heinrich Class), *Wenn ich der Kaiser wär' – Politische Wahrheiten und Notwendigkeiten* (Leipzig: Dieterich'sche Verlagsbuchhandlung, 1912), viii.

139. Ibid., 4.

140. Ibid., 9.

141. Ibid.

142. Ibid.

143. BAL, RlbPa, R8034 II, 7093, #35: *Die Post*, Nr. 154, March 31, 1912.

144. Retallack, *Notables*, 213–214; for the meeting between Class and the BdL, see Class, *Wider den Strom*, 271–273.

145. See Stegmann, *Die Erben Bismarcks*, 352–448; Retallack, *Notables*, 214–215; Geoff Eley, *Reshaping*, 316–334; Heinz Hagenlücke, *Deutsche*

Vaterlandspartei: Die nationale Rechte am Ende des Kaiserreichs (Düsseldorf: Droste Verlag, 1997), 40–48.

146. Eley, *Reshaping*, 317.
147. Ibid., 320; Chickering, *We Men*, 282–285.
148. Eley, *Reshaping*, 318.
149. Ibid.
150. Chickering, *We Men*, 283.
151. Bassermann, quoted in Eley, *Reshaping*, 318.
152. Hagenlücke, *Deutsche Vaterlandspartei*, 47.
153. Ibid.
154. Dirk Stegmann, *Die Erben Bismarcks*, 447.
155. Max von Schinkel quoted in ibid., 447.
156. Crown Prince quoted in Fischer, *War of Illusions*, 284.
157. Wilhelm II quoted in ibid., 284.
158. Jeffrey Smith, "The Monarchy versus the Nation: the 'Festive Year' 1913 in Wilhelmine Germany," *German Studies Review* XXIII (May 2000): 259.
159. Ibid., 257.
160. Ibid.
161. Ibid., 266.
162. Bernhardi quoted in Pflanze, *Bismarck*, III, 451.

–3–

Bismarck in the Crisis Decade, 1914–1923

> The simplest person hopes that a revolution will dethrone. Our revolution left in sacred glory all the idols that did not run away.
>
> Maximilian Harden, *Die Zukunft*, 1918[1]

In December 1923 Captain Felix von Woldeck von Arneburg unveiled to former Grand Admiral Alfred von Tirpitz a plan to overthrow the Weimar Republic. It called for Army Chief of Staff Hans von Seeckt to force President Ebert's resignation and appoint a dictator. After reading a 'Christmas message' on December 24, the new leader would proceed to the Berlin Bismarck monument, where he would throw the Versailles Treaty into a fire. Throughout Berlin church bells would peal, military units would go on parade, and patriotic youth would hold torch-light processions. On Christmas Day this would be repeated before the Bismarck monument of every German town.[2] While Woldeck's plan never materialized, coming at the tail end of a period of dramatic instability, it does shed light on Bismarck's continuing centrality in radical nationalist thinking. It is no coincidence that the destination of the putschists was the Bismarck monument, both in Berlin and across Germany. Thanks to the growing Bismarck Cult such locations had already been invested with mystical, quasi-religious qualities for decades.

Waldeck's plan also points to a new role for the Bismarck image in German political culture. The years from 1914 to 1923 marked a decade of crisis longer and more intense than anything the nation had yet experienced. August 1914 saw the Reich begin a four-year struggle against a world of enemies. In the heady atmosphere of the 'August days' Bismarck helped unite the nation as one of the key components of the 'spirit of 1914'. However genuine this spirit of national community was, it would soon break down as fatigue and frustration set in over a war that seemed to promise no end, but only ever-rising casualties. As Germans diverged over a variety of issues, Bismarck re-entered the political fray and found a role on both sides of the debates. The tension involved in this struggle over such a critical national symbol would once again contribute to the Right's further radicalization and a new expression of right-wing unity: the Fatherland Party. With Germany's defeat in 1918, an opportunity emerged for the nation to set out on a new path. Could the Weimar Coalition get beyond Bismarck and establish a new democratic political culture? If so, it would have to accomplish the feat during an initial period of intense instability and turmoil that would leave deep scars on the political land-scape. This civil war was a critical time for the fledgling regime, seeking to estab-lish its legitimacy in the face of crises as perplexing as those that ultimately felled the system in the early 1930s.

The challenge would be even greater than that faced by the imperial government before 1914. Thanks to this tumultuous decade, the crisis of leadership would reach its ultimate expression. Whereas earlier the leaders were attacked but the foundation of authority was questioned by very few, now it was both the leaders and the foundation upon which they based their authority that growing segments of the population called into question. After all, the Bismarckians, who saw them-selves as the traditional upholders of the German national idea, now found them-selves on the outside while Bismarck's enemies, the *Reichsfeinde*, were in control. The trauma of these changes helped transform Bismarck into a revolutionary anti-system figure. The crisis decade would help the Cult grow in intensity as its rituals, values, and mission were given new meaning. With years of established practice behind them, its followers now went into combat against a new system struggling to define itself. While Weimar's supporters sought to move forward into a new world of democracy and reconciliation, Bismarckians sought to move in another direction, towards authoritarianism and power politics.

Germany's 'Holy War': The Bismarck Cult and the Spirit of 1914

Three weeks after the start of the war, the *Tägliche Rundschau* wrote that "the great times of heroes, which had almost become a legend, have returned. So, too, did our sons and brothers march off into the holy war."[3] The Pan-Germans wel-comed the war, confident that such terrible challenges would bring "deliverance and blessing."[4] The choice of words here was not coincidental, nor should it come as a surprise. As Jeffrey Verhey points out, the collective memory of the 'spirit of 1914' was an historical myth developed primarily by Germany's middle-class nationalists.[5] If the experience of the August Days was not one of general 'war enthusiasm', those who did participate in the patriotic processions tended to be students and members of Germany's 'better society' – groups most closely associ-ated with the Bismarck Cult.[6] Not surprisingly, then, the crowds typically ended up at the Berlin Bismarck monument and the chancellor's office, where they sought to inspire the current occupant with memories of his glorious predecessor. It was here on July 25 that a high school teacher expressed the hope "that Bethmann Hollweg will show himself worthy of Bismarck."[7] Developing for more than a decade among Germany's middle classes, the Bismarck Cult had now found a new application. Inspired by their political god, these Germans viewed the con-flict as a kind of holy war, fought in defense of the Bismarckian Empire, of the values for which it stood and for which the Iron Chancellor fought throughout his career. If the 'spirit of 1914' was only a myth, it was a powerful one for this segment of society, for it developed into a vision of the fulfillment of Bismarckian prophecy. And Germany's academics continued their role front and center as they greeted the war enthusiastically.[8] Only one year later Professor Gustav Roethe declared that the Iron Chancellor achieved his greatest victory "in that wonderful hour of the German national spring, where the outbreak of war found all of Germany as one in the iron will of indissoluble unity to engage itself for the longevity and greatness of the Reich."[9] While certainly an exaggeration, Bismarck would play a critical role throughout the war for at least one group of Germans. Those steeped for years in the Bismarckian political religion entered the war with a clear understanding of why it erupted, what its purpose was, and how it had to end.

The war fitted well into the Bismarckian world-view. One of the most important lessons of the founding period was the positive value of military solutions to crises. After all, didn't Bismarck solve the Prussian constitutional crisis through three successful wars? And didn't those wars also have the salutary effect of ending the German national trauma of statelessness? Now a new generation of Germans found a new war forced upon them – a war clearly tied to their idol. According to popular understanding, the conflict resulted from the unjustified attack of Russia, supported by a vengeful France and a traitorous England. This was a war of jealousy – the countries encircling Germany envied its stature. As a result, these countries now sought to destroy what Bismarck had created. The war was therefore a fight for Germany's very existence, which, for Bismarckians, meant a fight for the Iron Chancellor's legacy. Professor Dr. Adolf Deißmann of the University of Berlin declared that "the battle that we fight is, because it is a battle for Germany, a battle for the creator of Germany. The world war is a battle for Bismarck."[10] And just like the legendary days of Bismarck, here again war would prove therapeutic. The Wilhelmine crisis period would end just as the constitutional crisis had ended. Germany would grow in size and strength just as Prussia/Germany did after the wars of unification. The war thus provided the opportunity for redemption through Bismarck by conducting the war in his spirit. If this was done, a "new, more powerful Germany, greater than the Germany of Prince Bismarck, will rise on the horizon ... Also this time, as in the years 1870/71, a new, glorious time for our fatherland will arise out of a bloody seed."[11]

The idea of Germans coming together to defend Bismarck's creation provided a powerful affirmation of the faith his followers had placed in him for years. Bismarckians' hopes seemed to have become reality – as they saw it, the nation had come together under the banner of the first chancellor. This became the Right's collective memory of the August Days, and what followed they interpreted through the lens of their political religion. General Superintendant D. Klingemann from Coblenz announced that a legacy of the Bismarck spirit had now arrived in the form of "the entire German nation that fights in holy determination."[12] For Bismarck and his creation, the people were to sacrifice all. "To live is nothing, but to live for the Fatherland and to serve it – that is great, that is German, that is Bismarckian."[13]

In most countries, the war had a particular meaning and sense of mission. For Germany, this involved spreading the 'ideas of 1914', which proclaimed German culture superior to both the unbridled individualism and materialism of the West and the bald despotism of the East.[14] Developed at the outset by the majority of Germany's intellectual elite – the high-priests of the Bismarck Cult – this almost religious faith in the nation's ideals tied in neatly with the Cult.[15] After all, whether it was the mix of authoritarian and democratic features, militaristic values, or attempts to solve social issues from the top down, the 'ideas of 1914' owed much to Bismarck's legacy. To give one example, Pan-German Professor Berthold Litzmann spoke of the 'spirit of militarism', "which through Bismarck flowed in our blood and became iron, that does not stand in contrast to the *Bürgertum*, but rather draws its nourishment from the consciousness of duty of the citizen, with which it was raised, and that has given us the duty and the right as a world power to follow our peaceful paths over the entire planet, to engage our national personality in peaceful world struggle everywhere, and, when it has to, to put it through with blood and iron."[16] And just as Bismarckians before the war looked to a new age when the 'spirit of Bismarck' would animate the nation and direct it to its destiny of world power, they now embraced the 'ideas of 1914' and saw the war as the opportunity to spread them around the world.[17]

The bond between the 'spirit of 1914' and the 'spirit of Bismarck' became clearer than ever in April 1915 when Germany celebrated the Iron Chancellor's one hundredth birthday. Bismarckians had been anticipating this date for years. They hoped for massive demonstrations of devotion and planned for the building of a national Bismarck monument on the cliffs overlooking the Rhine at Bingen. No one anticipated that the anniversary would coincide with a war. In the end, the monument was never built. That did not mean, however, that Germans failed to pay tribute to their hero. For many, the war itself, and the anticipated victory, would serve as the most proper Bismarck celebration. "So will the current world war, and the spirit in which it is led on our side, truly become a single, magnificent homage for our Bismarck, certainly not with joyous words, but rather with victorious action. We all feel it and know it: the German people's true Bismarck celebration will be Germany's victory."[18] While the heady optimism of the August Days steadily declined in the face of an increasingly bloody war, many thousands of Germans turned to Bismarck for leadership, guidance, inspiration, and hope. They did so by attending ceremonies held across the country, reading the numerous tribute articles and special editions of newspapers, or buying one of the hundreds of thousands of commemorative publications.[19]

As with the crisis situation of 1908, the occurrence of the Iron Chancellor's one hundredth birthday in the midst of a world war also resulted in an intensification of Bismarck idolatry. The *Reichsgründer* now stood at the height of his symbolic power. Gustav Stresemann declared that "[h]is stature already grows without limit. We see him before our eyes superhumanly large, as Roland and Siegfried combined."[20] To Professor Georg Bülow he was "a titan . . . a superman, like a people, indeed the whole of humanity only rarely brings forth."[21] The ceremonies of 1915 gave Germans the opportunity to signal their devotion to this superman who once led their fathers into battle for German unity.

The crisis situation to which the war gave rise and the resulting intensification of Bismarck hero-worship also led his followers to see in him the hope for the future. They called to his spirit to protect and guide them through the difficulties ahead and to a bright future. Bismarck historian Erich Marcks declared that "[h]e is with us, just like he was and how he lives on in our people, as power, as spirit, as flame that burns within us, as strength that breathes in us, that works for us and builds, that lives with us and through us, beyond his earthly days, far beyond our earthly days."[22] If Bismarckians could take comfort in his spiritual presence, the gospel also provided for more tangible hopes – for example, a new leader. The *Hamburger Nachrichten* expressed the wish that, after a German victory, God would give them, "if not again a genius, then still a man of great thoughts and pure heart, who will show the way out of the strife of the parties right to the midst of joyful, patriotic community! Then the dead Bismarck will live again for us."[23] If the Cult assured its followers that Bismarck's spirit watched over and protected Germany, it also provided a vision of how the war should be prosecuted and how it should end.

That vision provided by the Bismarckian gospel fitted well with the general understanding and expectations of Germany's annexationists. Just as the Pan-Germans had welcomed the outbreak of the war with a kind of spiritual exuberance, Heinrich Class also viewed the end in quasi-religious terms. With a vision of iron-hard politics and a dream of redemption in mind, Class announced what the Germans should bring back as "Siegebeute" after the conflict: "the outer security and the inner rebirth of our people."[24] To achieve victory and a 'German peace', Wolfgang Eishenhart declared that the nation again needed "to practice German politics with Bismarckian spirit. Today is the time to strike down our enemies with the full weight of Bismarckian state-craft and to break their power for the duration. Today our government, our whole nation, should hurl our enemies to the ground again with the firm strength of will of a Bismarck and at their expense erect the greater, more glorious, stronger German Reich, which, in extent and power, goes beyond the creation of our first statesman."[25] So despite the fact, then, that this was a defensive war, the nation's mission seemed to dictate that their goals must go beyond mere defense. Bismarck's inspiration translated into an increasingly firm and unyielding stance regarding the need for extensive annexations.

This had implications beyond the confines of the Cult, for war aims would prove one of the central political issues of the war. It was not yet, however, the *divisive* issue it would eventually become. At this point, the unity of purpose felt by most Germans in defending the nation shifted to one of unbounded confidence and a desire for aggrandizement as the army swept through Belgium and France in the west and into Russia in the east.[26] Whatever discussion there was at this point involved mainly the *extent* of German conquest. That there would *be* conquest was a given.[27]

One sees this clearly in the case of Bethmann Hollweg soon after the outbreak of war. Even the Chancellor could not avoid the fever that gripped so many Germans. He, too, had visions of a victorious Germany emerging dramatically strengthened through the annexation or indirect domination of large swaths of European territory and extensive colonial acquisitions. The broad outlines of Bethmann's chilling vision became clear through his September Program, drawn up in the face of an apparent German victory. With the defeat at the Marne, however, he pulled back, hoping to avoid commitment to any annexationist program while the war's outcome remained in doubt. So while he did not surrender his dreams of a greater Germany, he did resist the danger of showing his hand too early. There still remained the problem, though, of vocal nationalists showing *their* hand. Stifling those voices risked the appearance of insufficient devotion to the national cause. It was a dangerous balancing act and, despite the dearth of tangible political benefits, Bethmann tried to sustain it, hoping for a strong victory while restraining the hubris of the nationalists. In the hopes, then, of maintaining the domestic peace and the perception of fighting a defensive war, he sought to control public discussion of war aims, passing press guidelines forbidding criticism of the government, thus prohibiting public discussion of war aims. By 1916, however, those regulations were proving ineffective, and they were lifted before the year was out.

Still, even during the war's early phase, when government censorship and a general desire not to disrupt the tenuous domestic peace meant that explicit discussion of war aims did not easily find its way into the public discourse, possibilities for airing one's views did exist. The rituals of the Bismarck Cult, in particular, provided just such a forum. In the speeches and tributes to the Iron Chancellor during his hundredth birthday celebrations and after, Germans took the opportunity to speak out and in Bismarck's name put forward their own visions of a future, enlarged Empire. Here was a space, then, provided by their political religion, in which they could not only dream of the German future, but also, if the situation called for it, attack the government in the name of their political god.

But if the Iron Chancellor provided the inspiration for an extensive victory – a 'German Peace' – he also presented one of its biggest obstacles. A serious challenge for Bismarckians was the question of how to deal with their hero's well-known claim that Germany was 'satiated'. For the Pan-German Graf Reventlow, the issue went straight to the heart of whether or not one was properly in tune with Bismarckian politics. "We must not only understand Bismarck," Reventlow declared in 1915, "we may also not misunderstand him. And a misunderstanding allows the catch-phrase 'we are satiated' to be used so often today. We are not sati-ated in the sense that we do not desire anything, that we do not need anything. No, we want to hold firmly what we have, keep what we will need for the future. It may be now a securing of the borders or the freedom of the seas. Those are no fantastic plans."[28]

Equally important was the need to deal with Bismarck's supposed moderation during the wars of unification and, in particular, the peace he concluded with Austria in 1866. Annexationists scoffed at the notion that his peace settlements were models of moderation. Such characterizations were "legends."[29] One of the most vocal and dedicated annexationists, National Liberal Gustav Stresemann, often linked Bismarck to the goal of territorial conquest. With regard to his sup-posed moderation in 1866, Stresemann conceded that perhaps it was true. But he also stressed that such lessons did not necessarily apply to the current situation. It would be a false conclusion to draw from 1866, he said, since "with Austria it dealt with a brother nation; he would never have applied the same consideration to the current enemies."[30] Erich Marcks was even more succinct. There may well have been more than one side to Bismarck, but in the end "there is absolutely no doubt: he was the father of the great annexations, he alone."[31] Clearly then, beyond putting forward their own claims in Bismarck's name, these annexationists were justifying those claims in the face of what they perceived to be the false usage of their idol.

The "false Bismarckians" represented the few voices of reason seeking to fight back with what they knew was one of the Right's most significant symbols. One example was *Bund neues Vaterland*, a small organization consisting of pacifists from the middle classes, the aristocracy, and the intelligentsia dedicated to a quick end to the war through a peace without annexations or reparations. Beginning with a small circle of some ten members, it reached 135 by the fall of 1915. While its size proved a handicap, it did include the likes of Eduard Bernstein and Albert Einstein.[32]

In 1915 the Bund published a pamphlet entitled "What would Bismarck do?" It provided Bismarck-quotes which portrayed a moderate, realistic figure who, in the current situation, would have resisted the popular desire for annexations in favor of a 'peace of understanding'. "The image," they wrote, "that one gains by a really exhaustive study of Bismarckian foreign policy departs completely from the popular image of the Hun with cuirassier boots striding over the European stage, who ruthlessly does away with all resistance."[33] Whatever one thought of his ideas and his actions, they wrote, "one again and again wonders at the masterful moderation" of the man.[34] Still, unlike others in the war aims debate, those in the Bund were not willing to draw comparisons between Bismarck's era and the present. That did not mean, however, that they could not criticize the annexationists in Bismarck's name. The one thing they could say with complete certainty was that "[t]he greedy dreams of conquest of those politicians who swagger in the 'Post,' the 'Deutsche Tageszeitung' and other organs would not have been shared by him; he would have rejected them in the sharpest sense, and in the refreshing clarity that is peculiar to him, characterized them as they are: as the most wicked sin on the future of the German nation."[35]

The opposition that *Bund neues Vaterland* represented signified another way in which the Bismarckian political religion functioned. It provided enemies – those who would undo or destroy Bismarck's work. Clearly the Entente represented one such enemy. *Bund neues Vaterland* was another, but for different reasons. In arguing against territorial gain they exhibited a quality that Bismarckians hated and feared most: weakness. But there existed another, even more dangerous example of this problem: the government. The fear that Berlin would fail to attain a 'German', 'Bismarckian' peace, that it would prove too weak, haunted radical nationalists. Weakness – the opposite of their Bismarckian ideal – stood at the heart of their anti-government polemics and helped feed their progressive radicalization. But for them, the direst consequences of weak government leadership were not to be found solely in foreign policy, but also in domestic politics and in particular the call for democracy.

Wartime Radicalization: Leadership Crisis, Democratization, and the Emergence of the Fatherland Party

In the summer of 1918 Pan-German publicist Fritz Bley summed up the Right's frustration with Berlin when he wrote: "Surrendered are not only all healthy basics of Bismarckian tradition, but rather also all the foregone conclusions of healthy common sense. No longer shall the strength of weapons and the power of political prestige compel our enemies to peace, but rather with innumerable peace offerings one hopes to be able to lull to sleep an entire world that is part of a conspiracy aimed at the destruction of Germany."[36] For Bismarckians, that conspiracy included not just the Entente, but also those Germans promoting democracy. The two elements were closely linked, for the Right feared that a peace with minimal or no annexations would inevitably lead to democratic reform. Concern over such a double debacle quickly found its focus in the person of Bethmann Hollweg. If not an active participant in the conspiracy, he appeared to radical nationalists to be increasingly guilty of aiding and abetting it. How the chancellor's office had sunk in their eyes! From the glory of Bismarck, the respect and fear he inspired, to the weak, indecisive Bethmann Hollweg, who inspired in his enemies not the fear of a crushing German victory, but rather the will to hold out and the hope of winning. The crisis of leadership that Bethmann personified for the Right led them to see in his ouster the only hope for victory. It was a goal that drove Bismarckians further rightward.

Attacks on Bethmann focused on weakness in the face of relentless enemies, both within and without. Only a week after the outbreak of war, General August Keim wrote to Class about the need to replace both Chancellor and Foreign Minister. "Bethmann Hollweg and Jagow must disappear," he wrote. "They are not the people, in these terribly serious times, to lead the German people through to great goals. We need forceful men . . . otherwise we will bring endless sacrifice of life and property without getting for the German people that which it can demand."[37] For Bismarckians, Bethmann's policy of the diagonal betrayed an indecisive nature. Against it they contrasted "the compact unity of Bismarckian leadership, the superiority of his autocratic energy of will, the mastery of his handling of men and nations, his purposeful certainty."[38] Bethmann's tactics also appeared to favor the interests of those they considered to be the regime's traditional *enemies*. And their concerns were not completely without foundation. After all, the Chancellor was in a precarious position. Aware of the uncertainty of the situation, and thus of the irresponsibility of loudly publicizing grandiose plans, Bethmann tried to maintain a delicate balance. This involved conciliating the Right while not antagonizing the workers' movement (critical to industrial peace and thus military victory) or the Catholic Center (which, along with the SPD, held a majority in the Reichstag). The problem he faced involved the extent to which his enemies exaggerated the threat. And this did not require much effort on their part. As Raffael Scheck noted, for most loyalist Conservatives "even impartiality of the government toward organizations of the left and right appeared scandalous."[39] The fact, then, that the government had to make concessions was going to help make real the paranoid fears that shaped much of the Right's political understanding. There were a number of government actions that essentially confirmed for the Right the existence of a conspiracy. The most important was the dismissal of Grand Admiral von Tirpitz on March 19, 1916.

For most on the right, Tirpitz was the man to save the Empire. In fact, if the *image* of Bismarck was one of the few unifying elements tying together an otherwise fractured Right, then the *person* of Tirpitz should be seen to have served a similar function during the war. The most vocal advocate of unlimited submarine warfare, he was seen as a man of forceful action who would end the stalemate and bring about a decisive victory. In his study of the Fatherland Party, Heinz Hagenlücke wrote that: "The name Tirpitz always represented a kind of myth with the national-liberal *Bürgertum*. He was the man, in the view of many contemporaries, who, at the earliest, had Bismarck's prestige and could inherit his legacy."[40]

Supporters of a Tirpitz chancellorship included industrialists like Hugenberg and Ballin, radical nationalist groups including the Pan-Germans and the Agrarian League, political figures from Conservative Ernst von Heydebrand to Liberals Gustav Stresemann and Ernst Bassermann to the Center's Matthias Erzberger, the Crown Prince and the Kaiser's brother.[41] While the British jokingly compared his dismissal to Bismarck's, many Germans recognized such a parallel in all seriousness and feared its consequences. Raffael Scheck makes the point, in fact, that after his dismissal many on the right "began to consider changing the political system instead of solely demanding different policies."[42] As such, the dismissal of Tirpitz marked a critical stage in the radicalization of the Right.

Tirpitz's dismissal marked for some a turning point similar in magnitude to Bismarck's dismissal twenty-six years earlier. If men such as Heinrich Class and Diederich Hahn experienced March 20, 1890 as the event that converted them to radical nationalism, Wolfgang Kapp experienced the much more charged atmosphere surrounding March 19, 1916 as the factor that pushed him to the next stage of right-wing extremism.[43] The son of a '48er, Kapp turned fairly early to the right and found his inspiration in Bismarck.[44] Having heard about Tirpitz's departure, he wrote to a friend that the Grand Admiral "was the only one whom the English really feared ... With Tirpitz the single true statesman of the post-Bismarckian period is eliminated. The day of his dismissal is an unlucky day in the history of Germany and in the history of this war. The process calls to mind the dismissal of Freiherr v. Stein, and the analogy with Bismarck unfortunately lies only too close."[45] As a result of this trauma, Kapp helped forge a new kind of right-wing figure for the crisis decade – a populist, *bürgerlich* Conservative – and thus pushed further the transformation of German conservatism.[46]

Wolfgang Kapp's conservatism now bordered on the revolutionary. His nationalism, therefore, more closely resembled that of Heinrich Class than that of his party leader Ernst von Heydebrand. In a January 1917 memorandum he made it clear that if everything was not to be completely lost, an immediate change of system and without delay the "[r]eplacement of this chancellor with a strong, confident man of iron nerves and unbending decisiveness under all conditions is necessary."[47] The influence of the Bismarck Cult and its vision of salvation through leadership clearly made itself felt here as he wrote that a change in the chancellor's office and the calling of a true statesman would work like "a deliverance from evil" on the nation and would heighten its will to resist and its enthusiasm for the fight to the maximum.[48]

Meanwhile, as the war dragged on, more and more Germans, particularly workers and farmers, sought an end to the bloodshed. Responding to this sentiment, Bismarck's 'enemies of the Reich' – Social Democrats, Left Liberals, and the Catholic Center – passed a resolution in the Reichstag demanding a peace without annexations or reparations. Bethmann's inability to control the political situation that led to the Peace Resolution confirmed for the Right his utter weakness at a time that demanded iron hard leadership. In despair, Kapp wrote to the Agrarian League's Konrad Wanghenheim asking "[t]o what has it come with Germany, and what shall become of Bismarck's legacy?"[49] Pressure from the Right, the military leadership, and several key figures from the Reichstag led to Bethmann's fall in July 1917. Radical nationalists then looked on, hoping for the appointment of a strong man. Their disappointment was unmistakable as Wilhelm appointed the relatively unknown Georg Michaelis. Kapp's disillusionment was immediate. After Michaelis' first appearance before the Reichstag, Kapp wrote to Ulrich von Hassel: "I had not expected a speech so weak in form and content by the new man. Tactically, politically, statesmanlike, it was a complete failure . . . It is my full impression that yesterday he dug the first shovel of his grave. T[irpitz]'s hour will strike yet; in three months his name will be on everyone's lips."[50] Disappointment with Michaelis reinforced Kapp's belief in the need for a new party.

The continuing crisis of leadership and the fear of democratization thus combined to push the Right to another attempt at unity, different in scale and extent from the pre-war *Kartell*, similar in the inspirational symbol that guided it. Kapp worked through the summer of 1917 to develop a new right-wing party and by August he had a plan for a "Bismarckbund against Party Strife in War" (*Bismarckbund gegen den Parteihader im Kriege*). He hoped it would counter "a power-hungry democratic Reichstag majority" which "[i]n Germany's most difficult hour of destiny undertakes the malicious attempt to attack Bismarck's lifework through the weakening of the imperial power."[51] Under the banner of the name of the *Reichsgründer* and "in consideration of his titanic battles against the ruinous party spirit," people were to come together to win the war. Nothing substantial came of this initial plan, but Kapp did eventually achieve his goal with the founding of the Fatherland Party (*Deutsche Vaterlandspartei*), originally to be called the 'Bismarck Party', in September 1917.[52]

Despite the absence of Bismarck's name, his image remained prominent in the organization's rhetoric. As the ultimate nationalist organization, the Fatherland Party participated in that most German of all national festivities, the Bismarck celebration. They held numerous ceremonies across the country, usually making sure to anchor their legitimacy with the image of the first chancellor. As the speaker at one such celebration in Hamburg declared, "[a]ll our national thoughts, desires, and dealings take their starting point from Bismarck, who created for us a common national life, and also the German Fatherland Party, which wants to protect the German fatherland and keep it strong and secure, stands as a matter of course under his spirit, directs its view to him with their difficult work in the bitter struggle against lack of insight, effeminacy, and lack of dignity."[53] Frustration with a government considered too weak to hold back democracy at home and the enemy armies abroad thus combined with the Bismarck Cult to create a new and ominous political force.

The Fatherland Party, like the *Kartell* before, has been the subject of lively historical debate. Though often viewed as proto-fascist, the latest scholarship concludes that "[t]hrough its synthesis of old-style conservative groups and radical nationalist organizations, it appears both as a last manifestation of Wilhelmine *Sammlungspolitik* (though now against the state) and as a model for a broader rightist party, such as the DNVP, founded right after the end of the war."[54] As such it marks a significant stage in the Right's development. The party symbolized the continuing goal of right-wing unity and the radicalization of the movement. It marked a stage beyond that of the *Kartell* and closely approached the form of a mass party of the Right – a movement that could give voice to the new revolutionary conservative-populist nationalism personified by Kapp.

The marriage of conservative and radical nationalist politics can be seen in the inclusion of the Pan-German League as a key ingredient in the Fatherland Party. Heinrich Class played an important role in its founding, and, in accepting election to its executive committee, he hoped to channel the party in the most radical direction. He hoped that the party would "infect" the people with its *völkisch* ideology, ultimately taking it over at war's end, constructing out of it a right-wing people's party.[55]

But while Class worked behind the scenes, Kapp saw the Fatherland Party as a means of pushing Tirpitz – as a 'new Bismarck' – to the foreground of German politics.[56] In doing so, he was clearly tapping into that most central element of German political culture: the cult of leadership. "One longs for Bismarck-words," the *Pommersche Tagespost* wrote in January 1918, "one longs for a Bismarck, for a truly great one in the midst of the greatest time. Such longing for political leadership of Bismarckian greatness is today the key-note of *völkisch* voices. If only now a man like Bismarck would come!"[57] As it turned out, Tirpitz was not to be the man. Still, Germany did have another potential savior, a man perhaps more closely associated with blood and iron.

Field Marshal Paul von Hindenburg emerged early in the war as the most promising 'new Bismarck.'[58] His physical stature alone must have reminded people of the *Reichsgründer*, but his crushing victory over the Russians at the Battle of Tannenberg provided him with the critical aura of success. Taking a cue from the Bismarck Cult, many German cities began erecting Hindenburg towers. The first one, in Berlin's Königsplatz, was a massive wooden statue, into which people would drive an iron nail. In the shadow of the Iron Chancellor, thousands drove their nails home, thereby transforming the wooden figure into an 'Iron Hindenburg'.[59] It was an impressive display of the effectiveness of the Bismarck Cult in preparing the ground of German political culture in the years before 1914. The ritual and rhetoric of the Cult would prove flexible enough during the war to embrace a figure like Hindenburg and place him alongside the Iron Chancellor, seeing in him a possible fulfillment of the Bismarckian gospel of salvation through a god-given leader. At Bismarck ceremonies and in the press, Germans often connected the *Reichsgründer* and the Field Marshal in their dreams of a return to powerful leadership. At a Bismarck birthday celebration organized by the Fatherland Party, Dr. A. Hoche depicted Hindenburg as "the continuation of Bismarck."[60] The Pan-Germans expressed their thanks that "we have, in the military area, a divinely favored leader of Bismarckian style, a Hindenburg."[61] The Field Marshal's role within the wartime Cult was unmistakable.

In the end, Hindenburg proved to be no more of a 'new Bismarck' than Tirpitz. Meanwhile, the conspiracy the Right saw acting on Germany continued to press forward. By the summer, Ludendorff realized the cause was lost. And within the country the democratic conspiracy appeared to be gaining strength. Soon their victory would be complete. Bismarckians would find themselves in a world turned upside down. If and where they would find a place in that new world had yet to be determined.

Challenging the Iron Chancellor: Bismarck and the Revolution

The deification of Bismarck was never a one-sided process in which his disciples spread the gospel unopposed. Rather, there always existed a degree of resistance, in the form of negative or counter-images. It was therefore not only in discussion amongst themselves, but also against these alternative images that Bismarckians shaped their conception of their idol. Without a sense of this resistance, it is impossible to achieve a full understanding of the dynamics of the Bismarck Cult and its implications. The circumstances of 1918–19, when the Iron Chancellor's enemies temporarily gained the ascendancy, provide a perfect opportunity to study this 'other side' of the Bismarck phenomenon.

In November 1918 the war ended, a revolution erupted, and Bismarck's Empire collapsed. In its place arose a republic, whose leaders sought a new path. Having fought Bismarck for decades, Germany's political outsiders now had the opportunity to shape the nation, discarding the old myths and symbols for others more suited to a democracy. In seeking to get beyond the old authoritarian, semi-feudal system and the mindset it engendered, Weimar's leaders sought to infuse a spirit of freedom, equality, and brotherhood – a *Volksgemeinschaft* of a different sort. In place of the Kaiser, there would be a popularly elected president; in place of the imperial black-white-red flag, there was the black-red-gold of 1848; and in place of Bismarck, there were calls to Goethe and Schiller. It was a unique opportunity to reshape and redefine a nation, and its success or failure would help determine the republic's fate. Perhaps like no other issue, the question of legitimacy would dominate the history of Weimar, and looming ominously over that legitimizing process was the image of Bismarck.[62]

The victory of the revolutionaries signified the triumph of the *Reichsfeinde* over their arch-enemy and his followers. They would now determine Germany's future. It was a stunning reversal. Bismarckians, once the proud standard-bearers of the nation, retreated to the sidelines and looked on as their old antagonists chipped away at the once proud edifice of the German Empire. Once having confidently preached the gospel of Bismarck as self-evident truth, they now found themselves having to justify it in the face of those who considered it an intolerable impediment to democracy.

One of the best places to witness the process of national redefinition is in the constitutional debates of the National Assembly. While one side tried to build anew on the rubble of the Bismarckian Reich, the other side sought to preserve what it could of a system considered integral to its world-view. One can see the debates as a conversation in which visions of the ideal Germany competed for primacy. In these struggles Bismarck played a significant role, symbolizing for both sides the best and worst of recent German history. It was, in some ways, a protean moment, and if it did not last much more than a year, it still provides a valuable opportunity to analyze Bismarck's role in the thinking of the nation's new dominant political groupings.

As the war dragged on and fatigue and discontent grew, a new force emerged to the left of the Social Democrats – the Independent Social Democratic Party (USPD). As a more extreme expression of the radicalism that once defined Social Democracy, the USPD fought against any remnants of the Bismarck Reich in the new Germany. USPD Deputy Cohn opposed keeping the name 'Reich' at the top of the constitution. This was intolerable, an acceptance of what was, in his view, "an accidental appearance of history" – that is, the Bismarckian Reich.[63] He was clearly aware of the symbolic power that retention of the name Reich might have on Germans as they sought to accommodate themselves to the new circumstances. For Cohn, the issue was fundamental – the symbols of the past were still too powerful to be left untouched. Bismarck, as primary symbol of that past, would have to give way.

To a large degree, the Social Democrats could envision no real place for the Iron Chancellor in the new order. As one Socialist deputy declared: "We want to build for ourselves a new Germany on the broad foundation of freedom, justice and righteousness, a new Reich that has almost nothing in common with the old Reich other than the name."[64] The Bismarckian Empire embodied all that was negative for these groups – it was certainly no model upon which to build, especially since it contained within its own structure the seeds of its ultimate demise. "On blood and iron, with the forceful exclusion of millions of the best Germans, was the old Reich founded, and because it was built on blood and force, it collapsed in blood and force barely fifty years later . . . and survived its creator barely twenty years. Force and repression marked the old Reich during its entire duration."[65] Majority

Socialist and Interior Minister Eduard David sought to remind those in the Assembly who, in praising the glory of the old system, forgot that "this old glory collapsed . . . in a war whose cause was rooted in the old system."[66]

As part of the governing Weimar Coalition, the German Democratic Party (DDP) faced a somewhat different situation when confronting the Bismarck image. Emerging primarily out of the old Progressive People's Party, many of its members had felt the sting of his hostility and thus were often as eager as the SPD to discard the vestiges of their old nemesis. However, the party's new incarnation involved the absorption of part of the old National Liberal Party – a traditional Bismarckian stalwart. In addition, the DDP sought to position itself as the primary bourgeois people's party – supporter of the democratic republic, yet also a defender of bourgeois interests in the face of the power of Social Democracy. Its willingness to work closely with the SPD made it suspect in the eyes of many bourgeois nationalists. It therefore had to be careful in downplaying its nationalist credentials.[67] The result was a more ambiguous position regarding Bismarck, though at this point the consensus appears to have been one of fundamental rejection.

The Iron Chancellor received the most criticism from those on the party's left wing, such as Walther Schücking – wartime pacifist and member of *Bund neues Vaterland* – who had opposed the Cult for years. Schücking attacked the spirit of Bismarck and its disseminators, explaining how "in the last fifty years one portrayed Bismarckianism for us as the true German disposition, and thereby, in my view, falsified the true value of Germandom."[68] Not content merely to criticize, however, Schücking provided alternatives – better models, more closely suited to the new Germany that was emerging. He remembered twelve years ago, when he called to the German people, "less Bismarck and more Schiller!"[69] Of course, he said, he received a great deal of criticism for such a statement, particularly from the German professors. Still, he was confident that "the ways that have led us here to Weimar confirm that I was correct."[70] According to Schücking, Bismarck was simply the wrong model, lacking, as he did, the necessary attitude and attributes with which to develop democracy. Vom Stein, for example, had "the fundamental concept of democracy: trust in the people!"[71] Bismarck, however, lacked this trust. To build, Goethe declared, one needed a particular inclination; to build the new constitution, Schücking added, one needed an inclination towards democracy and towards justice. The two are inseparable, and thus how can Bismarck serve as a model? "Of Bismarck no one can really say, as much as one may want to glorify him, that he was a champion of the concept of justice . . . From Bismarck comes the lesson that the great questions of the day would be solved with blood and iron."[72] The German people, therefore, must leave him behind.

A more moderate voice from the DDP, Erich Koch-Weser, rejected the Bismarckian model, though he refrained from particularly harsh criticism.

Whereas the parties of the Right liked returning to 1866 and 1871 as their models, Koch-Weser preferred 1848. He saw a direct line between 1848 and 1918, while, "in the end, the gigantic work of Bismarck, in its ultimate goals, could not mature." [73] Unlike his colleagues to the left, however, Koch-Weser did not see this as being solely the fault of the *Reichsgründer*, but rather a reflection of the times and the situation within which he had to work. Even Bismarck was aware of these limitations. "The great and admirable opportunist Bismarck, who called politics the art of the achievable, did not create the constitution of 1866 and 1870 as something that at that time in his life he would have labeled as ideal, but rather he created it in order to achieve what was achievable at the time." [74] Trying to combine a number of disparate components, such as the unity of the Empire with the princely houses, parliament with the authoritarian state, or democracy with divine right, into a solid and effective structure, it should have come as no surprise to anyone that such a structure was extremely difficult to maintain. In this, Bismarck shared the blame since he had created a system that required all sorts of restraints to maintain it, "[r]estraints that loosened and dissolved when the strongest restraint was lacking, namely the mighty fist of Bismarck that held the whole work together." [75]

In the face of these challenges to a symbol so central to their world-view, Bismarckians offered spirited, though ineffectual, rebuttals. Rudolf Heinze, chairman of the German People's Party's delegation to the National Assembly, rejected the notion that the cause of the Second Empire's collapse lay in its own constitution. It was, in fact, according to Heinze, the element that allowed Germany to survive under such adverse conditions as long as it did. [76] The greatness of Bismarck's constitution – "genius of the highest measure" in the style and method of its construction – existed in the fact that he recognized the powers of the German people and through his constitution brought them to full development. [77] That constitution was "the outpouring of the Bismarckian spirit that was inclined to the facts . . . . that looked away from theories, that viewed dealing as the central point of statesmanlike effectiveness." [78] In contrast, the spirit that dominated the new Weimar constitution was a democratic spirit. "But more than a democratic spirit . . . it is the spirit of an extreme democracy . . . and that we reject." [79] Instead, if asked which spirit must dominate the constitution and the life of the state, Heinze had no doubt as to the answer: "the spirit of 1870/71 – that means the spirit of action, and not the spirit of 1848/49 – that means the spirit of ideology and of theorizing." [80]

Rather than defending the Bismarckian constitution itself, German National Peoples' Party (DNVP) deputy and former Vice-Chancellor Clemens von Delbrück attempted to defend their own history as well as their very conception of the state. Delbrück and his party had to reject the first article of the constitution, which declared: "The German Reich is a republic. The power of the state derives from the people." For them this meant "a revolution of our fundamental relationships."[81] Addressing those in the ruling coalition, he acknowledged that "[i]t means perhaps for you something self-evident (very true! Left) and something desired. (renewed agreement on the left) For us it means something else, (very true! Right) for us it means the departure from a great past, (lively agreement on the Right) the departure from arrangements that led Germany to a high measure of power, culture, and respect."[82] Responding to the assertion that the Second Reich was an "accidental appearance, an accidental form of state," as well as to heckling by DDP deputies calling the Second Reich an aberration, Delbrück declared that "[t]he German Reich of Bismarck was neither an aberration nor an accident, but rather it was a link in the chain of the difficult development of the inner political relationships of Germany and a link of a significance and of an efficiency that history has consistently recognized and will recognize in full measure."[83]

With their world-view under attack from the new national leadership, the two parties of the bourgeois Right acted in the spirit of their idol, backing their words with action and voting against the constitution. Bismarck was now becoming the symbol of national opposition to a degree unheard of in the Empire, for in his name the Right rejected the entire Weimar system. For the moment, however, they would have to be content with a futile vote of rejection, since the political climate was such that even Bismarck's symbolic power was not enough to effect significant change. In such an atmosphere there arose others, outside the National Assembly, who recognized the danger the Iron Chancellor posed for the new democracy and took the opportunity to add their voices to the effort to further his decline.

For years sociologist Max Weber acted as both admirer and critic of Bismarck. A liberal imperialist and intense nationalist, he too had called on the name of the first chancellor for a program of expansion.[84] The war found him a lonely voice of reason speaking out against the wave of irrational war-fever and the preaching of a particular 'German mission' emanating from the academy.[85] Towards the end of the war Weber assessed the nation's condition and, in particular, Bismarck's governmental system and its development since his dismissal. The articles that appeared in the *Frankfurter Zeitung* in the summer of 1917 left no doubt that one of the greatest problems facing the nation – a crisis of leadership – was due overwhelmingly to the Iron Chancellor's dominating influence and the cult that grew up around him.[86] In the cauldron of war, Weber saw the need to reshape German politics in a new, democratic form that would help it realize its world destiny. Initially, this involved criticism of the national hero in order to get beyond him.

Though a harsh critic of Bismarck, Weber never questioned his essential greatness. In praising the political abilities of German liberals of the 1860s, he made clear the distinction between them and their counterpart. "Of course," he wrote, "one cannot compare them to Bismarck with regard to diplomatic skill and intellectual energy; next to him, they appear at best as average, but this is true also of all other German politicians and of most foreign ones. At best a genius appears once in several centuries."[87] What he did criticize was the cult that developed after 1890 as well as the tangible political legacy he left behind. Specifically, he attacked those who "admired not the greatness of Bismarck's sophisticated and commanding intellect, but exclusively the admixture of violence and cunning, the seeming or actual brutality of his political approach."[88] After his death, this way of thinking had become the most prevalent and affected German politics in ways we have already seen. "For a long time now, this dominant attitude has shaped not only the historical mythology of Conservative politicians, but also of genuinely enthusiastic literati and, of course, of those intellectual plebeians who by imitating Bismarck's gestures seek to legitimate themselves as partaking of his spirit."[89]

Still, all of this was not solely the fault of the post-Bismarck generations. Much of the blame Weber laid at the feet of Bismarck himself. He never allowed the Reichstag to exercise significant political responsibility. He destroyed parties and individuals that could threaten him. He resorted to demagoguery to accomplish this and to get his policies passed. It was, therefore, in large part Bismarck himself who was to blame for the nation's poor level of political maturity after 1890.[90] Weber thus left no doubt as to the outcome of Bismarck's own actions combined with what he would have described as pathetic hero-worship. Interestingly enough, though, this would not be the last word. With the shape and character of the country's political institutions open to debate thanks to the revolution, he now had the opportunity to see his ideas implemented.

By mid-November 1918 Weber had begun to play a role in founding the German Democratic Party. He spoke on its behalf and was spontaneously nominated to head the DDP ticket in Frankfurt for election to the National Assembly. His candidacy ultimately fell through, and thus his role in the reconstruction of German politics remained an advisory one.[91] Still, despite his connection to the most liberal bourgeois party, his political ideas, as they stood at this point, seemed to be diverging from his more democratic recommendations of the previous year.

To solve the crisis of leadership, Weber now proposed what he called plebiscitary leadership democracy. Whereas before he had allowed for a strong parliament and a role for the people in the government's policy decisions, he now jettisoned such notions in favor of the overpowering figure of the plebiscitary *Führer*. This leader, emerging from the political battles of parliament and having been affirmed through a direct popular vote, would not follow the will of the electorate. He would lead it. He would set out a policy and then use his demagogic abilities to create a following within parliament and among the people in support of it.[92]

The resemblance between this new charismatic leader and Bismarck is striking. It would seem that Weber had made a dramatic turnaround – the object of his criticism appears to have become the model for a new system. Here he was, now praising those same features he had attacked so harshly in Bismarck. But was this really such a radical change? After all, Weber clearly admired the Iron Chancellor's strength and ability.[93] In addition, his concern with political reform had always had as its starting point the importance of increasing the nation's world power position. This being the ultimate end, all other issues relating to it served merely as means to that end. His commitment to parliamentarization and democratization, therefore, must be seen in this light. Parliamentary democracy was, according to Weber, the best means of producing leaders in the modern world of mass industrial society. His bitter disappointment with the political situation following the revolution and the dearth of qualified leaders in post-Bismarckian Germany certainly played an important role in his returning to a Bismarck-like ruler as the answer to the country's dilemmas.[94] Combining this with his desire to keep under control that central problem of modernity – ever-increasing rationalization – he ended up seeking refuge in a Caesarist form of leadership selection, approving of this method "even at the cost of rationality and objectivity in the formation of public opinion."[95]

In the end, Weber provides a further means of understanding the function and appeal of the Bismarckian political religion, now in the changed circumstances of post-revolutionary Germany. It was clearly a difficult time for Weber and the German middle classes more generally, as the nation plunged headfirst into the 'crisis of classical modernity'. Out of his critiques of Bismarck, Weber ended up returning to that very same figure as his model of the ideal leader. In the hopes of avoiding imprisonment in the 'iron cage' of rationalization, he escaped into the irrational world of charismatic leadership with its claims to supernatural abilities, its demagogic appeals to emotion rather than reason, and its idolization of the *Führer* figure at the expense of the role of the individual in politics. The Bismarck Cult as middle-class political religion had been providing just such a refuge for years. Though Weber clearly never became an adherent of the Cult, one can see a confluence of his political thought with perhaps the dominant mode of political understanding among the nation's middle-class nationalists. His nationalism, if perhaps more extreme than that expressed on the left of the DDP, was fairly typical of Germany's middle classes. Such nationalism, when combined with the chaos and uncertainty of Weimar's early years, made Weber's ideas much more tempting than the risks associated with the new democracy. Perhaps we can see in this some of the tendencies that would lead over the course of the 1920s to much of the Protestant bourgeoisie shifting its allegiance to groups that espoused a less rational solution to their problems.[96]

The years 1918–19 marked an important moment in the development of German political culture. The Right's retreat provided an opportunity to get beyond the burdensome symbols of the past and establish a climate more conducive to democracy. The efforts of those in the National Assembly were clearly a step in that direction. Yet even as they moved to bury Bismarck, the resistance refused to disappear and ominous portents remained. Considering the attitude of the vast majority of Germany's academic elite towards Bismarck and the cult of his leadership, if such perceptive and educated individuals as Max Weber could see no other way out than a return to the comforting reliance on great leaders, the task of those who set out to escape the Bismarckian past clearly required a great deal more time and effort. The need to 'overcome Bismarck' was apparent. Whether or not they would succeed is another question, for the forces arrayed against them were losing little time in adapting Bismarck to the new circumstances – the shift from defense to offense was underway.

A New Bismarck for a New Right: The Iron Chancellor as Counter-Revolutionary Icon in the Civil War Period

The Right found itself on the defensive immediately following the revolution. Waiting in the shadows, German nationalists sought hope for their eventual reemergence. Belief in Bismarck provided that hope in a quasi-religious sense.[97] If darkness and gloom marked the period following the revolution, the light could be found through faith and action in the spirit of Bismarck. "In him alone," wrote Heinrich Class in 1920, "lies the salvation, from him alone comes the deliverance."[98] The upheaval of the war, the shock of defeat, and the loss of position due to the revolution transformed the Iron Chancellor into a messiah-like figure longed for by many seeking escape from Weimar democracy and rebirth in a new national community.[99] Radical anti-Semite Alfred Jacobsen depicted German nationalists in a role reminiscent of Christ's disciples. Standing at Bismarck's grave in April 1919, he passionately declared: "Prince Bismarck, you suffer with us, but you are ours, and you must help us endure; we will not leave you. You shall comfort us and give us strength to bear the unspeakable shame of these days. Now we stand here, a line of German men and women, all ready to give their best for the furtherance of your work."[100] They had lost "a holy inheritance" and it was up to them to regain it and pass it on to their children. To do that, according to Jacobsen, to live in freedom, strength, and pride, meant struggle, toil, self-sacrifice. It meant learning to bear scorn and ridicule. "If we are called to that, to work together on this great undertaking, so let us lift up our hands and our hearts and in this completely solemn hour renew the vow at the feet of our Prince Bismarck, to set everything upon it, in order to win again for our people the strength and honor it has lost."[101] A new Bismarck was emerging, with an intense radicalism, with which it would carry out its new mission during a five-year civil war between Right and Left. But that was not all that was new.

Following their initial retreat, German nationalists reentered the political arena with a new array of parties and organizations to push through an agenda that represented a new level of radicalism. From a pre-war politics of national opposition, the German Right came away from the war and revolution with a program that no longer simply challenged government policy, but instead attacked the very legitimacy of the government itself. They were determined to confront the traitors whom they felt had undermined the war effort and replaced the Second Reich with a foreign-inspired democracy. In this emerging battle the Bismarck image helped lead the charge, having served as both inspiration in their hour of darkness and the embodiment of their hopes and dreams.

As the new party structure developed after 1918, the Right found itself divided again, with Bismarckians establishing several new parties. Gustav Stresemann carried the bulk of the National Liberals into the German People's Party (DVP). Unlike the liberals to the left in the German Democratic Party (DDP), those in the DVP refused to accept the democratic system and looked back longingly to the Bismarckian Empire. From this initial stance of 'national opposition' they refused to ratify the constitution, and though they gradually came to accept the new conditions, their support never rose particularly high.[102] If those around Stresemann eventually grew to support the system, there remained a strong faction that rejected their leader's moderation and continually pushed for right-wing unity.[103] That goal, however, proved as distant as that of liberal unity, for there emerged a new entity on the right to challenge the DVP's national credentials. The German National People's Party (DNVP), emerging from the Fatherland Party, was an amalgam of old German Conservatives, Free Conservatives, and smaller anti-Semitic parties, as well as some right-wing elements of the old National Liberals. In taking their stand against the Weimar system, both parties leaned on Bismarck for justification and inspiration. In 1920, for example, the DNVP called for the creation of a 'Bismarck-Fund' to provide the resources necessary for the "battle against crass self-interest and internationalism."[104] The tension between these two parties – each claiming the greater legitimacy as heirs of the first chancellor – played an important role in the Right's continuing radicalization.[105] It was not, however, the only factor in that process. Another crucial source lay just beyond the realm of the parties.

If the party-political Right emerged from the war and revolution in a radicalized form, so too did the world of radical nationalist organizations, and to an even greater degree. In this development, the Pan-German League played perhaps the most critical role. Among those most dedicated to a victorious, expanded Germany, its shock and disappointment upon learning of the defeat must have been immense. Add to that the revolution which ushered in a democratic republic led by the hated Social Democrats and the intensity of their anger and resentment should surprise no one. From its increasingly extreme position, then, the League took up the struggle against Weimar, and, as it had done before 1918, it claimed the Iron Chancellor as its own. Bismarck helped justify its fierce opposition, and the heightened invective in its language makes clear that the Iron Chancellor had moved to a level significantly beyond his pre-war incarnation. In its 1919 Bamberg Declaration, the League stressed that it was, after all, Bismarck himself who provided the example of true 'national opposition'. Now such a position was more urgent than ever. The only route to salvation lay in a return to Bismarckian principles. They had been preaching this for years. Whereas before such calls never went far beyond impassioned pleas for a change in policy, the dire situation in which the Reich now found itself meant that more was needed. Direct conflict with the government was the only option. "We are following the example of Otto von Bismarck, who found the Pan-German League worthy of the honor of being its first honorary member, in so far as . . . we take up the struggle against national corrupters, who deliberately destroy Bismarck's work and thereby commit the greatest political crime in the history of the world."[106]

The greater danger that the new Bismarck posed in the hands of this radicalized group can be seen in the Pan-Germans' relationship to both the parties of the Right and the world of radical nationalism more generally. In the tangled web of radical nationalist politics, the League stood at the nexus of the most dangerous organizations in Weimar. While it did emerge from the war dramatically strengthened in membership, its importance had always derived more from the intensity of its members and their message, rather than sheer numbers.[107] In a very real sense, the League can be seen as an incubator in which radical *völkisch* ideas developed and were then sent out by carriers, in the form of personnel, to germinate among other nationalist groups. During the tumultuous period of civil war that marked the republic's first years, there existed a certain community of thought among the radical Right – a milieu in which people and ideas circulated, all connected by the general desire to abolish the revolution and its results, though oftentimes never becoming more unified than that.[108] As facilitators of this exchange of ideas, the Pan-Germans played a key role, while their primary icon, Bismarck, proved a valuable tool for the task of transmission.

One example can be seen in the relationship between the League and the DNVP.[109] In terms of a fundamental rejection of Weimar, there existed an obvious connection between the two. As a symbolic expression of this radical opposition, Bismarck served as a powerful ideological link. The impressive list of Pan-Germans in leading positions in the party, including Alfred Hugenberg, Heinrich Class, Gottfried Gok, Axel von Freytagh-Loringhoven, Paul Bang, Konstantin von Gebsattel, and Leopold von Vietinghoff-Scheel, made this link more tangible. This is not to say, however, that their impact on the party was decisive. The DNVP was a somewhat unstable coalition that included groups with various shades of right-wing opinion, with the *völkisch* group simply one element among many.

The League's efforts within the DNVP represented one way in which it hoped to dramatically extend its influence – it had others. In 1919 the Pan-Germans founded the German Racial Defense and Defiance League (*Deutschvölkischer*

Schutz- und Trutzbund). Led by Pan-German Konstantin von Gebsattel and helped in its financing by Heinrich Class, it became, according to Hans Mommsen, "the most important expression of popular anti-Semitism in postwar Germany."[110] Before it was banned under the Law for the Protection of the Republic in 1922, it had achieved a membership of approximately 180,000. In 1920 alone it circulated 7.6 million pamphlets, 4.7 million handbills, and 7.8 million stickers.[111] While it shared the anti-Semitism of its parent organization, it also shared a reverence for the Pan-Germans' greatest hero. Thus, the League staged regular Bismarck celebrations, where, for example, Freytagh-Loringhoven could contrast the glory of Bismarck's time with what came later, when "the spirit of materialism, that Jewish spirit, spread far and wide, and whose influence has since become stronger and stronger."[112]

It was also out of this same Pan-German cauldron that the National Socialists would emerge. Their original incarnation, the German Workers' Party (DAP), had been founded in 1919 through the initiative of the Thule Society, itself the successor to the Order of Germans, which had originally emerged from the fringes of the Pan-German League.[113] By 1920 the DAP had renamed itself the National Socialist German Workers' Party (NSDAP), still a small *völkisch* fringe group, the majority of whose leaders, however, came from the Defense and Defiance League, as did many of its members.[114] The Pan-German connection manifested itself further as Heinrich Class met with Adolf Hitler several times in these early years, seeking to cultivate him, having recognized a strong community of interests.

The meetings between Class and Hitler were also significant for bringing to light another important aspect of Weimar political culture – generational change. As Nazi leader, Adolf Hitler represented a new generation of political players. For Hitler and many in the Nazi Party, the war and its violence were their formative experience. This generational element would help shape the republic's political culture, and would prove, over time, to be an important fault line within the Right. It did not, however, prevent Bismarck from serving as political god to some of these younger nationalists. As it did with the fractured Right in general, then, the Bismarck image can be seen to have served as a unifying element, helping at least in part to bridge the gap between old and young.

Adolf Hitler remained an ardent admirer of the first chancellor throughout his career. The "greatest stupidity . . . ever committed in national politics," he declared in 1921, "was the dismissal of the old Reich Chancellor Bismarck by Wilhelm the Last, already struggling on the leash of a few stock market Jews."[115] While such a position could hardly be considered unique among German nationalists, at other times Hitler did seem to be shaping his image of the Iron Chancellor to fit an idea of leadership more suited to his own situation. In April 1922, at a Bismarck celebration, Hitler set out his program for battle against the "Jewish democracy," equating his and his party's tasks for the present with those of the Iron Chancellor more than fifty years before. In this struggle, he said, "we want to think *today*: Bismarck."

> He had to fight as well against a worn out majority. His *Feuerkopf* knew, however, what benefits Germany; he forged for himself the great German army as the weapon of his political ideas. And after 1867 the majority came to him. Bismarck did without the praise of public opinion; he felt within himself the right to deal. In *his* tracks must we travel. Ruthless decisiveness to enforce our rights. We do not want millions of indifferent people, but rather 100,000 *men*, stubborn men. Success will compel the millions behind us. Indeed, we are instigators, we want the German people to once again learn to feel the whip as the whip and shame as shame and not as dignity, and say that we will not be governed by cowardice and scoundrelism together. We do not want to contribute to our prison castle, but rather to tear it down. And when the time comes, then we will want to say: we bow ourselves before you, Bismarck![116]

Though dramatically distorting the historical figure, this depiction of Bismarck as an unconventional outsider placed Hitler in a better position to eventually stake his own claim to a national leadership position. It also opened up the field of potential new Bismarcks to those outside his historical social position. It was just the start of a continuous effort by the Nazi leader to establish his legitimacy through a connection to Bismarck.

While Hitler certainly demonstrated the impact of the war on German political culture, the Stahlhelm, or League of Front Soldiers, did so in perhaps an even more tangible way. The Stahlhelm emerged out of the war and spirit of 1914, which, by years of combat, was transformed into the 'spirit of the front'. As both veterans' organization and paramilitary league, the Stahlhelm glorified the front experience as a brief glimpse of the cherished *Volksgemeinschaft*, and rejected the republic's establishment on the ashes of the Bismarck Reich. Initially, the Stahlhelm purposely eschewed party politics, focusing instead on organizing veterans and staging nationalist spectacles among the bourgeoisie. Its ability to resist the temptation of political involvement, however, would not last. The Stahlhelm helped inject a new militancy into the *Bürgertum* – a critical new ingredient in Weimar political culture. In the Empire, they had watched as Socialist demonstrators marched through the streets, while they remained on the sidelines of carefully staged official celebrations. As we have already seen, the ceremonies of the nascent Bismarck Cult represented some of the first signs of a change in middle-class political culture in this direction. Following the war and revolution, much of the bourgeoisie abandoned their previous reservations and, under the Stahlhelm banner, took to the streets to claim that public space. Such a transformation would prove crucial in the development of this group's fascist potential. With its impressive size – over 300,000 members by the mid-1920s – and effective organization, the League soon distinguished itself as a leader and custodian of the nationalist holidays. Prominent among these were the Bismarck celebrations.[117]

Claiming the Iron Chancellor as spiritual leader was natural for the *Stahlhelm*. Just as on the eve of the war, when the spirit of Bismarck met the spirit of 1914, so too did the League's essence match perfectly that of the Iron Chancellor. From the outset they sought to make clear the connection between themselves – a group that transcended parties and party politics – and the great leader. "Bismarck shall not have fought in vain for the soul of his people. May the political parties take positions towards him as they wish, may they set their love or their hate in Bismarck, their fear or their desire, we front-soldiers want to see in him the embodiment of the spirit of the front!"[118]

The Bismarck Cult had survived the war and revolution. Having suffered a series of psychic blows, his followers had regrouped, founding new organizations or carrying over others from the Empire. There were new followers, too – men for whom the violence and chaos of the crisis decade marked their formative years. The differences between old and new would reveal themselves over time. What they shared in common was Bismarck, now a symbol embodying total opposition to the republic. They also shared the Cult's ritual practices. Such rituals provided a forum through which they could voice their concerns and put forward their political visions. The Bismarck ceremony and tribute article became the sounding boards for vicious, virulent attacks on the republic. Whether it was democracy, the party system, socialism, internationalism, Jews, or Versailles, the celebration of Bismarck often meant the opportunity to attack one or more of these enemies. These attacks did not remain, however, solely on the verbal level. To understand the significance of the Bismarck phenomenon and its role in the radicalization of the German Right, one must examine how the Cult translated into political practice during this period.

Once the struggle between Bismarck and the *Reichsfeinde* had begun, the Right held little back. Frustration over several government decisions quickly led some on the right to seek to overthrow the republic by force. In a poorly planned and executed putsch, some of the very same Bismarckians we have already discussed, including Wolfgang Kapp of the Fatherland Party and then the DNVP, attempted to topple the republic on March 13, 1920. Heading the list of complaints in the leaflets announcing the coup was the crisis of leadership. "The government, without authority, powerless, wrapped up in corruption, is in no condition to exorcise the danger" facing the nation.[119] In preparation for the putsch, propaganda leaflets were distributed in which Ebert, Bauer, and Noske were juxtaposed against Wilhelm I, Bismarck, and Hindenburg.[120] Not all those in the Bismarckian camp agreed with Kapp's tactics or timing, but they certainly did not mind the intended outcome.[121] Even a somewhat more moderate Bismarckian like Gustav Stresemann chose to go along with the putsch. In fact, Henry Turner has pointed out that Stresemann's attitude changed little even after the coup. He did not want anyone in his party to attach any "sanctity" to the Weimar constitution. Such a response would cover over the fact that "what has come came against our wish and will, while the ideal of our life lies in ruins." Just how far he was willing to go to recapture that ideal he made clear when he declared: "No parallels with the happenings of 13 March, but if our Lord God and destiny sends us a man who, without holding to all the paragraphs of Weimar, builds us a great Germany again, then our party would – so I hope – grant him the same indemnity which the fathers of the National Liberal Party granted to Bismarck."[122]

In fact, the aftermath of the coup saw little change in the Right's thinking. If, for the moment, they refrained from further putsch attempts, their verbal assaults lost nothing in their intensity, putting Bismarck's symbolic force to full use as counterrevolutionary icon. The Pan-Germans saw the triumph of "[t]he three parties that today make our people the laughingstock of humanity" as the inexorable result of developments which followed Bismarck's dismissal in 1890.[123] "His fall opened for them the way to power, and in a direct line led the inner development of Germany from year to year to that so-called democratic course, which ended with the back-stabbing of the front, with the fall of the Empire and the smashing of the Bismarck-nation."[124] Hitler traced the nation's downfall, "[b]eginning with the mighty head of a Bismarck to the half-negroid Hebrew-skull of Bethmann-Hollweg, to the balloon-head of a Max von Baden and the dark, badly burning oil lamp of a Herr Simon, in between that, the rubber ball of the famous small town teacher from Buttenhausen [Erzberger], in short, a collection of glorious, incomparable heads."[125] Clearly the new leadership could never match Bismarck's greatness. Such contrasts with Weimar's leading figures appeared frequently in the Right's propaganda.[126]

Kapp's failure to end the crisis of leadership did little to discredit the belief in the need for a Bismarckian leader. In fact, the inept nature of the putsch may actually have helped reinforce such a belief. Less than two weeks later, DNVP leader Westarp announced that things could only improve if destiny once again sent Germany a great man. "This one, our leader, shall unite in himself intent, ability, will, strength of character and moral greatness and free his people and lead it upwards to the development of the best powers of the German essence."[127] The Thule Society as well decried what was happening to the nation and saw salvation in the arrival of a new leader. "What the enemy left us of the Reich will be completely destroyed through the weakness and stupidity of the leaders if, in the last hour, a man does not arise for us who once more with Bismarckian spirit and Bismarckian power leads us out of the dark."[128]

If the leaders could not compare with Germany's first chancellor, the system established by the *Reichsfeinde* fared little better. Democracy was anathema to the national opposition, and, just as the leadership continued to suffer the

Bismarckians' relentless scorn, so too did this 'foreign implant' come under vicious assault. Only weeks after Kapp's demise, Conservatives at the DNVP's *Kreuzzeitung* declared that Bismarck was "[i]n every inch and in every word a living reproach and an immortal opponent of this democracy."[129] The General Strike that helped defeat the attempted seizure of power gave the Right added fuel. The DNVP took the opportunity provided by Bismarck's birthday to blast the Democrats for their cooperation with the two socialist parties in such a radical endeavor. Through an advertisement in the *Hamburger Nachrichten* entitled "Prince Bismarck against democracy and its forerunner," they made it clear that Kapp's failure changed little in the thinking of the DNVP.[130]

Following Kapp, Bismarckians clung to their hero with the hope of eventual triumph. Paying tribute to the *Reichsgründer* in April 1920, the *Hamburger Nachrichten* stressed the importance of keeping his memory alive and remaining conscious of the fact that

> Bismarck must be and remain our model. In his sense we must work further if we want to strive for a better future; his spirit shall bring us solace and give back the balance of the soul, which it has lost in the chaos of the present. Like a brilliant star the image of Bismarck greets us in the dark night. When we look up to him and hold his memory in honor, a sprout will develop once more out of the seed now sleeping in the winter frost, with the fruit of which our whole nation can revive itself.[131]

As it turns out, they would not have long to wait before that seed began to sprout and bear fruit. Already the nation had witnessed attempted coups from the left in the Spartacus uprising of January 1919 and from the right with Kapp in March 1920. From a middle-class perspective, the Spartacus uprising raised the horrifying specter of a Bolshevik Germany, as did the General Strike that helped bring down Kapp. The terrible vengeance meted out by right-wing *Freikorps* units, on the other hand, met with toleration, if not approval, by the bulk of the middle classes. For them, the danger always seemed to come from the Left, while the Right stood for law and order. So despite the proximity in time to the attempted right-wing overthrow, it was the red shadow that haunted Germany's middle-class voters when elections approached in June 1920.

These elections put the system to the test as the Bismarckian parties faced off against a Weimar Coalition they blamed for Germany's chaotic and weakened state. Both the DVP and DNVP ran under the banner of Bismarck. While the DVP was not completely intransigent, its attitude towards the regime could at best be described as luke-warm. Aside from publicly muting its monarchism, how little the Kapp Putsch had affected the party's attitude can be seen in the fact that they entered the campaign under the slogan "The enemy is on the left."[132] The DNVP fought a much more definitively oppositional campaign. The results would seem to indicate the growing popularity of their position, or at least the increasing disillusionment with the parties of the Weimar Coalition and the system they had established barely one year earlier. The Bismarckian parties gained dramatically at the expense of their bourgeois rivals in the DDP, nearly doubling their vote from the previous year's National Assembly elections, while the Democrats lost more than half their total vote from 1919. The Majority Socialists also lost nearly half their 1919 vote, and the Center lost one-third. The other big winner was the left-oppositional Independent Socialist Party, which nearly tripled its total. Such a devastating defeat for the Weimar Coalition, combined with dramatic increases for parties fundamentally opposed to the system, led Larry Jones to comment that "[a]s a referendum on the policies and accomplishments of the Weimar Coalition, the outcome of the 1920 Reichstag elections clearly established the extent of popular disillusionment with the new republican order."[133]

While the June election results had to be reassuring to many on the Right, it was by no means the end of the crisis period, and thus hope and faith in the spirit of Bismarck continued to grow.[134] Middle-class alienation from the republic continued apace, even gaining strength from such a horrific act of violence as the murder of Foreign Minister Walther Rathenau in 1922, the culmination of a string of killings resulting directly from the radical anti-Semitism propagated by the *Schutz- und Trutzbund*.[135] Unlike the situation following Matthias Erzberger's assassination the previous summer, Germans across the political spectrum expressed genuine grief and regret. However, the protests organized by the Left, during one of which a bust of Bismarck was toppled and destroyed – apparently these groups could see from what kind of political culture such murderous acts could spring – once again sparked fear in the hearts of the bourgeoisie.[136] As Peter Fritzsche points out, "when the assassination resulted in tough laws designed to protect the republic rather than safeguard frightened burghers, bourgeois opinion was outraged."[137] Chancellor Wirth's declaration in the Reichstag that "the enemy stands on the Right," while pointing to the DNVP deputies, confirmed for many that the measures were clearly aimed at repressing the Right while protecting the Left. Rathenau's murder, followed by the merger of the Independent and Majority Socialists, "left German towns more polarized and the republican state more illegitimate in the opinion of burghers."[138]

The longing for salvation through Bismarck reflected the chaotic and tumultuous times which many Germans experienced during the civil war. For many, the route to salvation would be revealed by a great leader. We have already seen how the Bismarck image helped feed and develop the *Führer* idea in middle-class circles before 1914 and how that developed further with the war and the opportunity thus provided for heroic leadership. With the end of the war and the trauma that followed, such ideas gained even wider currency among an expanding nationalist public. Ian Kershaw has noted that the "spread of fascist and militaristic ideas in post-war Europe meant that 'heroic leadership' images were 'in the air'," and thus not simply confined to Germany.[139] He went on to say, however, that the ideas within Germany naturally "had their own flavor" due to the particular features of German political culture, and that "the crisis-ridden nature of the Weimar state, detested by so many powerful groups in society and unable to win the popularity and support of the masses, guaranteed that such ideas, which in a more stable environment might have been regarded with derision and confined to the lunatic fringe of politics, were never short of a hearing."[140] We have seen, however, that in the much less crisis-ridden years before the war the Cult of Bismarck as ideal leader was by no means limited to the lunatic fringe, but rather was becoming increasingly shared by some of the most powerful groups in society and politics, including the nation's academic elite. The events of the war and revolution, then, can be seen to have reinforced and intensified the Cult dramatically among groups already devoted to it, while expanding its appeal to newer segments of the German nationalist public.

One commonality that marked the future visions of most groups within the national opposition throughout Weimar was a striking *lack* of commonality. Beyond their shared devotion to Bismarck, it seemed that all that connected them was their agreement that Weimar had to be destroyed. With regard to what would replace it, the answer depended upon who was asked and when. Visions of the future ranged from a restored Bismarckian Reich with a Hohenzollern monarch, to authoritarian dictatorships based upon military or plebiscitarian foundations, or some combination of all of these. Clearly tied to these proposals was an image of the ideal leader – the new Bismarck. This, too, ranged from a Bismarckian successor leading a restored Hohenzollern Empire, to a new incarnation of Bismarck as dictator.[141] Such variation indicated divisions amongst these groups that proved crucial in keeping them from uniting for extended periods, thus sparing Weimar the full force of their wrath – the strength of which might have brought it down much earlier than was actually the case.

If no precise image could emerge at this point, the power of the Iron Chancellor in these years made his shadow no less dangerous. In fact, one could argue that it was this very indeterminate character that made it a much more ominous threat. If the image was vague enough in its particulars, then there existed many more potential 'new Bismarcks' than if there had been one universally agreed upon form. As Weimar experienced no shortage of 'new Bismarcks', the potential threats were that much greater, since most sought to drape themselves in the legitimacy of the Iron Chancellor. The flexibility of an amorphous Bismarck made their claims easier to stake, while making the task of their detractors correspondingly more difficult.

If the crisis-ridden years up to 1922 did little to quell middle-class despair over the government leadership and the corresponding desire for a savior, the events of 1923 would only serve to strengthen such feelings. During that year, the frustrations of the recent past would overflow and once again threaten to sweep away the whole Weimar system. In January 1923 the French occupied the Ruhr in response to Germany's failure to comply with particular terms of the Versailles Treaty. The unanimous outrage this move evoked throughout the country brought Germans together from left to right. Through passive resistance they hoped to defeat what Gustav Stresemann called a French attempt at the "annihilation of Germany."[142] Indeed, it all seemed reminiscent of that spirit of 1914 to which many Germans still longed to return. As was the case then, so too in 1923 did this spirit of national community become connected with memories of the Iron Chancellor.

The power Bismarck displayed in unifying the nation in 1914, inspiring perseverance, and the hope that he came to symbolize through the republic's chaotic early years worked to galvanize his followers in this fight. The common connection between Bismarck and the Ruhr struggle tended to be one of positive inspiration to hold out and triumph.[143] The conjunction of his birthday in April with Easter and its symbolism of rebirth and redemption gave the image an added boost. In *Der Tag* Friedrich Hussong called Bismarck "the holy German Easter legend" and "the hero of German Easter fairy tales."[144] The twenty-fifth anniversary of Bismarck's death in July 1923 once again provided the opportunity to seek and find inspiration in his spirit. "Bismarck is dead," declared the *Schlesische Zeitung*. "But if his earthly remains rest under the murmur of the Saxon forest, so his spirit lives nevertheless. His spirit is the spirit of 1914, is the spirit of passive resistance in the Ruhr, is the steady longing and burning in millions of German hearts, the longing and burning for freedom from shame and disgrace."[145] It would not be long, in fact, before that desire for freedom was acted upon in a last attempt to destroy Weimar.

If Bismarck's spirit inspired Germans to persevere in their resistance, it could not do so indefinitely, and most importantly it could not solve the crisis by itself. As passive resistance continued, the government's policy of paying striking workers in the occupied area through ceaselessly printing money led to hyperinflation. With the Mark's value reaching the unimaginable level of 4.2 trillion to the dollar, the prospects for Germany's stability grew dimmer. Under such harrowing circumstances, the desire for salvation grew and found expression in calls to the Iron Chancellor. In July the Nazi *Völkischer Beobachter* expressed the hope that the people's desire, "which today looks back to the spirit of Bismarck, will embody itself in a new statesman who shall lead us out of the trouble of the present."[146]

As the crisis continued, President Ebert named Gustav Stresemann Chancellor. He was immediately faced with the prospect of a right-wing putsch in Bavaria and a possible Communist uprising in central Germany. Stresemann was aware of the peril facing the country, having spoken in the Reichstag in April about the danger of political extremism. Such strengthening of the extreme was natural in times of crisis. What he found ridiculous was "those who believe here to be able to solve the entire issue by calling for the strong man against the allegedly weak natures who try in vain to solve these problems. Curiously, those who refer to Bismarck and the *Realpolitik* of this great statesman take not the slightest notice in their judgment of the foreign and domestic relationships."[147] Though his comments seem to have been directed more towards the Right than the Left, the course of action he chose appeared to favor the former. While deposing the state governments of Saxony and Thuringia where Communists had joined coalitions with the SPD, he responded much more mildly to the threats emanating from the radical nationalist cauldron of Bavaria.

Stresemann's accession to the chancellorship meant the end of passive resistance. Acting on what in the future he and his friends would regularly refer to as a cornerstone of Bismarckian politics, Stresemann displayed "the courage to be unpopular" in calling off the struggle with the French.[148] Seeing their opportunity to take advantage of the chaos disappearing before their eyes, many on the right felt it was time to act before it was too late. Plans had been hatching among right-wing figures for some time, and it just became a question of who would act first. The Army Chief of Staff Hans von Seeckt, for example, found himself under pressure from DNVP leaders Oskar Hergt and Count Kuno von Westarp to take power at the head of a three-man directorate.[149]

It was in the midst of this conspiratorial frenzy that Adolf Hitler chose to act. For months he had been making political capital by attacking the "November criminals" and the "Berlin *Judenrepublik*." In an August speech in Munich he noted with pride that the Nazis had been the only ones to consistently oppose Cuno's chancellorship. For that position, he said, they were "persecuted from all sides, from all parliamentary parties because we 'stirred up trouble'.[150] All this, Hitler declared, pointing to the current occupant of the chancellor's office, "even though now finally a man, 'the man' is there! A kind of second Bismarck!"[151] It was an attack by one aspirant to Bismarckian greatness on another. Whatever his aspirations, though, his feeble grab for power ended in failure. Despite his ignominious defeat, Hitler saw himself in a Bismarckian situation. During his trial, he pointed to Bismarck's actions during the conflict period in order to justify the putsch. What Bismarck did back in the 1860s in ruling without parliament may have been high treason, he declared, "if out of this act had not come the blessing that led the German people to unity, to its highest perfection and freedom. On the day on which, before Paris, the crown was set upon the German Emperor, the high treason was legalized before the German people and the whole world."[152] Bismarck's violation of the law was therefore justified, and since Hitler, too, had Germany's best interests in mind, so was his. If he was coming to see himself as a new Bismarck, his judges had not yet come around. Still, his argument did not fall on completely deaf ears. His imperial-era judges, having found him guilty of treason, sentenced him to only five years' imprisonment. At the end of the crisis decade, when

Bismarckians were fighting to restore or redesign a world turned upside down, Hitler's actions fit within the general confines of the Cult and the political culture it had helped shape.

Following threats from both left and right, Stresemann succeeded in ending the hyperinflation. The government had weathered a terrible storm, but had it won over the hearts of most Germans? The end of 1923 may have marked the twilight of putschism, but that did not mean that dreams of such action had vanished, as Woldeck von Arneburg's Bismarck-inspired plan of December makes clear. The period that followed has often been referred to as the years of stability, marking a brief moment of tranquility in Weimar's otherwise turbulent history. This, however, was more illusion than reality, as the forces of destruction had not gone away, nor had the basic political inclinations that signified fundamental opposition to the system. The 'years of stability' can perhaps be seen more accurately as 'years of possibility', as contending visions of the future fought for supremacy. And it was not solely a contest between right and left. Bismarckians would fight amongst themselves for Germany's future with differing images of their political god before them. This struggle for supremacy, for the survival or destruction of the republic, reflected in its ferocity the uncertainty of the times.

Notes

1. Young, *Maximilian Harden*, 224.
2. Woldeck's plan cited in Raffael Scheck, *Alfred von Tirpitz and German Right-Wing Politics, 1914–1930* (New Jersey: Humanities Press, 1998), 119.
3. Quoted in Jeffrey Verhey, *The Spirit of 1914: Militarism, Myth, and Mobilization in Germany* (Cambridge: Cambridge University Press, 2000), 109.
4. Pan-Germans quoted in Hagenlücke, *Deutsche Vaterlandspartei*, 50.
5. For the 'spirit of 1914', see Fritzsche's *Germans into Nazis* and Wolfgang Mommsen, "The Spirit of 1914 and the Ideology of a German 'Sonderweg'," in *Imperial Germany 1867–1918: Politics, Culture, and Society in an Authoritarian State*, trans. Richard Deveson (London: Arnold, 1995), 205–216.
6. Verhey, *Spirit of 1914*, 31–32, 60.
7. Sikoski, quoted in ibid., 30.
8. See Ringer, *Decline of the German Mandarins*, 180–181; Hans-Ulrich Wehler, *Deutsche Gesellschaftsgeschichte. Bd. 4. Vom Beginn des Ersten Weltkriegs bis zur Gründung der beiden deutschen Staaten 1914–1949* (Munich: C. H. Beck, 2003), 14–16.
9. Gustav Roethe, *Zu Bismarcks Gedächtnis. Rede gehalten bei der Bismarckfeier des Vereins für das Deutschtum im Ausland am 30. März 1915* (Berlin: Weimannsche Buchhandlung, 1915), 42.

10. "Bismarck und sein kämpfendes Volk" in *Der Tag*, Nr. 167/77, Ausgabe A, April 1, 1915; see also "Zum hundertsten Geburtstag des Fürsten Bismarck" by Wolfgang Eisenhart, in BAL, RlbPa, R8034 II, 7102, #81: *Hallesche Zeitung*, Nr. 152, April 1, 1915; see also Julius Aßmann, *Bismarck – der Erfüller deutscher Sehnsucht und der Wegweiser deutscher Zukunft. Festrede bei d. Feier d. 100. Geburtstages Bismarcks zu Bromberg* (Bromberg: Jahne, 1915), 4.

11. Eisenhart, quoted in ibid.

12. "Bismarcks Erben" by Generalsuperintendant D. Klingemann-Koblenz, in Sonderbeilage des *Deutschen Kuriers*, in BAL, RlbPa, R8034 II, 7102, #63b: *Deutsche Kurier*, Nr. 91, April 1, 1915.

13. Aßmann, *Bismarck*, 11.

14. See, for example, Erich Marcks in *Vom Erbe Bismarcks. Eine Kriegsrede* (Leipzig: Quelle & Meyer, 1916), 50.

15. Machtan, "Bismarck Kult," 30; see speech by Professor Ulrich von Wilamowitz-Möllendorff, in 1915 to university students in *Der Tag*, Nr. 168, Abend-Ausgabe, April 1, 1915.

16. Professor Berthold Litzmann, *Bismarck und wir. Rede bei der Bismarckfeier des liberalen Bürgervereins in Bonn am 31. März 1915* (Bonn: Friedrich Cohen, 1915), 15; see also Professor Dr. Hunziger, *Bismarcks Werk und Geist. Gedächtnisrede* (Hamburg: Herold'sche Buchhandlung, 1915), 9–10.

17. See the speech by Berlin University Professor Otto von Gierke, September 18, 1914, "Krieg und Kultur," in *Deutsche Reden in schwerer Zeit* (Berlin: Carl Heymanns Verlag, 1914), 77–101.

18. Professor Dr. Gutzmer (Rector of the University of Halle) at the celebration of the German universities for Bismarck's 100th birthday, March 31, in BAL, RlbPa, R8034 II, 7102, #77: *Vossische Zeitung*, Nr. 167, April 1, 1915; see also "Des deutschen Volkes Bismarckfeier" in *Neue Preußische Zeitung*, Nr. 167, Morgen-Ausgabe, April 1, 1915.

19. For example, Bruno Garlepp's *Bismarck-Denkmal für das Deutsche Volk* was reprinted in a special edition for 1915 in a run of 120,000 copies. Paul Liman's *Bismarck in Geschichte, Karikatur und Anekdote* and the massive anthology from Erich Marcks and Max Lenz entitled *Das Bismarck-Jahr* also achieved impressive print totals. See Machtan, *Bismarck und der deutsche National-Mythos*, 31.

20. Speech by Stresemann at Sagebiel on April 1, 1915 in BAL, RlbPa, R8034 II, 7102, #18: *Hamburger Nachrichten*, Nr. 156, April 2, 1915; see also "Bismarck-Gedenktag" in *Deutsche Tageszeitung*, Nr. 167, Morgen-Ausgabe, April 1, 1915.

21. Professor Dr. Georg Bülow, *Unser Bismarck. Festrede, gehalten bei der von der Stadt Schweidnitz veranstalteten öffentlichen Bismarckjahrhundertfeier am 1. April 1915* (Schweidnitz: Reisse, 1915), 6.

22. Erich Marcks, "Bismarck und unser Krieg," in *Suddeutsche Monatshefte*, September 1914, 784; see also Erich Marcks, "Gedächtnisrede zu Bismarcks 100. Geburtstag," in Erich Marcks, *Männer und Zeiten. Aufsätze und Reden zur neueren Geschichte*. Second volume (Leipzig: Quelle & Meyer Verlag, 1922); Litzmann, *Bismarck und wir*.

23. "Bismarck. Genie und Politik – eine Betrachtung," in "Zum 1. April 1915" Sonder-Beilage der *Hamburger Nachrichten* in BAL, RlbPa, R8034 II, 7102, #71a-c: *Hamburger Nachrichten*, April 1, 1915; see also Graf Reventlow at the Berlin Bismarckkommers, April 1, 1915, in *Neue Preußische Zeitung*, Nr. 167, Morgen-Ausgabe, April 1, 1915; Paul Vogel, National Liberal, quoted in BAL, RlbPa, R8034 II, 7102, #63b: *Deutsche Kurier*, Nr. 91, April 1, 1915.

24. Class quoted in Verhey, *Spirit of 1914*, 50.

25. "Zum hundertsten Geburtstag des Fürsten Bismarck" by Wolfgang Eisenhart, in BAL, RlbPa, R8034 II, 7102, #81: *Hallesche Zeitung*, Nr. 152, April 1, 1915; see also Richard Jacobi-Zehlendorf, "Bismarck," in *Nationalliberale Blätter* (*Deutsche Stimmen*), March 28, 1915, vol. 27, Nr. 13: 243.

26. Jarausch, *Enigmatic Chancellor*, 186.

27. Ibid., 187.

28. Graf Reventlow at the Berlin Bismarckkommers, April 1, 1915, in *Neue Preußische Zeitung*, Nr. 167, Morgen-Ausgabe, April 1, 1915; see also Reventlow, "Mißverstehen Bismarcks," in *Deutsche Tageszeitung*, Nr. 178, Abend-Ausgabe, April 8, 1915.

29. "Bismarcks Mäßigung" by Conrad Bornbak, in BAL, RlbPa, R8034 II, 7095, #32: *Der Reichsbote*, Nr. 610, November 15, 1915; see also "Bismarcks Kriegszielpolitik," in *Deutsche Zeitung*, Nr. 633, December 16, 1917; Dr. W. Beumer, *Bismarcks Friedensschlüsse. Vortrag . . . gehalten im Industrie-Club, Düsseldorf am 6. April 1918* (Düsseldorf: Düsseldorfer Zeitung, 1918), in BA Koblenz, NL 1231/112, Nachlaß Hugenberg, #167–176.

30. Gustav Stresemann, *Bismarck und wir. Rede . . . zum 25. Bismarck-Kommers des Berliner Bismarck-Ausschusses, 1. April 1916* (Berlin: Reichsverlag, 1916), 8–9; speech by Stresemann in BA Koblenz, ZSg 1 252/5, Unabhängiger Ausschuß für einen deutschen Frieden, Satzungen, Veröffentlichungen, Mitteilungen und Flugblätter: Dietrich Schäfer, Graf Westarp, Dr. Pfleger, Dr. Stresemann, D. Traub. *Durch Deutschen Sieg zum Deutschen Frieden. Mahnruf ans Deutsche Volk* (Berlin: Verlag von Karl Curtius, 1917; speeches given on January 19, 1917 in der Versammlung des "Unabhängigen Ausschuß für einen Deutschen Frieden" im Sitzungssaale des Abgeordnetenhauses zu Berlin).

31. Erich Marcks, *Vom Erbe Bismarcks* 20.

32. Dieter Fricke, "Bund Neues Vaterland," in Dieter Fricke, ed., *Lexikon zur Parteiengeschichte*, I, 351–360; see also Arthur D. Brenner, *Emil J.*

Gumbel: Weimar German Pacifist and Professor (Boston: Humanities Press, 2001).

33. *Was täte Bismarck? Realpolitik gegen Gefühlspolitik* (Berlin: Verlag "Neues Vaterland," 1915); Flugschriften des Bundes "Neues Vaterland" Nr. 2 in BA Koblenz, ZSg 1 13/6, Bund neues Vaterland, Flugblätter, 8.
34. Ibid.
35. Ibid.
36. Fritz Bley, "Ohne Bismarck!" in BAL, RlbPa, R8034 II, 7096, #116: *Deutscher Volkswart*, Nr. 25, July 26, 1918.
37. Keim to Class on August 8, 1914, quoted in Hagenlücke, *Deutsche Vaterlandspartei*, 51.
38. "Zum Bismarcktage" in BAL, RlbPa, R8034 II, 7095, #193: *Tägliche Rundschau*, Nr. 167, April 1, 1917; for more criticism in Bismarck's name, see "An der Gruft Bismarcks" in *Deutsche Tageszeitung*, Nr. 383, Abend-Ausgabe, July 29, 1918; "Zum Bismarcktage" in BAL, RlbPa, R8034 II, 7095, #193: *Tägliche Rundschau*, Nr. 167, April 1, 1917; "Zwanzig Jahre ohne Bismarck" in *Deutsche Zeitung*, Nr. 372, July 24, 1918; "Dem größten Deutschen! Zu Bismarcks 20. Todestage" in BAL, RlbPa, R8034 II, 7096, #124: *Pommersche Tagespost*, Nr. 209, July 30, 1918.
30. Scheck, *Tirpitz*, 43.
40. Hagenlücke, *Deutsche Vaterlandspartei*, 219.
41. Scheck, *Tirpitz*, 40–43.
42. Ibid.
43. Hagenlücke, *Deutsche Vaterlandspartei*, 124.
44. In 1909 he became head of Königsberg's Bismarck Society. Ibid., 118.
45. Kapp to Schinckel, 2 April 1916, quoted in ibid., 124.
46. Ibid., 119.
47. Ibid., 133.
48. Ibid., 133–134.
49. Wolfgang Kapp to Wangenheim, June 25, 1917, quoted in ibid., 143.
50. Kapp to Hassel, July 20, 1917, quoted in ibid., 145.
51. "Aufruf der Bismarckpartei" quoted in ibid., 149, fn. 44.
52. Ibid., 151–164.
53. "Bismarck-Feier der Deutschen Vaterlands-Partei" in BAL, RlbPa, R8034 II, 8868, #163: *Hamburger Nachrichten*, Nr. 161, April 3, 1918.
54. Scheck, *Tirpitz*, 67; this is also Hagenlücke's conclusion in *Deutsche Vaterlandspartei*.
55. Scheck, *Tirpitz*, 70.
56. Ibid., 70.
57. "Bismarcksehnsucht" in BAL, RlbPa, R8034 II, 7095, #158: *Pommersche Tagespost*, Nr. 28, January 29, 1917; "Dem größten Deutschen! Zu Bismarcks

20. Todestage" in BAL, RlbPa, R8034 II, 7096, #124: *Pommersche Tagespost*, Nr. 209, July 30, 1918.

58. Wehler has noted Hindenburg's connection to the "collective memory of the 'superhuman' figure of the charismatic '*Reichsgründer*'." *Deutsche Gesellschaftsgeschichte, Bd. 4*, 23.

59. Fritzsche, *Germans into Nazis*, 49–50.

60. Dr. A. Hoche, at a Bismarck celebration by the Fatherland Party, Magdeburg Chapter, in BAL, RlbPa, R8034 II, 7096, #99: *Magdeburgische Zeitung*, Nr. 250, April 5, 1918; see also BAL, RlbPa, R8034 II, 8868, #164: *Badische Landeszeitung*, Nr. 154, April 3, 1918.

61. *Deutsche Zeitung*, Nr. 164, March 31, 1918.

62. Thomas Childers, "Languages of Liberalism: Liberal Political Discourse in the Weimar Republic," in Konrad H. Jarausch and Larry Eugene Jones, eds., *In Search of a Liberal Germany: Studies in the History of German Liberalism from 1789 to the Present* (New York: Berg Publishers, 1990), 323–359.

63. Deputy Cohn, USPD, *Stenographische Berichte über die Verhandlungen der verfassunggebenden deutschen Nationalversammlung*, February 28, 1919, vol. 327, 1208–1210.

64. Fischer (Berlin) SPD, *Stenographische Berichte*, February 28, 1919, vol. 326, 371–372.

65. Ibid., 372.

66. Dr. David, SPD, Minister of the *Interior, Stenographische Berichte*, July 2, 1919, vol. 327, 1219.

67. See, for example, Larry Eugene Jones, *German Liberalism and the Dissolution of the Weimar Party System, 1918–1933* (Chapel Hill: The University of North Carolina Press, 1988), 37–43.

68. Walther Schücking, DDP, *Stenographische Berichte*, March 3, 1919, vol. 326, 475–476.

69. Ibid.

70. Ibid.

71. Ibid., 476

72. Ibid.

73. Erich Koch-Weser, DDP, *Stenographische Berichte*, February 28, 1919, vol. 326, 390.

74. Ibid.

75. Ibid.

76. Rudolf Heinze, DVP, *Stenographische Berichte*, February 28, 1919, vol. 326, 396; July 30, 1919, vol. 329, 2093; Heinze was a member of the delegation's executive committee.

77. Ibid.

78. Ibid.

79. Ibid.

80. Ibid.

81. Delbrück, *Stenographische Berichte*, July 2, 1919, vol. 327, 1216.

82. Ibid.

83. Ibid.

84. Wolfgang Mommsen, *Max Weber and German Politics 1890–1920*, translated by Michael Steinberg (Chicago: The University of Chicago Press, 1984), 391.

85. Wolfgang Mommsen, "The Spirit of 1914 and the Ideology of a German 'Sonderweg'," in *Imperial Germany 1867–1918*, 210–211.

86. Max Weber, "Parliament and Government in a Reconstructed Germany," I, "Bismarck's Legacy," in Max Weber, *Economy and Society: An Outline of Interpretive Sociology*, eds. Guenther Roth and Claus Wittich (New York: Bedminster Press, 1968), 1385.

87. Ibid., 1387.

88. Ibid., 1385.

89. Ibid.

90. Ibid., 1392.

91. Mommsen, *Max Weber and German Politics*, 332–380; also Marianne Weber, *Max Weber: A Biography*, translated by Harry Zohn (New York: John Wiley & Sons, 1975), 638–641.

92. Mommsen, *Max Weber and German Politics*, 187–189.

93. Ibid., 187.

94. Marianne Weber, *Max Weber*, 653; see also his January 1919 lecture "Politics as a Vocation," in Max Weber, *From Max Weber: Essays in Sociology*, eds. H. H. Gerth and C. Wright Mills (London: Routledge, 1991), 113–114.

95. Mommsen, *Max Weber and German Politics*, 186.

96. Ibid., 424, 426.

97. Conservative leader Kuno Graf Westarp discusses the importance of faith in salvation through a Bismarck-like leader in Westarp, *Konservative Politik im Übergang vom Kaiserreich zur Weimarer Republik*, edited by Friedrich Freiherr Hiller von Gaertringen with Karl J. Mayer and Reinhold Weber (Düsseldorf: Droste Verlag, 2001), 556–560.

98. "Bismarcks Schatten," *Alldeutsche Blätter*, Nr. 12/15, March 27, 1920.

98. See "Bismarck" in *Hamburger Nachrichten*, Nr. 167, April 1, 1919.

100. Alfred Jacobsen, April 1, 1919, in *Hamburger Nachrichten*, Nr. 169, April 2, 1919. For Jacobsen's radical nationalist connections, see Uwe Lohalm, *Völkischer Radikalismus. Die Geschichte des Deutschvölkischen Schutz- und Trutz-Bundes 1919–1923* (Hamburg: Leibniz-Verlag, 1970), 8.

101. Ibid.

102. Thomas Childers, "Languages of Liberalism," 331–338.

103. Jones, *German Liberalism*, 155–156.

104. *Bismarckhort der Deutschnationalen Volkspartei* (before the June 6, 1920 elections), in Stadtsbibliothek zu Berlin, Sammelband: "Reichstagswahl 1920. Flugschriften und Plakaten," #35.

105. See Deutsche Volkspartei, *Mitteilungsblatt für den Wahlkreisverband Berlin*, Nr. 1, April 1920, in Stadtbibliothek zu Berlin, Sammelband: "Reichstagswahl 1920. Flugschriften und Plakaten," #97; for the DNVP, see *Blätter für das Münsterland. Organ des Landesverbandes Westfalen-West der Deutschnationalen Volkspartei*, Nr. 17, April 1, 1924.

106. "Erklärung des Alldeutschen Verbandes," Feb. 16, 1919, Landesarchiv Berlin: Rep 240 (Zeitgeschichtliche Sammlung)/Acc. 243/Nr. 161.

107. In 1918 membership totaled 36,377 and peaked in 1922 at 52,000. Edgar Hartwig, "Alldeutscher Verband (ADV) 1891–1939," in Dieter Fricke, ed., *Lexicon zur Parteiengeschichte*, I, 13–47.

108. Ian Kershaw, *Hitler: 1889–1936: Hubris* (New York: W. W. Norton, 1998), 136–137.

109. For the significance of the Pan-German League in the Weimar Republic and, in particular, its relationship with the DNVP, see Barry Jackisch, "'Not a Large, but a Strong Right': The Pan- German League, Radical Nationalism, and Rightist Party Politics in Weimar Germany, 1918–1933" (Ph.D. diss., State University of New York at Buffalo, 2000).

110. Mommsen, *Rise and Fall*, 156–157; see also Lohalm, *Völkischer Radikalismus*.

111. Willi Krebs, "Deutschvölkischer Schutz- und Trutzbund (DSTB) 1919–1922 (1924)," in Dieter Fricke, ed., *Lexicon zur Parteiengeschichte*, II, 562–568; see also Kershaw, *Hitler: 1889–1936: Hubris*, 137–138.

112. Freytagh-Loringhoven, at a *Schutz- und Trutzbund* Bismarck ceremony in Halle, in BAL, RlbPa, R8034 II, 7098, #177: *Hallesche Zeitung*, Nr. 156, April 1, 1922.

113. Mommsen, *Rise and Fall*, 156–157; Detlev Rose, *Die Thule-Gesellschaft. Legende – Mythos – Wirklichkeit* (Tübingen: Grabert Verlag, 1994), 67.

114. Mommsen, *Rise and Fall*, 157; Kershaw, *Hitler: 1889–1936: Hubris*, 137–138.

115. Adolf Hitler, "Dummheit oder Verbrechen," speech at Nazi gathering, Munich, January 4, 1921, in Eberhard Jäckel, ed., *Hitler. Sämtliche Aufzeichnungen 1905–1924* (Stuttgart: Deutsche Verlags-Anstalt, 1980), 294.

116. Hitler at a Nazi Bismarck celebration in the Bürgerbräukeller in Munich, April 2, 1922, in Jäckel, ed., *Hitler. Sämtliche Aufzeichnungen 1905–1924*, 598–599.

117. For the history of the Stahlhelm, see Volker Berghahn, *Der Stahlhelm. Bund*

der Frontsoldaten 1918–1935 (Düsseldorf: Droste Verlag, 1966); for the Stahlhelm's role in transforming Weimar's burghers, see Peter Fritzsche, *Rehearsals for Fascism: Populism and Political Mobilization in Weimar Germany* (New York: Oxford University Press, 1990).

118. "Bismarck" in *Der Stahlhelm: Halbmonatsschrift des "Bundes der Front-soldaten,"* Nr. 7, April 1, 1920.

119. "Der Aufruf des 'Reichskanzlers Kapp' vom 13. März 1920," in Johannes Erger, *Der Kapp-Lüttwitz-Putsch. Ein Beitrag zur deutschen Innenpolitik 1919/20* (Düsseldorf: Droste Verlag, 1967), 324.

120. Erger, *Der Kapp-Lüttwitz-Putsch*, 90.

121. See "Der versuchte Staatsstreich," in ADB, Nr. 12/13, March 27, 1920.

122. Stresemann quoted in Henry Ashby Turner, Jr., *Stresemann and the Politics of the Weimar Republic* (Princeton, New Jersey: Princeton University Press, 1963), 66–67.

123. "Bismarck" in *Deutsche Zeitung*, Nr. 136, April 1, 1920.

124. Ibid.

125. Adolf Hitler, "Das Schaufmännchen" from *Völkischer Beobachter*, May 19, 1921, in Jäckel, ed., *Hitler. Sämtliche Aufzeichnungen 1905–1924*, 401.

126. Further examples: Max Dreßler, "Ein ernster Gedenktag," in BAL, RlbPa, R8034 II, 7098, #47: *Deutsche Zeitung*, Nr. 174, April 16, 1921; Alfred Roth at Friedrichsruh, April 1, 1920, in *Hamburger Nachrichten*, Nr. 169, April 2, 1920; "Zum 1. April" in *Hamburger Nachrichten*, Nr. 155, April 1, 1922; *Deutscher Volkswart*, Nr. 3, March 1920.

127. Graf Westarp at DNVP Bismarck celebration at Conventgarten in Hamburg, April 1, 1920, in *Hamburger Nachrichten*, Nr. 169, April 2, 1920.

128. "Zu Bismarcks Gedächtnis" in *Völkischer Beobachter*, Nr. 27, April 3, 1920; see also *Hamburger Nachrichten*, Nr. 151, April 2, 1921; other examples: "Bismarck und unser Volk" from speech at Bismarck celebration of the Alten-Herrenvereinigung des Weinheimer S. C. zu Darmstadt, by Rudolf Kindt, Darmstadt in BAL, RlbPa, R8034 II, 7098, #46: *Deutsche Zeitung*, Nr. 173, April 15, 1921; Freytagh-Loringhoven, at Bismarck ceremony of the *Deutschvölkische Schutz- und Trutzbund* in Halle, in BAL, RlbPa, R8034 II, 7098, #177: *Hallesche Zeitung*, Nr. 156, April 1, 1922; Rechtsanwalt Dr. Berger at Pan-German Bismarck celebration in Friedrichsruh, April 2, 1923, in *Hamburger Nachrichten*, Nr. 157, April 3, 1923; "Otto von Bismarck" in *Völkischer Beobachter*, July 31, 1923.

120. "Bismarcks Geburtstag" in *Kreuzzeitung*, Nr. 150, April 1, 1920.

130. DNVP advertisement in Hamburger Nachrichten, Nr. 167, April 1, 1920; see also *Hamburger Nachrichten*, Nr. 151, April 2, 1921; "Bismarck und Wirth" in *Blätter für das Münsterland. Organ des Landesverbandes Westfalen-West der Deutschnationalen Volkspartei*, Nr. 7, March 1, 1922.

131. "Zum 1. April" in *Hamburger Nachrichten*, Nr. 167, April 1, 1920; see also "Zu Bismarcks Gedächtnis," *Völkischer Beobachter*, Nr. 27, April 3, 1920.

132. Childers, "Languages of Liberalism," 338.

133. Jones, *German Liberalism*, 67–80.

134. BAL, RlbPa, R8034 II, 7098, #48: *Deutsche Zeitung*, Nr. 148, April 1, 1921; see also "Bismarck" in the Deutschbund's *Deutscher Volkswart*, Nr. 3, March 1920, 76.

135. Mommsen, *Rise and Fall*, 157.

136. Dr. Hugo Preuß mentioned the incident with the Bismarck bust in a speech in the Prussian Landtag, July 6, 1922, in Herbert Michaelis and Ernst Schraepler, eds., *Ursachen und Folgen. Vom deutschen Zusammenbruch 1918 und 1945 bis zur staatlichen Neuordnung Deutschlands in der Gegenwart.* Vol. 4, *Die Weimarer Republik, Vertragserfüllung und innere Bedrohung 1919/1922* (Berlin: Dokumenten-Verlag Dr. Herbert Wendler & Co., 1960), 226–227.

137. Fritzsche, *Rehearsals for Fascism*, 65–66.

138. Ibid.

139. Kershaw, *Hubris*, 181–182; see also Kurt Sontheimer, *Antidemokratisches Denken in der Weimarer Republik: Die politischen Ideen des deutschen Nationalismus zwischen 1918 und 1933* (Munich: Deutscher Taschenbuch Verlag, 1968), 214–222.

140. Kershaw, *Hubris*, 181–182.

141. See, for example, Graf Yorck von Wartenburg, "Bismarcks Vermächtnis," in *Die Tradition*, July 3, 1920; BAL, RlbPa, R8034 II, 7098, #177: *Hallesche Zeitung*, Nr. 156, April 1, 1922; "Bismarck und unsere Zeit," by Heinrich Class in BAL, RlbPa, R8034 II, 7098, #36: *Deutsche Zeitung*, Nr. 148, April 1, 1921; "Bismarck, wach auf!" in BAL, RlbPa, R8034 II, 7098, #46: *Deutsche Zeitung*, Nr. 150, April 1, 1922.

142. Stresemann quoted in Mommsen, *Rise and Fall*, 129–131.

143. See "Reichsgründung," *Kreuzzeitung*, Nr. 18, January 18, 1923.

144. "Deutsches Ostermärchen" in *Der Tag*, Nr. 78, April 1, 1923.

145. BAL, RlbPa, R8034 II, 7099, #126: *Schlesische Zeitung*, July 29, 1923.

146. "Otto von Bismarck" in *Völkischer Beobachter*, July 31, 1923.

147. Henry Bernhard, ed., *Gustav Stresemann. Vermächtnis. Der Nachlass in drei Bänden*. I (Berlin: Ullstein Verlag, 1932), 54.

148. Turner, *Stresemann*, 119.

149. Mommsen, *Rise and Fall*, 141; for more putsch plans, see Scheck, *Tirpitz*, 95–109.

150. Hitler in Munich, August 21, 1923, in Michaelis and Schraepler, eds., *Ursachen und Folgen. Vol. 5, Die Weimarer Republik, das kritische Jahr 1923*, 181.

151. Ibid., 181.

152. Hitler quoted in Herbert Andrews, "Hitler, Bismarck, and History," *German Studies Review* 14(3): 516–517.

–4–

A Hopeful Interlude
Bismarck and the 'Years of Stability', 1923–1930

General Ludendorff: *What is your idea of a democracy, then?*
Max Weber: *In a democracy the people choose a leader whom they trust. Then the chosen man says, "Now shut your mouths and obey me. The people and the parties are no longer free to interfere in the leader's business."*
General Ludendorff: *I could like such a "democracy"!*
Conversation between Erich Ludendorff and Max Weber, 1919[1]

In the spring of 1924 Gustav Stresemann, Germany's Foreign Minister since August 1923, discussed his country's political situation with the British Ambassador, Lord D'Abernon. He had been talking with representatives of the German National People's Party, the largest non-socialist party in the Reichstag following the recent May elections. In tortuous negotiations, Stresemann had been trying to get them to join a coalition government. Despite the utter intransigence of die-hard opponents of Weimar, there was a group willing to participate in the government of the republic they so detested. During negotiations, however, it became clear that their understanding of current politics was still deeply colored by the myths that had shaped their world-view since 1918. As a condition of their entry into the government, they demanded Stresemann's resignation. In doing so, they were calling for the head of the man responsible for ending the Ruhr crisis, successfully repressing both left- and right-wing threats to the state, stabilizing the currency, and attempting to regularize the system of reparations payments on a basis favorable to Germany. It reflected political immaturity and an unwillingness to deal with political realities divorced from emotions. Faced with such intransigence, Stresemann could only throw up his hands and complain to the ambassador: "In other countries the successful conduct of foreign affairs brings about confidence in the Minister. Here it only produces envy . . . Events like this . . . make one realize what Bismarck meant when he said, 'I hated all night long'."[2]

Historians often characterize the period from the stabilization of the system until the Depression in 1929 as perhaps the most hopeful opportunity for the survival of a democratic Germany. Certainly in comparison with the chaos of the crisis decade that preceded it and the misery of the Depression that followed, these 'years of stability' do, in fact, appear to represent a hopeful interlude – a possible alternative to what actually came to pass in 1933. Recently, however, historians have come to question the stability of these years, seeing them instead as the period during which the foundation of democracy was undermined due to the effects of the crisis decade that preceded it. Looking at the struggle over the Bismarck image in these years, one can see further evidence of this undermining process, but also the promise of an alternative future. For these years would be marked by the confrontation between the realism and moderation of Stresemann and the emotional, often irrational politics of the national opposition. Each had a vision of Bismarck that corresponded to their own world-view – Stresemann of a leader who understood the realities of his situation and sought to achieve only what could be achieved without risking all, and the radical Right of an Iron Chancellor utterly opposed to the republic, ready to do anything necessary to speed its destruction. Each believed their Bismarck to be the most genuine. It was a struggle for all or none, for the system, imperfect though it may be, or for some idealized vision of a future Reich, stripped of all liberal, democratic values. The battles fought between these two opposing Bismarcks help illustrate one of the last hopes for the future of German democracy. While it was not the sole, decisive factor, an investigation of the dynamics of the Bismarck image can help us better understand both the process that ultimately led to Weimar's demise and the way in which it helped determine what might replace it.

Gustav Stresemann and the Pursuit of a Moderate Bismarck

The notion that Gustav Stresemann would become perhaps the greatest hope for the salvation of a democratic German republic would have tested the imagination of many if suggested only a few years before. Though having stood on the National Liberal Party's left-wing on domestic issues before 1918, he gained a reputation as a rabid expansionist during the war, even gaining the title of "Ludendorff's young man."[3] He was a loyal monarchist and remained so into the republic's early years. In fact, as late as 1922, Stresemann was still clinging to dreams of a restored monarchy. "The sharp criticism," he declared in Hamburg, "which Bismarck leveled at the Kaiser in the third volume of his reminiscences was not directed against the dynasty, and if Bismarck had had his way, then Germany today would still be a monarchist country."[4] That devotion to the Hohenzollerns made it diffi-cult for him to adjust positively to the republic.

Stresemann's intense wartime nationalism also carried over into the republic as he declared his outrage at the new international system with a rhetoric nearly indistinguishable from the radical Right. At a Bismarck celebration in 1922 he took issue with the idea of German war-guilt and the restrictions that then bound Germany. He announced that "[h]istory will duly describe the World War and set the peace of Versailles down as a document of disgrace. The world owes Germany reparations, the Treaty of Versailles must fall. Let us not lose our belief in the future!"[5] As much as he criticized the Allies' treatment of Germany, Stresemann also attacked his own government for what he saw as weak-kneed subservience to the enemy powers. From the start, he opposed the government's policy of fulfill-ment of the Versailles Treaty. At a Bismarck speech in April 1919 he complained that much of the problem lay in the attitude of the new leadership towards what he viewed as the successful political formula of the past. "The spirit of Bismarckian *Realpolitik* which characterized his domestic and foreign policy today becomes the most often attacked. One sets it up as an outpouring of evil power consciousness" and contrasts it with an idea that must lead "to world reconciliation and to a union of equal nations."[6] Condemning this Weimar substitute for Bismarckian politics, he had no doubt that "the exuberance of this politics of illusion will soon be fol-lowed by disenchantment."[7] For Stresemann, the answer lay with the Iron Chancellor. "When the dream is completely dreamed out, then we will have to return to the simple and robust Bismarckian conception with all means of *Realpolitik*, above all to fight for one's own people's space and development of their life chances, and to achieve its place among the nations, supported by its own power."[8]

As leader of the second largest Protestant-bourgeois party, such vocal opposi-tion did not bode well for the survival of democracy, especially after the shift to the right that followed the June 1920 Reichstag elections. As it turns out, though, his trajectory was not simply one of continuous intransigence. While the Kapp Putsch did little to alter his attitude, the events of the summer of 1921 and 1922 helped bring about a gradual acceptance of the current conditions. In the end they contributed to the transformation of an opponent into a *Vernunftrepublikaner* and ultimately into a determined defender of the Weimar Republic. The assassinations of Matthias Erzberger and Walther Rathenau by right-wing extremists led Stresemann to renounce the dangerous political rhetoric of groups to which he had once stood close. Already before Rathenau's killing, his growing realism was beginning to distinguish him from most others in the national opposition. With a Bismarck that was changing to reflect his evolving outlook, Stresemann in 1922 attacked the "call for the strong man."[9] Bismarck's greatness, he declared, "lay not in his cuirassier boots and the clenched fist. Bismarck knew how to deal with foreign countries in noble fashion."[10] While clearly not entirely enthusiastic about the regime, his model of a moderate Bismarck led Stresemann to demand support for the government in its rejection of the latest Allied demands. Such support, he stressed, reflected a love of fatherland greater than that of the intransigents to his right.

With his accession to the chancellorship in August 1923, his conversion was essentially complete. His ultimate goal remained Germany's return to its previous world power position. In that sense he retained some of the features he shared with the national opposition. The means with which he hoped to attain that goal, however, diverged significantly. His strategy continued in many respects the policy of the previous governments – 'fulfillment' or *Erfüllungspolitik*. By demonstrating to the Western Allies Germany's goodwill, he hoped to undermine the more onerous provisions of the Treaty and thereby gain the opportunity to revise its provisions.[11] Whereas the Right often based its position on a dream world of instant rejuvenation and an immediate war of revenge, Stresemann was aware of the country's military position and knew such a policy was folly.[12]

Interpretations of Stresemann's motives have ranged from cynical opportunism to genuine conversion to a reasonable foreign policy based on cooperation and reconciliation.[13] Certainly ministerial responsibility helped dampen his more aggressive instincts. In seeking to demonstrate Germany's goodwill, presenting a Bismarck image that contrasted with the popular foreign conception of the Iron Chancellor in cuirassier boots could help in gaining trust. If the symbol of Germany was not the warrior Bismarck, but the Chancellor of peace, Stresemann's ultimate objective of regaining lost territory and restoring Germany's previous position might be easier to achieve. Along with this went a realization that the stability of the political system was critical for the attainment of his goals. As a result, for the rest of his life Stresemann fought against his one-time allies with a moderate Bismarck for the survival of the republic.

Domestically, such a policy of patient diplomacy for consistent, though limited gains had several disadvantages in comparison to the radical Right's program. First of all, the concept of fulfillment was already associated with the Weimar Coalition – Bismarck's *Reichsfeinde*. Even Stresemann himself had been an energetic opponent of what he once derisively labeled *Illusionspolitik*. In addition, the fulfillment policy relied on patience and reasoned argument to justify the limited gains that were to accrue over a longer period. In contrast to the glorious visions of immediate revenge and sweeping territorial revision put forward in emotional appeals by the national opposition, such a cautious policy had to seem much too meek for a former world power. As Bethmann Hollweg did before him, Stresemann would find it difficult to make his moderation more appealing than the Right's fantastic visions.

Confrontations between the radical nationalist Bismarck and the moderate Bismarck were not long in coming, for in the May 1924 Reichstag elections fulfillment served as one of several critical issues. One month before, the German National People's Party set out its position at a party congress in the shadow of its hero in the Bismarck city of Hamburg. The events and speeches of the congress itself and simultaneous Bismarck celebrations blurred to the point where they were barely distinguishable from one another. The opening event of the party meeting was, in fact, a parade of the DNVP Bismarck Youth to the gravesite at Friedrichsruh. There, before the tomb, spoke the party's newest Reichstag candidate, Prince Otto von Bismarck, the Iron Chancellor's grandson. In perfect step with the party, he set out his program as a "fight against the treaty of shame and defense of national honor through a strong government."[14] Reichstag deputy Wilhelm Laverrenz concluded the pilgrimage with a summation of the party program, declaring: "We want out of the Weimar Constitution; we want to live in a Bismarckian world-view: Back to Bismarck, that is our slogan!"[15]

'Back to Bismarck' did indeed become the party slogan, both in 1924 and for the rest of the republic's existence. At speech after speech during the congress, representatives acknowledged the first chancellor as inspiration and model for their assault on the republic. 'Back to Bismarck', though, meant several different things. With regard to foreign policy, it meant a break with the timid, un-German practice of fulfillment and a return to an assertive position that sought to regain Germany's freedom of maneuver. According to DNVP leader Oskar Hergt, Chancellor Wilhelm Marx's claim that the government's policy was not one of fulfillment, but rather of liberation, was simply untrue. What the German people had before them was merely an illusory freedom, which they traced back to the earliest manifestation of "*Stresemannpolitik*." "More than ever have the government measures in this period been draped in the national mantle although they are only a second version of the old *Erfüllungspolitik* in more careful form."[16] The German Nationalists demanded an immediate and forceful offensive for revision of Versailles – the exact opposite of Stresemann's tactic. Concern for how other countries might react to the composition of parliament or the government can no longer concern the German voter. "For the new government of the right, only the old word of Bismarck may be valid: 'We Germans fear God and nothing else in the world'."[18]

Stresemann and his German People's Party, however, were not about to leave the field to their rivals unchallenged. Perhaps like no other individual in Weimar, Gustav Stresemann tied himself, his politics, and his party to the image of Bismarck. Aside from the Nazis, few other parties had such a dominant personality as leader and few, if any, other parties used the image of their leader in election propaganda to the extent that the DVP did. In one election poster after another, Stresemann's image stood front and center, often with Bismarck's somewhere in the background. In 1924 Stresemann graced one poster in the image of a blacksmith – the forger of a *new* Reich – with a shadowy Bismarck behind him, placing his hand on his shoulder and proclaiming, "So it is correct, Stresemann, you are doing it!"[18]

When, on the eve of the May 1924 elections, the DVP sought to present the electorate with the issues as it saw them – a struggle between realism and emotionalism – it should come as no surprise that they chose to do so in an election flyer entitled "Bismarck and our times." In it, the DVP set out its position along with criticism of its right-wing rival. "In the election battle," they wrote, "much will be said of Bismarckian politics, loudest and most often by people who hardly understand him correctly." The DNVP, from its position of intransigent opposition, found it easy to contrast the current conditions with those of the glory days of the Second Empire and framed its criticism of the ruling parties accordingly. By willfully ignoring the changed circumstances, the Nationalists attacked the government for not carrying out that firm, aggressive politics that they claim Bismarck would have. What they did not understand was that "[t]he statesman Bismarck always carried out a policy that took into account the power relationships . . ." Even "in the days of the highest expansion of power, he rejected a policy of the great word as political stupidity." Resting on the Iron Chancellor's authority, the DVP cited his declaration that "[t]he extreme parties in Germany are not capable of governing." The German Nationalists, they asserted, had no right to use Bismarck. "They possess no trace of Bismarckian *Realpolitik*, but rather practice an agitation of the catchphrase and promises, a foreign policy which they themselves know in the current power relationships is completely impossible without causing the greatest misfortune for people and fatherland." Rather than the DNVP, it was Stresemann's DVP that was the "party, carried by the Bismarckian spirit of love of fatherland and national responsibility, the party, which carries through history the famous title of the party of the founding of the Reich, the party that also consciously serves for the maintenance of the Reich at the cost of sacrifice – that is the German People's Party."[19]

The DNVP responded with a flyer of its own entitled "Against the Stresemann Party – in the Spirit of Bismarck." In it they clearly set their sights on the DVP leader and his willingness to join in governmental coalitions with Bismarck's enemies, particularly the Democrats and SPD. In what could be read as an attempt to split the right-wing members of the People's Party, the German Nationalists dismissed the DVP's historical claims to a Bismarckian pedigree. They made a clear distinction between the 'true' National Liberals of the tradition of Bennigsen, Miquel, and von Heyl – those genuine German patriots who stood with Bismarck back in the early days of the Reich – and the line that split off from them, the followers of Lasker and Bassermann. With this last group they associated Stresemann. This triumvirate of Lasker–Bassermann–Stresemann, they asserted, led the National Liberals into

> the swamp of the "great liberal party" . . . of which those men always warned; to them the Fatherland really went above party; to them, like Bismarck, every connection with democracy appeared disgraceful; they, like Bismarck, led a bitter struggle their entire life against bourgeois and social democracy. Lasker–Bassermann–Stresemann, however, always sought and drove the path to the "great liberal party," and with it to that which Bismarck and the great National Liberals held to be fatal and essentially degenerative.[20]

This degeneration showed itself in the path down which Stresemann chose to lead his party – not against "the democratic-socialist international, not against

Marxism, no! Against the German National People's Party!"[21] The German Nationalists had thereby declared themselves to be opponents of the DVP. In contrast to the Democratic-SPD-tainted German People's Party, the DNVP portrayed itself as the truest embodiment of German nationalist politics and the nearest manifestation of that ultimate Bismarckian dream – right-wing unity. It was, they claimed, "the Bismarckian cartel concept made real, as in an organization which encompasses all elements and groups, which is prepared for the *Volksgemeinschaft* on the basis of the national world-view."[22]

When the polls closed the DNVP had registered a dramatic victory. With 106 seats, they had become the second strongest party in the Reichstag. Unburdened by the stigma of government responsibility, their emotional appeals for an aggressive policy of resistance to Stresemann appear to have struck a chord. Among people still recovering from the trauma of the previous years, a Bismarck in cuirassier boots with sword at the ready for the reassertion of their interests likely had more appeal than a realistic, patient leader, willing to accept in much smaller increments what could be achieved at any given time. In denouncing Stresemann for his willingness to cooperate with *Reichsfeinde*, his weak foreign policy, and bowing to the wishes of the enemy – in short, his insufficiently German, un-Bismarckian politics – the German Nationalists were sounding a note that resonated among the nation's middle-classes.

In contrast to the rewards reaped by the emotional politics of the DNVP, preaching a moderate course from the seat of government cost Stresemann and his party a good deal of support. They lost twenty seats.[23] While the defeat must have been disappointing, it did not come as a surprise to the Foreign Minister – it was the price of responsibility as he saw it, of being willing to live up to that Bismarckian dictum of daring to be unpopular for the sake of the nation. It was a price he would continue to pay, for the German Nationalists had found a formula that worked, and the effects of their political rhetoric would batter the champion of moderation not only from without, but also from within.[24]

For many national-minded Germans, not just those within the DNVP, the Foreign Minister's political turnabout must have seemed perplexing. Soon after the party's 1924 setback, in fact, he would have to defend his position against members of his own party's right who accused him of betraying his principles. At a party congress in May 1924 he responded, and, just as he had done against the German Nationalists, he defended himself with the image of a moderate, reasonable Bismarck. "If one questions the correctness of the policy we have followed from 1920 to 1924," he asserted, "of seeking allies where we could find them, where the most productive work could be accomplished, then I must ask whether the greatest German statesmen . . . have not done the very same. He who elevates principle above all else must lay his wreath not on the monument of Bismarck, but rather on the monument of Eugen Richter. The idea of holding unflinchingly to principle is an aspect of political philistinism . . . Bismarck knew how to take things as they were and make allowances for circumstances."[25]

Despite the obstacles, Stresemann continued along the path he felt corresponded to the spirit of Bismarck. His efforts to get the French to begin evacuating the Rhineland showed no signs of progress by early 1925 and so, hoping to accelerate the process, he proposed a security treaty between the two neighbors. What would become the Treaty of Locarno marked an important stage in the improvement of Franco-German relations and a further step in Germany's road back to Great Power status. For Stresemann, Locarno was meant to demonstrate German goodwill, thereby deflating French fears and obviating the need for continued occupation of the Rhineland. While guaranteeing the territorial status quo in the West, the treaty did not commit Germany to a similar guarantee in the East – something Stresemann was not about to accept and which he took great pains to stress when justifying the agreement back home.[26]

The task of justifying the treaty would not be easy, for Stresemann came under immediate assault from the right once the negotiations became public. For much of the national opposition, Locarno was the opposite of what they felt was needed. Rather than the aggressive reassertion of German interests, the 'spirit of Locarno' promised continued cooperation and therefore acceptance of the Versailles system. In particular, two aspects of the treaty proved especially onerous to the radical Right. First, Locarno specifically committed Germany to renounce its claims to Alsace-Lorraine. Second, Germany was required to enter the League of Nations, an organization the Right viewed with intense suspicion. While some German Nationalists agreed with some of Stresemann's arguments, most strongly objected to the renunciation of Alsace-Lorraine and demanded unreasonable conditions be put to the Western Allies before negotiations could begin. Meanwhile, further right the Pan-Germans and Nazis launched a vitriolic attack, calling the plan a "third Versailles" and demanding Stresemann's indictment for treason.[27]

In January 1925 the DNVP joined the government for the first time. It proved, however, to be an uneasy relationship which did not last long. Intransigence among the party's right wing spread, particularly through the local branches, as the Locarno negotiations dragged out, making Stresemann's task more difficult. While the party leadership maintained a truce with the DVP and its leader, instructing local branches to refrain from open criticism, the far right refused to obey. When the coalition collapsed in October 1925 and Germany failed in its attempt to gain a permanent seat on the League Council, all bets were off and the attacks resumed, led by the party's *völkisch* wing and in particular Heinrich Class and the Pan-Germans.

Opposition to Stresemann formed one of the primary pillars of radical nationalist political rhetoric after Locarno.[28] To the Right, the notion that Stresemann could claim to be the truest incarnation of the Bismarckian spirit was laughable at best, treasonous at worst. The Nazis relentlessly attacked him, derisively labeling him "the 'Bismarck' of the November Democracy" for such pretensions.[29] A Nazi paper in Karlsruhe noted that "[t]he times of misery of a people, which often end with its complete collapse, always then appear when the state succeeds from the hands of the great into the hands of the small, from the hands of the strong into those of the weak, from the hands of the fighter into those of the dealer. The German state has been passed out of the hands of the fighter Bismarck into those of the bottled-beer dealer Stresemann. The result is clear for all to see."[30] Hitler himself devoted a good deal of time to attacking Stresemann for his un-German, un-Bismarckian foreign policy.[31] He criticized his acceptance of the democratic system. "Bismarck," he claimed, "had once fought against the majority and succeeded against it, founded Germany against the majority, while Herr Stresemann is a child of the majority."[32] The implication was clear. Just as Bismarck had known what was right for Germany, Hitler knew what was right for the country now. He knew this because he, not Stresemann, was the true Bismarckian, most in touch with his spirit. He could therefore assert that "if Bismarck came today and he had to cast a criticism over the foreign policy of the current German Reich, so would that criticism either eliminate this foreign policy or land Bismarck in prison. He could not speak otherwise than thousands and thousands of German patriots today speak about this foreign policy."[33] For Hitler, the greatest historical right to lead a nation goes to the one most hated by the enemy. The French wanted the Nazis arrested, "because we are the representatives of the other spirit, of the other Germany." [34] This was the Nazis' greatest justification. In considering Stresemann's path of reconciliation, Hitler knew, therefore, under which banner he was leading his fight as he declared in 1930: "I can place myself here with pride in the shadow of a greater one. What do you believe if Bismarck were among us today: would France love Stresemann more, or Bismarck? Would France wish more that Stresemann be arrested or Bismarck?"[35]

Others on the radical Right also took up the fight against Stresemann's conception of Bismarckian politics. In March 1926 the *Hamburger Nachrichten* lamented the fact that "all political stupidities of the last thirty-six years are to be traced back to the inadequacy of the leaders, the leading circles, from the Sanzibar Treaty up to the Satyr play in Geneva. With grim humor would Prince Bismarck pillory the occurrences of recent times if he still lingered among us."[36] At a birthday ceremony in 1927 former General Karl Litzmann spoke to the Berlin Bismarck Society and expressed the hope that the men governing them at the moment did what they did for the fatherland and truly wished for its well-being. This, however, was doubtful, since "they do not travel Bismarckian paths with the more than modest policy of cooperation and the so-called 'understanding'." These paths have led us beyond London, Locarno and Thoiry to Geneva and up to today have registered endless humiliations and disappointments." [37] With a Bismarck at the helm, things certainly would have been different. "Could you imagine," he asked, "that a Bismarck would have gone to London in order to approve the ruinous Dawes Plan? Or to Locarno in order to voluntarily recognize the shameful Treaty of Versailles – the 'monstrosity of filth and fire' born of hate and lies? Or to the – ah, so competent, wise and just – League of Nations in Geneva in order to sit with obligatory smiles with our mortal enemies at the negotiating table? . . . It is, for me, as if I could hear out of the rustling of the oaks in the Saxon Forest a defiant, derisive laugh of the dead giant Bismarck!"[38]

For the next several years Stresemann would continue to justify his chosen path against such hostile opposition, trying to demonstrate the wisdom of cooperation and reconciliation in the face of admittedly few tangible benefits. While Germany improved economically, evacuation of occupied territory came much slower than Stresemann would have preferred. Nevertheless, he was convinced that his way was the best. To an audience in Stuttgart in 1926 he expressed his frustration towards his opponents on the right. Sounding very much like his imperial predecessor, von Bülow, he declared that it would be good "to write a book about the misunderstood Bismarck, in which it would be depicted how he, at the height of power, was most careful in the use of power, how he succeeded in 1866 and 1870 against those who could not receive enough. He wanted to maintain the peace of Europe. That would be a better image of him than that of the legend made of him when he is depicted as the man with the cuirassier boots."[39]

In the years following Locarno, Stresemann pursued the path he felt to be most in accordance with Bismarckian principles. In 1926 Germany entered the League of Nations with a permanent seat on the League Council, and soon thereafter talks between the German and French Foreign Ministers were held in the French town of Thoiry for a complete resolution of all disputes between the two countries. Thoiry did not resolve all outstanding differences, and as time went by it became clear that the fruits of fulfillment would indeed be slow in coming. For a while, though, it did seem that Stresemann's insistence on paying attention to the realities of Germany's foreign policy situation was having some effect on his former enemies as the pragmatists within the DNVP appeared to be gaining the upper hand within the party.[40] Once again they joined in a Cabinet coalition in 1927, this time based on acceptance of the policy of reconciliation.

This veering away from party principles, however, did not suit everyone in the DNVP. Frustration with the course of cooperation, along with continued virulent hostility to Stresemann, led the party's right wing to defy orders and resume its assault on the government. At a 1928 election rally in Dresden, DNVP and Pan-German member Paul Bang complained angrily that the Germans had a "spirit of London", a "spirit of Locarno", a "spirit of Thoiry", a "spirit of Geneva", but the one thing they no longer had was "the spirit of Bismarck, the spirit of Potsdam!"[41] Soon discontent among the right wing led them to launch a full scale assault, masterminded by Heinrich Class, which resulted in Alfred Hugenberg's election to the party chairmanship in October 1928. Without a split in the party, this effectively ended Stresemann's chances of finding further cooperation with his neighbors to the right.

The trend towards the right in German politics that Hugenberg's triumph symbolized also found expression in the Center Party – an original member of the Weimar Coalition – when it elected Monsignor Ludwig Kaas to the party chairmanship in December 1928. Kaas had already established himself as an opponent of Stresemann's foreign policy and now set himself the goal of pursuing a nationalist and authoritarian course. In October 1929 he declared his belief in "leadership on a grand scale."[42] The Foreign Minister had lost one more potential ally.[43]

The DNVP's declining electoral fortunes led Hugenberg to develop closer ties to other, more radical right-wing elements. Increasingly close relations with the Stahlhelm amplified the force of Hugenberg's attacks on the government. Seeking to bring unity to the national opposition, he turned to the National Socialists, thereby providing critical legitimacy to a man and a party whose stock and trade had been virulent verbal abuse of the national leadership. If one could still not talk of a unified national opposition, there could be little doubt of the increased determination to undo all that Stresemann had achieved.

While the DNVP's 1928 electoral setback was its first since 1919, the DVP continued its trend of diminishing vote totals and decreasing Reichstag representation. Stresemann's efforts to focus the people on the critical national issues as he saw them, through rational, moderate debate, failed to show results in the face of the increasing appeal of splinter parties playing to limited economic issues.[44] Their success ate away at the support of the DVP and DDP, underscoring the decreasing legitimacy enjoyed by the traditional ideological parties.[45] While their success rested more clearly upon bread-and-butter issues, though playing on the dissatisfaction with parliamentary democracy generally, even some splinter parties could not resist the temptation to drape themselves in the Bismarckian mantle, as his image graced the election propaganda of the *Wirtschaftspartei*, one of the most successful splinter parties.[46]

Despite his disappointment, Stresemann and his few remaining allies continued their efforts to promote their program and counter right-wing attacks as best they could. In April 1928 Stresemann's ally in the DVP, Albrecht Graf zu Stolberg-Wernigerode, answered the criticism leveled at the Foreign Minister by the DNVP's Graf Westarp.[47] Westarp had written in the *Kreuzzeitung* that: "The illusions from Locarno, Geneva, and Thoiry have evaporated. The policy characterized by these names has suffered a fiasco, has not brought success for Germany."[48] On the contrary, Stolberg wrote, Stresemann had actually taken away French Premier Poincaré's best weapon in eliminating the need for direct intervention in German territory. While Stolberg-Wernigerode had to concede Westarp's point that the policy took too long, this was not Stresemann's fault. It takes time, he stressed, to change world opinion. What was needed was "a policy of wise moderation," such as with Locarno and Geneva, "thus precisely that which, in your article, you condemn."[49] The arguments in Westarp's article proved once more to Stolberg-Wernigerode, "how right Bismarck was when he said: 'The best is often the enemy of the good.' Nationalist politics is often the enemy of the achievement of national goals."[50]

Stresemann too, in spite of failing health, continued to defend his policies and the republic. To university students in May 1928 he stressed that the "maintenance of the peace and the efforts directed towards that are not cowardice, are not weaknesses, they are real political recognition of our own national interests."[51] At a Constitution Day celebration in late 1928 he spoke of how "one quotes these days many a Bismarck word that says that after an unlucky war Germany could become great again, but to be sure only on the basis of a republic."[52] Noting how "the great Chancellor of the old Reich had a nearly visionary way of seeing the future," he hoped that such a prediction would prove to be true. He warned, however, that they had to be clear "that neither dreamy resignation nor over-exuberant force of words where actual force is lacking will bring us there, but rather only the sober, conscious work of a whole generation."[53]

Stresemann's struggle to combat the problems he saw on both the left and right would consume him to the end of his life. For the last great, towering figure in German politics who stood firmly in the camp of the republic's defenders, this lonely fight proved beyond his powers. As his strength faded due to illness, his presence appeared to fade from the stage already before his death. Some of his last, most significant acts in defense of the system came, in fact, through telephone or telegraph from his place of convalescence. His passing in September 1929 dealt the democratic republic a blow from which it never recovered. Whether he could have saved democracy in Germany had he lived can never be answered. Certainly his work seemed an uphill fight even at the height of his strength. For his efforts at bringing Germany back to a position of respect, if not power, in the world, he failed to gain the appreciation of much of the middle class, most of whom had already deserted his party for the extremists before he died.[54] His admiration of Bismarck had guided his politics throughout his career, and in Weimar he often portrayed himself as a Bismarckian figure, fiercely nationalist, misunderstood, yet always working for what he felt was best for Germany. In one of his last Bismarck speeches, Stresemann criticized his countrymen for their treatment of his idol. "It is a weakness of the Germans that they so often only recognize greatness when the bearer of the work no longer lingers among the living."[55] How easily he could have been describing himself! And just as Germans after 1898 came to regret the loss of the man who first gave them their nation, many would eventually have cause to bemoan the passing of perhaps the last man who could have saved it.

The Radical Bismarck and the Undermining of Weimar Democracy

As Stresemann faded from the scene in the late 1920s, his vision of a moderate, liberal Germany seemed to be going along with him.[56] The liberal parties were in disarray, having suffered a steady decline in votes as their constituency continued a steady pilgrimage rightward. From the right, the forces of destruction pressed on, spreading their anti-democratic rhetoric of salvation. A speaker for the Berlin Bismarck Society in 1928 declared that "only radical nationalism can save us." Victory could come "only through conscious rejection of all that is today."[57] Heinrich Class and his fellow Pan-Germans had come to this conclusion years before. From 1924 on, he set out to gain control of the DNVP through its provincial organizations, transforming it into an instrument of his radical vision for the future German Reich. Even before he achieved this goal, Class began plotting for fellow Pan-German and Bismarckian Alfred Hugenberg's appointment as chancellor and dictator in 1926. Sending a steady stream of visitors to Hindenburg, including the Field Marshal's own son, Oskar, whom he had won over to the idea, Class hoped to put into practice his still rather amorphous vision of his longed-for German dictatorship.[58] It was yet another salvo in the Right's battle to end the crisis of leadership on its own terms. The difficulty lay in deciding just what those terms actually were.

What the Right was fighting for, beyond an end to Weimar and its replacement by some form of authoritarian government, no one could say with certainty. But if this purely negative goal could prove enough of a unifying element for the elimination of what existed, it provided no such unity for what was to follow. To understand the German Right in Weimar, one must first realize its remarkably fractured nature and its often powerful embrace of a politics of the irrational. It is taken for granted that the German Left was the traditional home of factionalized politics. While this is certainly true, the mistake is to assume an hegemony and a consistency on the right which simply did not exist. Examining the rhetoric of Bismarckians provides ample evidence to support this conclusion and enables us to see this phenomenon in all its confusion. In doing so, we will look further at the process of the Right's progressive radicalization as parties and organizations succeeded one another in their quest to destroy the republic.

While the lack of commonality is indeed striking, one constant can be found: an image of Bismarck and a brand of radical politics embodied in it. This is not to say, however, that the specifics of the Bismarck image were common to all groups – quite the contrary. The truth is that a remarkable diversity existed between and even within different groups. To talk, then, about a 'Stahlhelm Bismarck', a 'Pan-German Bismarck', and a 'Nazi Bismarck' would be to grossly oversimplify an astonishingly complex phenomenon. Nevertheless, the general features could be said to provide enough of a unifying vision to signify a serious threat to the republic. As groups rose and fell and personnel transferred from one to the other, the image of Bismarck and its associated ideas went with them. While certainly not the cause of this process, the image of the Iron Chancellor must be seen as an important facilitating factor. Even in the so-called period of stability, impatience with the leadership in Berlin grew and would increase dramatically with the Depression. During this time, the politics of destruction embodied in the Right's Bismarck image would spread as the supporters of the bourgeois parties fled their traditional homes for those with more radical solutions. It was in this period that the crisis of leadership would reach its crescendo, and its solution, through the emergence of a 'new' Bismarck, would find ever greater numbers of advocates.[59]

Despite the growing temporal distance from the Iron Chancellor's era, the mid-1920s witnessed an increase in the size and frequency of Bismarck celebrations.[60] The Hamburg monument was the sight of powerful demonstrations of devotion to the Cult as thousands participated in torch-light processions under the motto "Struggle against everything un-German, struggle against the insanity of the International, because only from the firm national will will the salvation some day come for us!"[61] Such spectacles would continue throughout the remainder of the decade. Also prominent were the yearly "German Bismarck Day" celebrations put together by the newly refounded Association for the Establishment of a Bismarck National Monument.[62] As the years of stability turned into the years of crisis, the continued use of the traditional sites and rituals of the Bismarckian political religion would provide important outlets for nationalist frustration with the continuing problems of German leadership.

For many within the national opposition, the key to victory lay in a unified movement that could topple Weimar through the force of its combined strength. Bismarck therefore continued his pre-war role as inspiration for right-wing unity, but now with a mission far more radical than before and with the added weight of an additional decade of established ritual. In a 1924 article in the Pan-German *Deutsche Zeitung*, fittingly titled "Bismarck's Resurrection," Max Maurenbrecher expressed hope for radical nationalist unity through devotion to the Iron Chancellor. While blame for Germany's weakness in the face of the French occupation lay with the government, the national movement itself had to shoulder some responsibility. Through its own division it had proven unable to provide the leadership necessary to save the country from disgrace. Maurenbrecher called for a renewal and reorganization of the national movement and, to do this, he declared that "for the national Germany of the future, the real hero of the Germans, Bismarck, will become the master under whose thoughts we all bow and from whose roots we will all strive to grow further."[63] This "genuine, original . . . living Bismarck" offered "the basis on which the *völkisch* state of the future will be able to build itself. In this Bismarck rests the heart of all that we try today to establish as the *völkisch* state of the Germans in contrast to the western democracies."[64]

Here we see the continuation of pre-war populism expressed through the language of Bismarckian political religion. For, according to Maurenbrecher, it was in the ideas of this "undemocratic and anti-parliamentary" Bismarck that lay the heart "out of which the new anti-democratic state of free German burghers, farmers, and workers has to grow."[65] It was for this purpose that the national, *völkisch*-minded people had to organize and work together. When laying their wreaths at the feet of Bismarck, they should be thinking about this work. "Not the dead one, but rather the living one it is whom we seek and believe, not the old one, but rather the eternal-youth, not the one who was, who one time in the past created a glorious Reich, but rather the future one, out of whose wisdom we will be able to create a new Reich. He shall once again rise from the dead for us and point to the new creation!"[66]

Clearly, one of the main elements of the radical Bismarck that could unify the disparate elements of the national opposition was his embodiment of anti-parliamentary, anti-democratic politics. Historian and radical Right sympathizer Karl Alexander von Müller described Bismarck at a birthday celebration in April 1924 as "by nature undemocratic down to his foundation."[67] The radical Right often saw itself as a besieged minority calling for national renewal against the initial popularity of the Weimar Coalition. Instead of despair, von Müller drew strength from this position, a position he equated with that of Bismarck, claiming that, while Bismarck ruled, "he stood, often as the only one, in the breach for a German royalty against parliamentary government, domination by the masses, political democracy."[68] Echoing von Müller's characterization, Heinrich Göppert declared the Iron Chancellor to be "by his entire essence undemocratic."[69] In fact, according to Göppert, the German people as a whole were by nature undemocratic. It was, indeed, their strength. "The greatest times of German history were those when the leadership lay in the firm hands of chosen leaders. Then one saw what a magnificent people we actually have."[70] Heinrich Class drew the logical conclusion from such ideas when he called for the "elimination of parliament-domination."[71] In doing so, he made clear that freeing Germany "from the unbearable domination of parliament . . . must be tied to a recognition of Bismarck."[72] If putschism was fading from the scene, the ideal that this anti-democratic Bismarck represented provided a vision for the national opposition that signified continued struggle against a 'foreign', 'un-German' system. During a time in which some had hoped that the period of post-inflation stability would reinvigorate the legitimacy of the parliamentary system, the anti-party rhetoric of radical Bismarckians indicated a trend that was just the opposite. Antipathy and mistrust of the traditional parties led to their breakdown, particularly those of the bourgeois middle. For Bismarckians, this could not have been a disappointment.

If, for the vast majority of the national opposition, Bismarck served to inspire out and out opposition to democracy, he also worked to galvanize the drive for its replacement by some form of authoritarianism. For at least one segment of the Right – the DNVP – the slogan 'Back to Bismarck', which guided them throughout their existence, also meant a devotion to monarchism. Their desire for a return to the imperial structure remained an important part of their political rhetoric. The connection between monarchism and Bismarck here was self-evident, though writers and speakers never seemed to tire of enunciating it. During a speech at the 1924 DNVP congress in Hamburg, Graf Westarp stressed that "whoever declares himself to Bismarck must declare himself to the idea of a constitutional monarchism out of an historical right, otherwise he did not understand his Bismarck."[73] Speaking the previous day before the DNVP's Bismarck Youth, the young Prince Bismarck declared that the organization of German national youth embraced the fundamental principles of the party, including "Christian conviction," "*völkisch*-national outlook," and "social community." But "we profess ourselves above all things to the national monarchy. To the national monarchy, which under the flag black-white-red may become the carrier of our national consciousness, of our national community."[74] Despite the increasing distance in time, the rhetoric of a surprisingly large segment of the Right retained an element of monarchism, and for the promotion of that system the Iron Chancellor was ideal.

If many still spoke as if they longed for the return of the Hohenzollerns, they realized that this was a distant dream. More directly, they called for a leader who would either rule as a new Bismarck, or, for monarchists, hold the place for the ultimate return of the dynasty. In either case, the Bismarck Cult played a critical role in fostering the cult of the leader that marked such a significant feature of Weimar political culture, what Kurt Sontheimer has called "the most striking leitmotif of public opinion in Germany during the Weimar Republic."[75] Just as in the period before 1923, a great deal of Bismarckian rhetoric centered on the belief in the necessity and inevitability of a coming leader and savior. Historian Karl Alexander von Müller continued the trend of giving intellectual absolution to the *Führer*-desire in general and to the radical-revolutionary Bismarck image in particular when he noted in April 1924 that it was the German people's ungratefulness, their contempt towards "true god-given leaders," that led to the nation's fall. Relegated to a state of powerlessness and mediocrity, the people were crying out for the one that should lead them. Looking to Bismarck, von Müller took hope in the fact that, since "his spirit is not yet dead, we are allowed the hope that one day he will rise anew for our people."[76]

In early 1925 radical nationalists received the opportunity to realize their dreams for the coming leader legally. With the elections to replace the recently deceased President Ebert, they could begin the process that might usher in the next Bismarck. In discussing the Right's goals, Noel Cary points out that: "The campaign's organizers had planned to nominate a candidate with the political shrewdness of a Bismarck, who, like the Iron Chancellor, would use his office to confound the parliament and refashion the Weimar state from above."[77] For the first round of the election the DVP–DNVP Block chose Karl Jarres as its potential 'new Bismarck.' Once on the campaign trail, Jarres tried to tie himself to the image of the Iron Chancellor, speaking at one point in the shadow of the Hamburg Bismarck monument, calling to the crowds gathered before him for a 'return to Bismarck'.[78] When Jarres proved unable to win on the first ballot, the Protestant bourgeois Right turned to Hindenburg as the man they hoped could beat the candidate of the Weimar Coalition. In the old Prussian General they had found someone invested with the kind of stature that could evoke memories of the Iron Chancellor.

Once again Bismarck and the Field Marshal found themselves tied together. For DVP Reichstag deputy Dr. Runkel, the Reich's founder had to be the model for the new leader, and thus, in choosing the new President, "we look more than ever to the man who lifted Germany into the saddle, to the founder of the Reich, to Bismarck. What made him great and qualified him for his national accomplishment is also determinant for the one who stands at the head of the Reich, determinant for his work and for his success."[79] Of course the particular tasks were specific to the times in which they were living, "but the spirit out of which they spring must remain the same; it indicates the direct line which must be observed. And so Bismarck will become the standard for the worth or unworthiness of the men who run for the highest office in the Reich, the test for the general validity of the program they represent."[80] At a Bismarck celebration of patriotic organizations in April 1925, the president of the Breslau Veterans' Association hoped that "the vote falls to a man who is mindful of the great past and is in a position to lead the fatherland to a bright future; to a man who will fundamentally do away with the godlessness, the filth and rubbish, the corruption and who wants to know nothing of miserable groveling."[81] He had no doubt who the model for this new leader was to be. "With thoughts of Germany's great past comes to us the image of the Iron Chancellor before our eyes as the great statesman, as the man in which, as it were, all glorious and great virtues of our people were embodied. So he also stands today before our spiritual eye. Through all of Germany today goes the call for a Bismarck."[82]

There was, however, an important difference between the role many expected Hindenburg to play, and the Right's understanding of Bismarck's historical role. At his age, and with his very limited understanding of politics, few expected the Field Marshal to be the dynamic man of action, much less super-human action, that corresponded to the Right's conception of the Reich's founder. In this sense, then, he could be seen more as an 'ersatz Kaiser' rather than as a true 'new Bismarck'. What is important, however, is that other hopes were also tied to a Hindenburg presidency that were no less threatening. If he himself was not to be the great man of action, many in the national opposition hoped that Hindenburg would facilitate the rise of the actual new Bismarck. They wished to manipulate him and thereby bring about the desired changes to the system.[83] A Hindenburg victory, then, signified for many the first step on the road to national rebirth and the eventual emergence of a true dictator. Still, despite such hopes, at this stage the President took his oath to the constitution and proved loyal in word, if not in spirit, to Weimar.

If, however, Hindenburg's impact on German politics was not as dangerous as many feared it would be, neither was it so benign. Still, despite his work for the Right in the 1920s, the Field Marshal was not the leader many were waiting for. The crisis of leadership continued, and within the radical Right so too did the search for the new Bismarck. Stahlhelm leader Franz Seldte spelled out his own thoughts before a huge crowd on the organization's annual Front Soldiers' Day in May 1927. He and his comrades hoped to place themselves as soldiers at the disposal of a leader. But, he complained, "we have found no statesman and no leader who wanted to lead and command us as soldiers."[84] Seldte knew, however, that Germany's fate rested on whether or not "Germany once again carries through German tradition, German strength and German clear behavior in the Bismarckian sense."[85] While organizing the masses and educating them in "national spirit," they were waiting for "the great leader or statesman who is ready to lead this willing band and this willing army of the Stahlhelm. We will place ourselves with pleasure at the service of the one whom the Lord God has favored to be the leader of Germany."[86] Such vague generalities regarding the coming leader typified much of the Right's rhetoric.

The indistinct nature of the coming *Führer* meant that no possibilities were excluded. In Potsdam in 1928 a writer for the *Stahlhelm* observed how overall among the people there existed the desire for genuine leadership, though no one knew "out of which class the ultimate leader will arise."[87] No matter, he continued. "Wherever he comes from shall be irrelevant to us, whether from the aristocracy, from the bourgeoisie or the proletariat plays no role. History goes thereby its own secret ways. One thinks only of Napoleon, Bismarck, Lenin, or Mussolini in order to see out of which different social classes genuine state leaders can arise."[88] At the third national Bismarck Day in September 1929 in Munich, Karl Alexander von Müller described Bismarck as the closest, most trusted of all Germany's political geniuses. "His image floats before us when we hope that this political creative energy is not extinct in our people and will one day, once again, like lightning in the clouds, condense into a guiding leader. Whenever and from what class of our people he may come, whichever the next goal of his dealings will be: over the generations and beyond he will greet, as his relative and predecessor, the man whom today we remember."[89]

While the Iron Chancellor continued to be the model for the coming leader, as time continued to separate his day from the present, the less appeared the need for the closest possible duplicate. What was most important was that the next leader would be infused with the spirit of Bismarck. The key, then, would be the ability to recognize that Bismarck-inspired leader, and those most in tune with his spirit would be in the best position to do that. As a speaker at a Stahlhelm Bismarck celebration in Stolp in 1929 put it, "today the German people must find its way from within itself. In each individual, the spirit of Bismarck must come to life."[90] When it did, they would find their new leader.

For many Germans in the mid-1920s, the role of infusing the spirit of Bismarck throughout the nation's middle classes fell to the Stahlhelm. In Weimar the Stahlhelm took to the streets in a manner that resembled the Social Democrats more than the traditional liberal parties. Increasingly militant, and increasingly ready to do battle with the Left, the activities of the League of Front Soldiers reflected the growing violence that marked Weimar politics, while they also prepared and demonstrated the fascist potential of Germany's middle classes.[91] As they grew more vocal, they came to dominate the middle-class public sphere, claiming custodial rights over the nationalist calendar and the nationalist icons, marking a transfer of national legitimacy from the traditional parties to the Stahlhelm. League celebrations were larger in scale than previous Bismarck events, while the rhetoric reflected the concerns of much of middle-class Germany – anti-party, anti-parliament, anti-Marxism, anti-democracy, anti-Versailles.

The Stahlhelm cut across party lines, attracting large numbers of DVP and DNVP voters, and played a significant role in the breakdown of the parties of the bourgeois middle. If Stresemann could, early on, praise the League's idealism, he soon grew concerned over what he felt constituted the nucleus of a German "fascist party" and so, in 1928, he ordered all DVP Reichstag members out of the organization. Such a clean break was not possible, however, as the Stahlhelm's ties to everyday bourgeois society were extensive, and so some local branches found themselves stretched between the two poles of Stahlhelm radicalism and Stresemann moderation.[92] As the 1920s progressed, the Stahlhelm developed closer relations with the DNVP at the expense of a DVP shrinking into obscurity. The radicalized German Nationalists under Hugenberg found the Stahlhelm's size a valuable asset. Both shared largely the same political vision, both were determined to destroy the democratic republic, and both saw the necessity of a leader, a new Bismarck. Whether the new Bismarck would be Hugenberg or Seldte was still unclear. By decade's end, though, the likelihood that he would emerge from the Stahlhelm was growing less likely, for while its size remained impressive, its political impact was declining.

The Stahlhelm's paradoxical relationship to party politics would prove, in part, to be the cause of its downfall. In becoming Germany's largest political pressure group, they made great capital out of blasting the Weimar party system. Such rhetoric, a staple of radical Bismarckians, found fertile ground among the nation's middle classes. Yet at the same time their cooperation with the traditional bourgeois parties, most notably the DVP and DNVP, made them highly vulnerable to attack from farther right. And as they began to descend, there arose an even more radical group to take up the battle.

By the end of the decade the Weimar Republic found itself at a crossroads. The stabilization following the crisis decade seemed to bring hope for the future of German democracy. Overt threats to the republic had ended and the economy began to revive. If governments continued to change at a disturbingly high rate, some sense of stability was found in the continuity of individual cabinet members. In particular, Gustav Stresemann's presence in every cabinet from 1923 until his death in 1929 provided a reassuring air of continuity both for Germany's neighbors and for those at home who placed their hopes for the future in the survival of democracy. Stresemann's conversion from opponent to ardent supporter of the republic was one of the most positive developments in German politics during this time and should have served as a hopeful indicator of the system's prospects.

This potentially positive outcome, however, faced serious challenges in the form of a current of radical nationalist thought that continued to rail against the system and, if at this time only on the rhetorical level, continued to undermine its legitimacy. The stabilization that in one sense brought hope also had its darker side in the economic devastation it brought to Germany's middle classes. Their disillusionment with the republic continued and, as the decade progressed, they followed a path of steadily increasing radicalization, seeking answers ever further to the right. From the splinter parties to the DNVP and Stahlhelm they were lured by a vision of politics symbolized by an increasingly radical image of their hero, Otto von Bismarck. As the decade ended, several possibilities remained. If the survival of democracy looked improbable, what would replace it also remained uncertain. Men like Hugenberg, Seldte, and Tirpitz had their visions, but what they were was anything but clear. But with the Bismarck image as a unifying symbol – and the general tenor of politics that it represented – one could be fairly sure that authoritarianism would reign once again in Germany. The opening years of the next decade, then, would prove critical in determining just what path the nation would follow and thus what it would look like.

Notes

1. Marianne Weber, *Max Weber*, 653.
2. Stresemann quoted in Turner, *Stresemann*, 168.
3. For Bismarck's pre-war influence on Stresemann, see Wright, *Gustav Stresemann*, 57.
4. *Der Tag*, nr. 155, April 2, 1922 (Stresemann speech at Bismarck day in Hamburg).
5. Ibid.
6. Stresemann at Bismarck ceremony in the Herderkirche, 1919, in BAL, RlbPa,

R8034 II, 7097, #10: *Thüringer Landeszeitung*, nr. 81, April 1, 1919.

7. Ibid.

8. Ibid.

9. *Der Tag*, nr. 155, April 2, 1922 (Stresemann speech at Bismarck day in Hamburg).

10. Ibid.

11. This policy he called *Nationale Realpolitik*, making clear his debt to Bismarck. Gustav Stresemann, *Nationale Realpolitik. Flugschriften der Deutschen Volkspartei*, vol. 56 (Berlin: Staatspolitischer Verlag, 1924), 6.

12. See, for example, Hans W. Gatzke, *Stresemann and the Rearmament of Germany* (Baltimore: The Johns Hopkins Press, 1954), 12.

13. For the historiography of Stresemann, see Karl Heinrich Pohl, "Gustav Stresemann – Überlegungen zu einer neuen Biographie," in Karl Heinrich Pohl, ed., *Politiker und Bürger: Gustav Stresemann und seine Zeit* (Göttingen: Vandenhoeck & Ruprecht, 2002), 13–40. The latest work on the subject is Johnathan Wright's biography, *Gustav Stresemann*, in which he defends him as a man who truly transformed himself into a devoted defender of Weimar.

14. Bismarck quoted in "Die Bismarck-Jugend in Friedrichsruh," *Kreuzzeitung*, nr. 154, March 31, 1924.

15. Laverrenz quoted in ibid.

16. Party Chairman Oskar Hergt at DNVP congress in Hamburg, March 31, 1924, in "Deutschnationaler Parteitag" in *Kreuzzeitung*, nr. 156, April 1, 1924.

17. Ibid.

18. Mappe #3 (RTW 1924), "So ist's recht Stresemann, Du schaffst es!" in BA Koblenz: ZSg 1 42/7, Deutsche Volkspartei, Flugblätter 1919–1933).

19. "Bismarck und unsere Zeit" in BAL, RlbPa, R8034 II, 5132, #104: DVP Flugblatt from May 1924.

20. "Gegen die Partei Stresemann – im Geiste Bismarcks," May 1924, in BAL, NS 5 VI, 695, #63.

21. Ibid.

22. Ibid.

23. See Jones, *German Liberalism*, 220–222.

24. For internal DVP criticism, see speech by Dr. Otto Hugo, "Große vaterländische Kundgebung der Deutschen Volkspartei" in *Hamburger Nachrichten*, nr. 157, April 1, 1924.

25. Turner, *Stresemann*, 159–160.

26. Ibid., 186–191, 203–219.

27. Ibid., 203.

28. One exception was the Young German Order (*Jungdeutsche Orden*), which

supported Stresemann and his policy of reconciliation with France. Mommsen, *Rise and Fall of Weimar Democracy*, 231–232.

29. "Der 'Bismarck der Novemberdemokratie'," in *Völkischer Beobachter*, (Munich) nr. 14, January 19, 1926.

30. "Bismarck und Stresemann," in *Der Führer. Das badische Samstagsblatt für national-sozialistische Politik und deutsche Kultur*, May 19, 1928; the label 'bottled-beer dealer' refers to Stresemann's dissertation, a study of Berlin's bottled beer industry. See Manfred Berg, *Gustav Stresemann. Eine politische Karriere zwischen Reich und Republik* (Göttingen: Muster-Schmidt Verlag, 1992), 18.

31. See, for example, "Geist und Doktor Stresemann?" Speech to NSDAP Versammlung in Munich (also published in *Völkischer Beobachter*, May 5, 1928), in Institut für Zeitgeschichte, eds., *Hitler: Reden, Schriften, Anordnungen. Februar 1925 bis Januar 1933* (Munich: K. G. Saur, 1992), Volume II, *Vom Weimarer Parteitag bis zur Reichstagswahl. Juli 1926–Mai 1928. Part 2: August 1927–May 1928*, 805. See also "Das Ende des Völkerbunds-Schwindels" speech to NSDAP Versammlung in Munich, September 21, 1928, in Volume III, *Zwischen den Reichstagswahlen, Juli 1928–Februar 1929, Part 1: Juli 1928–Februar 1929*, 103.

32. Ibid., 826.

33. "Die jüdisch-marxistischen Zentralisationsbestrebungen zur Erleichterung der einheitlichen Begaunerung und Ausbeutung der Kolonie Deutschland zugunsten der internationalen Hochfinanz," speech to NSDAP Versammlung in Munich, December 7, 1928, in ibid., Volume III, *Zwischen den Reichstagswahlen, Juli 1928–Februar 1929, Part 1: Juli 1928–Februar 1929*, 334.

34. "Fort mit dem Parlamentarischen 'Führer'- Brei Schäffer – Auer'scher Prägung!" Speech to NSDAP Versammlung in Munich, August 12, 1930 (also published in *Völkischer Beobachter*, August 17/18, 1930), in ibid., Volume III, *Zwischen den Reichstagswahlen, Juli 1928–September 1930. Part 3: Januar 1930–September 1930*, 335.

35. Ibid., 335.

36. "Bismarck" in *Hamburger Nachrichten*, nr. 152, March 31, 1926.

37. Karl Litzmann, "Die Tragik des deutschen Schicksals und ihre Überwindung durch bismarckischen Geist," in *Berliner Bismarck-Ausschuß, Bismarck-Kommers am 2. April 1927*, 7.

38. Ibid., 7; see also *Hamburger Nachrichten*, April 4, 1928.

39. "Kein Kreuzzug gegen Rußland," speech by Stresemann in Stuttgart, April 18, 1926, in Henry Bernhard, ed., *Gustav Stresemann. Vermächtnis. Der Nachlass in drei Bänden*, II (Berlin: Ullstein, 1932), 504.

40. Robert P. Grathwol, *Stresemann and the DNVP: Reconciliation or Revenge in*

German Foreign Policy 1924–1928 (Lawrence: The Regents Press of Kansas, 1980).

41. Paul Bang in *Deutsche Zeitung*, nr. 106a, May 5, 1928. Thimme, *Flucht*, 55.

42. Kaas quoted in Mommsen, *Rise and Fall*, 262.

43. Ibid., 261–262.

44. Lothar Albertin, "Die Auflösung der bürgerlichen Mitte und die Krise des Parlamentarischen Systems von Weimar," in Eberhard Kolb and Walter Mülhausen, eds., *Demokratie in der Krise. Parteien im Verfassungssystem der Weimarer Republik* (Munich: R. Oldenbourg Verlag, 1997), 85–90.

45. Jones, *German Liberalism*, 302–305.

46. See the collection of political placards at BA Koblenz. One such poster for the *Wirtschaftspartei* showed a picture of Bismarck along with the following text: "So he spoke to the middle-class: 'I could not do anything for you in parliament; organize, become a power, and then come back!' Therefore vote *Reichspartei des deutschen Mittelstandes (Wirtschaftspartei)*."

47. Stolberg-Wernigerode was a consistent proponent of the Stresemann image of Bismarck. Examples are numerous: "Der liberale Bismarck," *Deutsche Stimmen*, September 20, 1925, Nr. 18, Bd. 37; *Zurück zu Bismarck* (Berlin: Staatspolitischer Verlag, 1926); "Bismarcks Kriegspolitik" in BAL, RlbPa, R8034 III, 450, #46: *Der Herkules*, Nr. 22, June 5, 1926.

48. Westarp quoted in Albrecht Graf zu Stolberg-Wernigerode, "Offener Brief" in BAL, RlbPa, R8034 III, 450, #42: *Nationalliberale Correspondenz*, Nr. 75, April 26, 1928.

49. Ibid.

50. Ibid.

51. Stresemann at the University of Heidelberg in *Deutsche Allgemeine Zeitung*, nr. 211, May 6, 1928.

52. "Stresemann zum 9. November" in BAL, RlbPa, R72, 1342, #123: *Vossische Zeitung*, November 10, 1928.

53. Ibid.

54. Appreciation was shown for Stresemann after his death, though this did not translate into success for his party. See Wright, *Stresemann*, 492–494.

55. Gustav Stresemann, "Zu Bismarcks Gedächtnis," Rede, gehalten bei der Bismarck-Geburtstagsfeier der Arbeitsgemeinschaft Ostpreußischer Regimentsvereine am 1. Januar 1928. In *Deutsche Stimmen*, April 5, 1928, Nr. 7, vol. 40: 199–200.

56. For Stresemann's last-gasp attempts to revive a unified Liberal party, see Jones, *German Liberalism*, 309–342, and Turner, *Stresemann*, 251–256.

57. Bismarck-Kommers in der Philharmonie zu Berlin am 31. März 1928 (Berlin: Verlag vom Berliner Bismarck-Ausschuß, 1928), 15.

58. Grathwol, *Stresemann and the DNVP*, 171.

59. Kershaw, *'Hitler Myth'*, 13–21; Sontheimer, *Antidemokratisches Denken*, 214–222.

60. Lothar Machtan, "Bismark-Kult," 44.

61. General Freiherr von Lebedour quoted in ibid., 44.

62. It also published a newsletter, the *Bismarck-Blatt*, containing all sorts of Bismarckiana. Reflecting the heterogeneous nature of the Cult, the leading members included moderates like Stresemann and Karl Jarres, and more radical figures like Field Marshal von Mackensen, Graf von der Goltz, leader of the United Patriotic Associations, Otto Sieveking, leader of the DNVP Bismarck Youth, Franz Seldte, leader of the Stahlhelm, and Prince Otto von Bismarck, the grandson.

63. Max Maurenbrecher, "Bismarcks Auferstehung," in *Deutsche Zeitung*, nr. 156, April 4, 1924.

64. Ibid.

65. Ibid.

66. Ibid.

67. Karl Alexander von Müller, "Bismarcks Sturz," in Karl Alexander von Müller, *Deutsche Geschichte und deutsche Charakter. Aufsätze und Vorträge* (Stuttgart: Deutsche Verlags-Anstalt, 1926), 219.

68. Ibid., 231.

69. Heinrich Göppert, *Bismarck und die deutsche Demokratie. Zum 1. April 1924* (Bonn: Kommissionsverlag von Albert Falkenroth, 1924), 5.

70. Ibid., 19.

71. Heinrich Class, "Mit Bismarck – über Bismarck hinaus," in BAL, RlbPa, R8034 II, 7099, #143: *Deutsche Zeitung*, nr. 149, March 31, 1924; see also "Die Feier der Vaterländischen Verbände Berlins" in BAL, RlbPa, R8034 II, 8873, #13: *Deutsche Zeitung*, nr. 27, January 17, 1926.

72. Class, "Mit Bismarck."

73. Westarp quoted in "Der Ausklang des deutschnationalen Parteitages" in *Hamburger Nachrichten*, April 2, 1924.

74. Otto von Bismarck II quoted in "Der Ausklang des deutschnationalen Parteitages" in *Hamburger Nachrichten*, April 2, 1924.

75. Sontheimer, *Antidemokratisches Denken*, 215.

76. Karl Alexander von Müller, "Bismarcks Sturz" in von Müller, *Deutsche Geschichte und deutsche Charakter*, 236; see also Major a. D. Kurt Anker, "Das deutsche Bismarck-Sehnen," in *Der Stahlhelm*, April 6, 1924.

77. Cary quoted in Scheck, *Tirpitz*, 191.

78. Otto Pflanze, *Bismarck*, III, 450.

79. "Bismarck und die Reichspräsidentenwahl" by Geheimrat Dr. Runkel, MdR, in BAL, RlbPa, R8034 II, 7100, #9: *Die Zeit*, Nr. 130, March 31, 1925.

80. Ibid.

81. "Bismarckfeier der Vaterländischen Verbände" in BAL, RlbPa, R8034 II, 7100, #27: *Schlesische Zeitung*, Nr. 163, April 6, 1925.
82. Ibid.; see also "Der Aufruf der Bismarckjugend" in BAL, RlbPa, R8034 II, 8872, #86: *Deutsche Tageszeitung*, Nr. 176, April 16, 1925.
83. Thimme, *Flucht*, 56.
84. "Der neue Weg des Stahlhelms. Seldtes Appell an das nationale Berlin" in *Der Stahlhelm*, May 15, 1927. GStA PK, I. HA Rep. 77, Ministerium des Innern, Tit. 4043, Nr. 328, Bd. 1, Bl. 281 (M); Stahlhelm, Bund der Frontsoldaten, Allgemeines.
85. Ibid.
86. Ibid.
87. "Führergedanke und Demokratie" in BAL, *Stahlhelm*, R72/407, #225–226: "Nachrichten-Blatt des Gaues Potsdam des Stahlhelm," nr. 11, November 1928.
88. Ibid.
89. Karl Alexander von Müller, "Bismarck und die heutige Zeit," in *Bismarck-Blatt. Zeitschrift des Vereins zur Errichtung eines Bismarck-National-Denkmals E.V.*, nr. 1, January 1930.
90. "Bismarck-Tag in Stolp" in BAL, *Stahlhelm*, R72/407, #397–398: *Pommersche Grenzwacht*, May 1929.
91. Fritzsche, *Rehearsals*, 167–189.
92. Ibid., 178–186.

–5–

Beyond Bismarck
The Iron Chancellor in the Third Reich, 1930–1945

So long as men worship the Caesars and Napoleons, Caesars and Napoleons will duly rise and make them miserable.

Aldous Huxley, *Ends and Means*, 1937[1]

In early July, 1944, Ulrich von Hassel, a member of the conservative conspiracy to assassinate Hitler, strolled through the grounds of the Bismarck estate at Friedrichsruh. As the dreams of German greatness attached to Hitler's thousand-year Reich appeared to be crumbling, von Hassel reflected upon the first chancellor and bemoaned what had become of his legacy. "It is regrettable," he thought, "what a false image we ourselves have produced of him in the world, as the power politician with cuirassier boots, in the childish joy that someone finally made Germany a force once again."[2] It must have been a painful realization for someone who had so heartily welcomed the Nazi takeover back in 1933, having seen in it the best chance for a revival of German power.[3]

Back in the early 1930s, though, such support for the Nazis was by no means unusual. The crisis conditions of that time had combined with a bourgeois-nationalist political culture heavily influenced by the Bismarck Cult to make a radical nationalist solution much more popular than it had once been. If the mid-1920s witnessed the rightward exodus of Germany's middle-classes from the DDP and DVP, the harrowing first years of the new decade saw a shift even further to the right as the German National People's Party steadily lost support to that ultimate radical nationalist movement, the Nazis. Guided to varying degrees by an image of Bismarck, these exiles from the more traditional parties sought a solution to the crisis of leadership. They saw the Nazis as perhaps their last, best hope. Just how much of Bismarck they saw in Hitler cannot be determined with any certainty. What is clear, however, is that Hitler actively sought to portray himself as an heir to the Iron Chancellor, and, as it had with Heinrich Class and Diederich Hahn before, the Bismarck Cult provided legitimacy to a previously marginal figure, helping him move to center stage in national politics. Having emerged from the milieu of the Cult, and having participated continually in it, meant that the similarities between Bismarckian and Nazi rhetoric, differing mainly in degree, must have been recognizable and must, therefore, have helped smooth the transition of the German middle classes from their traditional parties to the Hitler movement, as it scored repeated triumphs at the polls beginning in 1930.[4]

While Germany's middle-class voters made the National Socialists a force to be reckoned with, the ultimate decision to make Hitler chancellor was made by just a few. Though these power-brokers may not have seen in Hitler the next Bismarck either, they did recognize a community of interest, and at least viewed him as a means to achieve their Bismarck-inspired goals of destroying Weimar while restoring Germany's world-power position. The fact that he could sit with these men and be considered for such a position he owed at least in part to the Cult's radicalizing effects on German political culture. In the euphoria that followed the naming of the cabinet of 'national concentration', many felt that Germany had regained its footing and was now back on the path towards national rebirth. If some would ultimately find their victory a hollow one, few could see this in the immediate aftermath of triumph, for a Hitler chancellorship has to be viewed as one of the possible paths forged by the logic of Bismarckian political culture.

That some did not immediately see the nature of their 'victory' could possibly be explained by the fact that many people – including much of the academic elite, those high-priests of the Bismarck Cult – actively portrayed the Nazi triumph as the continuation of German history that led directly from Bismarck. The ease with which the Iron Chancellor fitted as a legitimizing symbol for the Nazi regime, and its acceptance as such, during the Third Reich's early years point tellingly to such a conclusion. From the 'Day of Potsdam' through the birthday celebrations of April 1933, the new government sought to drape itself in the mantle of traditional Prusso-German nationalism. In doing so, it firmed up its support base among those who might at first have been unsure as to the connections between the new leader and the Iron Chancellor. As the Nazi hold on power grew tighter, and Hitler's own stature and megalomania grew, the Bismarck image found itself pushed to the sidelines. In a truly remarkable testament to the effectiveness of Nazi propaganda and the Hitler myth, even the mighty Bismarck Cult had to give way before the power of the new god. In the end, what the Weimar Coalition could not do in the name of democracy, Hitler and the Nazis did in the name of tyranny. This chapter will examine the last significant years of the Bismarck image in German politics, from 1930, when Hitler emerged to score a dramatic electoral victory and provide hope to Bismarckians for a solution to the crisis of leadership, through the first half of the Third Reich, when Bismarck still had a role to play in granting legitimacy to the regime, and finally through the years of decline, when Hitler truly went 'beyond Bismarck', causing him to fade further and further within the *Führer's* own ever growing shadow.

'Solving' the Crisis of Leadership: Bismarck in the Last Years of Weimar

As the 1920s wound down and a new decade began, the Right appeared no closer to finding the leader it so desperately sought. If Hugenberg still fancied himself as an option, this became increasingly less realistic, particularly in view of his party's losses in the 1928 elections. The Stahlhelm's Franz Seldte might still have considered himself a possibility, but his organization, despite impressive membership numbers, seemed to have exhausted its revolutionary potential. Something new was needed. When Hugenberg reached out to a still marginal Adolf Hitler at the close of the decade, he opened the door to a man who shared with him a significant community of interests, however much he might complain of his crude style. Few could have imagined that within a remarkably short time Hitler would emerge as the man to whom a majority of the German nationalist public would turn for ultimate salvation from the country's seemingly endless crisis of leadership. In this section we will look at Hitler's dramatic rise, his conscious connection to Bismarck, and the end of Weimar democracy.

Even before the Depression, Hitler's National Socialists were showing ominous signs of growth. Their intense activism at the local level reflected the dynamic spirit of the movement.[5] For years Hitler had been placing himself in Bismarck's shadow, hoping to tap into the national legitimacy it bestowed. From his pre-putsch days to his court defense, and in numerous subsequent speeches, the Nazi leader repeatedly associated his name and his cause with that of the great national icon. Shaping history to suit his own purposes, Hitler stressed the importance of the individual – the effect that a single man can have in the face of an entrenched opposition. Speaking to the National Socialist Student Bund in November 1927, he asked who had made Germany: "The majority, or was it not the single brilliant head of a Bismarck who created Germany against the majority?"[6] Ever since his imprisonment, Hitler had come to the conclusion that he was the one chosen to make history for a new Germany.[7] The situations in which the two "great men" found themselves at the critical moment were, in Hitler's opinion, strikingly similar. Following a period of defeat, one man led the nation back up to a position of power and glory.

Today we can hardly measure what it meant for that time, that after a period of the deepest decay, of the decay of the German imperial majesty, of the decay of the German nation, of the disappearance of a German national honor, yes, of a German national sentiment, in such a time suddenly a German Reich emerged once more. The name of the one who founded this Reich, you know it, it is not called majority, not democracy, but rather Bismarck. An individual had given the German people a new Reich and, what is perhaps more valuable than the pure outer form, gave the German people with this new Reich also once again a new national idea, gave it a new national honor, a new comprehension of national honor.[8]

That message, that desire to give the German people a new sense of national honor, would resonate much more powerfully with the economic turmoil of the Depression. In a system already on the defensive, Hitler's message and the image he cultivated found fertile ground in the German nationalist political culture of the late 1920s, in which the issue of leadership held paramount importance.

The rise of the Nazis also coincided with a political situation that suited their rhetoric perfectly. The establishment of the Great Coalition in 1928 meant that once again Bismarck's *Reichsfeinde* were in control. With the onset of the Depression, criticism of the government grew even harsher. The Bismarck Cult provided a perfect outlet for middle-class German frustration with this latest manifestation of the crisis of leadership. Writing in Hugenberg's *Deutscher Schnelldienst*, W. S. Eckewart declared that it was "only in the current time of national emergency" that they "completely understand the greatness of the Bismarckian life accomplishment!"[9] It was during this time that Germany had become a laughing stock for the outside world, robbed as it was of its national freedom and national power. Because of that, he wrote, those who were "truly conscious of their Germanness and of German blood" felt a "deep, deep desire right on the day of Bismarck's death for a new leader for our German people, who will unite it in the spirit of Bismarck and experience a new national self-consciousness."[10]

When, in 1929, the Bismarckian triumvirate of Alfred Hugenberg, Franz Seldte, and Adolf Hitler joined forces to defeat the Young Plan – the latest international effort to regulate reparations payments – it marked a high point, at least on the surface, in the struggle to achieve right-wing unity. The implications for the future of Weimar democracy were ominous. At a Bismarck celebration in 1930, Nazi sympathizer Rudolf Beinert declared that those who honor the Iron Chancellor as the nation's greatest political teacher must be clear about the fact that Hindenburg's refusal to sign the Young Plan was "only the first part of a great struggle, a struggle against the *Erfüllungspolitik* of the last ten years, a struggle against the ruling system, against Social Democracy and its partners, that is, against the majority of the parliament. That means, therefore, a struggle similar to that which Bismarck in the year 1862 in the full strength of his years took up and led through successfully."[11] Once again, the national opposition cast itself in the Bismarckian role of lonely defender of the national interests. Although the struggle against the Young Plan failed, the ultimate struggle, of which it was just one part, moved forward. Hitler's popularity increased dramatically through the exposure of the anti-Young campaign. He would not have to wait long to reap the benefits.

Already by Easter 1929 those around the President were taking the first tentative steps towards the elimination of parliamentary government. They sounded out Center Party leader Heinrich Brüning about heading up a right-leaning cabinet.

Taking office on March 30, 1930, it signified the beginning of the end of parliamentary democracy in Germany. In May 1930 the recently revived Society for the Building of a National Bismarck Monument took the opportunity of the Iron Chancellor's 115th birthday to declare the warning of the day: "Beyond the petty strife of parliament, to find the way that leads out of the dark, the way to unity of people, nation, and Reich!"[12] In the months that followed, Brüning planned to lead the country in just such a direction. No longer ruling through a Reichstag majority, this first 'Presidential Cabinet' slowly but surely ate away at the prerogatives of the parliament, passing its first decree against the express wishes of that body by July 1930. The first moves towards authoritarian rule had been made. Through emergency decree, Brüning dissolved the Reichstag that very same month and scheduled elections for September. The results signified a further step away from democracy.

In the elections of 1930 the Nazis finally broke through. In an astonishing electoral turnabout, they transformed their dismal 1928 results of 2.8 percent of the vote into 18.3 percent and 107 seats, making them the second largest party. In attempting to explain this dramatic revival, no one single factor can suffice. Certainly the Depression was vital. In terms, though, of a shift in the middle-class electorate away from their traditional parties to the Nazis, the power of the Bismarck Cult must be considered a contributing factor. Many in this group had been seeking a return to their previous position in society since the revolution. With an image of Bismarck as one of their primary unifying bonds, they sought the party or organization best suited to accomplishing that goal. Certainly the rhetoric of Bismarckians all along, from Stresemann to the radical Right, had stressed above all a return to previous German power and glory. As Stresemann failed to deliver enough, while at the same time compromising his nationalist credentials through cooperation with Bismarck's enemies, many looked further right. Some turned first to the DNVP, with its offers of fantastic solutions through the sheer force of Bismarckian will. The Stahlhelm, with its strong anti-party rhetoric, helped in the process of dissolution, while the splinter parties drew off a great many as well. Most ended up with National Socialism.[13]

Here was a party untainted by governmental responsibility, that promised national rejuvenation through an end to party democracy, and that promised to restore national greatness. By no means original, Nazi rhetoric tapped into a verbal arsenal widely used by Bismarckians, a rhetoric that had been developing and radicalizing for decades within the milieu of the Right. Whether it was the inherent malignancy of political parties, the un-German character of parliamentary democracy, the promise of a future *Volksgemeinschaft*, or the need and desirability of a god-given leader, all had appeared before as fundamental concepts within the Bismarck Cult and had prepared the ground for further acceptance when presented in the dramatic style of a highly charismatic leader.

In Hitler, Germans had a man who consciously positioned himself as a Bismarckian figure, in a situation he depicted as strikingly similar to that of his hero. Certainly when looked at objectively, there was little to recommend the Austrian corporal as a 'new' Bismarck. But those susceptible to the Cult of Bismarck, who held a quasi-religious belief in German destiny and the inevitability of a new god-given leader, were not necessarily looking at the situation objectively. As increasing numbers of the middle classes flocked to him, they were coming with a conception of politics and leadership shaped by years of Bismarck adulation. The similarities in rhetoric had to make such a shift in allegiance that much easier. Radical as Hitler was, he still worked within the confines of this critical element of German political culture, the Bismarck Cult. Thanks to the distance in time and the dramatically changed circumstances brought about by the crisis decade, he could bend and push out the boundaries of that political culture – in terms of what the next Bismarck would look like, for example – without breaking them.

Following the Nazi breakthrough, the crisis that contributed to that success continued to grow, and as it did, the Bismarck image continued to embody the political aspirations of the German nationalist public. As those aspirations grew more radical, so too did the rhetoric associated with the Iron Chancellor. While groups certainly continued to speak of going 'back to Bismarck', one also heard complaints in these troubled times from those who demanded more. Speaking before the German Officer's League in Berlin in April 1931, retired Lieutenant General von Metzsch noted that "only today, in the depths of our collapse, does everyone recognize what the youth feels in the new Germany, that it stands in battle in a clear front with Bismarck against all liberal and Marxist lifelessness. Certainly the solution may not be called 'Back to Bismarck!' "[14] It no longer sufficed, as he saw it, to reestablish what was, but rather; to begin anew, though in doing so being sure not to leave the Iron Chancellor behind.

The Nazis, too, with their revolutionary rhetoric, felt the need to go beyond the old slogans. They complained of what they considered the old style of Bismarck worship, which contrasted with their own activist philosophy. The Bismarck image, they claimed in a *Reichsgründungstag* article in the *Völkischer Beobachter*, "is the only one which shines above us National Socialists, when the others hold the celebration of the founding of the Reich with hurrahs and cheers, as they have always done, as though the lessons of the World War have not yet stormed by them."[15] It was the Nazis' activism, and the hatred it aroused in others, that placed them in a position similar to that of their hero back in his time of struggle. For them, therefore, he served as a continued source of inspiration for the coming fight. What they were fighting for, however, was something new. Though he continued to serve as a powerful inspiration for the movement, the desire to destroy what existed while not returning to what had been meant that they needed to surpass their hero. "The

National Socialist Germany that will attain the new Reich through struggle therefore also rejects the slogan 'Back to Bismarck'. Our solution is called: Beyond Bismarck to greater Germany that will finally be the homeland of all Germans, territorially and politically."[16] Whether they sought to go 'back to' or 'beyond' Bismarck, it is clear that the Iron Chancellor remained the model against which they measured both the present situation and their hopes for the future.

Just as the Bismarck Cult provided meaning and direction for the faithful in a time of crisis, it also provided hope for the arrival of a savior. That Germans needed a leader was clear to Dr. Albert Vögler, a man whose own political trajectory symbolized the progressive radicalization of Germany's middle classes.[17] At a Bismarck celebration in Westphalia in 1931, he spoke of the country's need for a leader. That the new leader had to arise out of Bismarckian essence was clear, for "in all great questions, Bismarck was always, always correct."[18] Germans had to recognize this truth, and Vögler assured the crowd that: "There will come a time, and it is no longer distant, when Bismarck will stand in all German hearts."[19] His confidence reflected the combination of an ever-deepening crisis with a quasi-religious faith that had been building for decades. It can be seen, in fact, as a return of that sense of despair that plagued middle-class Germans during the last years of the crisis decade. As that situation appeared to sink to its darkest moments, followers of the Cult sought comfort in the belief that a new Bismarck would soon arise to save them. Vögler conveyed a similar sense of faith that not only would the savior arrive, but he would arrive soon. It was only through such faith in their political god that the resurrection of Germany and its people was possible. "When Bismarckian spirit and Bismarckian confidence once again fill German hearts, then will the tomb in the Saxon Forest become empty, Bismarck is then resurrected, he will live in the midst of the German Volk."[20]

If the desire for a new Bismarck and the nation's subsequent rebirth was widespread among the Right in the crisis-ridden Germany of the early 1930s, not everyone agreed on just what the new Germany would look like. For while the Nazi juggernaut was still gaining momentum, some took exception to a Bismarck-inspired National Socialist Germany. The DNVP's Bismarck Youth, for example, spoke out against the reinvigorated Hitler movement, remaining, in many ways, true to their original 'Back to Bismarck' position. At the eleventh annual meeting of the Berlin Bismarck Youth in November 1930, the organization's leader Otto Sieveking demanded a new Third Reich. The Bismarckbund, he pointed out, had demanded a Third Reich before the Nazis. Furthermore, he declared, "the Third Reich shall also look somewhat different than that of the NSDAP. The Bismarckbund wants to be led by a King and Kaiser established by God."[21] In most respects, the Bismarck Youth often sounded quite similar to the Nazis. But their monarchism distinguished them and probably helps explain their ultimate ineffectiveness against the Nazi onslaught.

For while Hugenberg gave the impression of an older, more restrained time, the Nazis' youth and dynamism was proving irresistible to more and more Germans. Hitler continually spoke of the coming Germany, and if his words failed to betray much in terms of details, the impression he gave was one of vitality and action. As he had done throughout the 1920s, the Nazi leader traveled under a Bismarck image tailored to his own specifications. His ability to connect old and new and transform it into an effective propaganda tool to draw Bismarckians to his movement continued throughout the crisis. Speaking before a Nazi gathering in Coburg in January 1931, Hitler tied together the themes of race and youth with Bismarck to make clear the connection between the Iron Chancellor and himself. The idea of race, he declared, was the new platform through which the Germans would come together. Under the swastika flag they would fight to regain that which Bismarck had given to them and which they had thrown away. The future, he announced, would justify their work.

> The Reich will arise in new, rejuvenated form. And the recognition of the racial laws to which science, philosophy, and poetry have brought us close will found the new basis. From that we will overcome the decay. In 10 years we will have a united German front of rejuvenated German people. *If Bismarck came back again today with his fellow fighters – they would all stand today by us!* We have high respect for the actions of this great one, for the exalted colors of the old Reich. Our flag is the symbol of the new Reich![22]

Hitler, thus, continued his efforts at claiming Bismarck and his symbolic power to further legitimize his movement and provide greater force for his attacks on the government.[23]

The youthful, dynamic image that characterized Nazi propaganda suited Hitler perfectly when he chose to run for president against Hindenburg in early 1932. Portraying himself as representative of the 'new, young' Germany, the Nazi leader went into battle against the aging Field Marshal, representative of the failed Weimar Republic. The dramatic turnabout in electoral support from the 1925 presidential elections to those of 1932 reflected the radicalization of German politics, while the rhetoric on both sides indicated the utter bankruptcy of the republican system. Whereas in the 1925 contest, it was the conservative and radical Right which helped elect Hindenburg, it was, largely, those same groups that ultimately opposed him in 1932.[24] Mention of the political parties or the Reichstag never appeared in Hindenburg's campaign, amounting to "an implicit abdication of responsibility by Germany's republican system."[25] Instead, as Hans Mommsen points out, "it was the venerable field marshal's role as the guarantor of national unity and the need to overcome the factionalism of political parties that received primary emphasis. Adapted to the tenor of National Socialist and DNVP propaganda, the campaign for Hindenburg called for an end to 'party rule' in what represented the swan song of parliamentary liberalism."[26] Instead of 'Nazi' or 'DNVP', Mommsen very easily could have described the tenor of the rhetoric as 'Bismarckian'.

For both sides, in fact, the Iron Chancellor made an appearance. Hitler took great pride in the fact that some were concerned about the effect of a Nazi victory on foreign opinion. Speaking before a party rally in Dortmund in March 1932, he announced that "Poland objects to my candidacy. France objects to it. Yes, I am proud that they object to it! I do not know whether either France or Poland, whether they would have welcomed a Bismarck candidacy."[27] Meanwhile, the remnants of the self-proclaimed Bismarck party, the DVP, sought to combat the anti-Hindenburg propaganda, in one case through a similar usage of the national idol. Working, one might say, in the 'spirit of Stresemann', Stolberg-Wernigerode defended the President against the criticism that he had signed the Young Plan. History would justify Hindenburg in his decision to take an unpopular position. One need only look back to the judgment leveled against Bismarck by the anti-Semitic parties early in the Second Reich. "He too would be attacked personally in the most hateful manner and was seen as no longer national because he did not follow those of the *Sturm und Drang*."[28]

In an election campaign in which the propaganda of both sides seemed to be tapping into the arsenal of the Bismarck Cult, the prospects for the republic's survival could not appear very great. For the traditional Bismarckians in the DVP, the best they could muster in a direct comparison between their hero and the President was the concept of 'maintenance of the Reich' – a less than inspiring rallying cry. In an article in the party newsletter, the coincidental timing of Bismarck's birthday during the second round of elections led to memories of the Iron Chancellor's dismissal and the resulting disaster. Could the German people allow it to happen again? To learn from history, then, meant to reelect Hindenburg, a man connected in so many ways with the founder of the Reich. Comparisons in personality "lead a clear and direct line from the one to the other."[29]

However forced the comparison, the most striking features of the 1932 Hindenburg/Bismarck are its defensive nature and its failure to mention the parties, democracy, or even the republic. When the election results came in, therefore, and the Germans 'avoided the mistake of 1890', reelecting Hindenburg, the victory was certainly not a cause for joy among the republic's remaining supporters. The attitudes towards the system became painfully obvious during a campaign which displayed the bankruptcy of that very system. Shortly after Hindenburg's victory, he dismissed Brüning and appointed Franz von Papen as chancellor. The momentum given to democracy's decline under Brüning increased under the newest Presidential Cabinet. The Reichstag declined to near insignificance as the emergency powers of Article 48 of the constitution provided the means to rule as the leadership saw fit. Hindenburg's triumph, then, signified merely a brief respite until the republic's ultimate fate could be determined.

If, in the end, they found the solution in a Hitler chancellorship, that was by no means preordained. By the early 1930s the Right was perhaps even more fractured than ever. Despite DNVP leader Hugenberg's repeated efforts to build a united front of radical nationalist opposition to Weimar, the unity of the anti-republican forces remained no more than a dream. Even the rally staged by the ominous 'Harzburg Front' in 1931, when the German Nationalists, Stahlhelm, and Nazis came together for a dramatic display of opposition, was, in reality, an extraordinarily precarious grouping that displayed fissures before the event was even over. Hitler's public and private snubs and insults directed at Hugenberg reflected the changed power relationship following the Nazis' 1930 election victory. Whereas before Hugenberg could graciously reach out to a less significant group of brutal and unsophisticated, though well-meaning, radical nationalists, now it was Hitler who could decide the next steps to be taken. The divisions within the Right came to a head before the presidential elections of 1932, when Hugenberg's efforts to find a suitable candidate for the entire national opposition foundered in the face of Hitler's decision to run as a candidate. Throughout 1932 and its remarkably active schedule of elections, both the DNVP and NSDAP engaged in brutal campaigns aimed at discrediting each other. For their part, the Nazis continued their self-portrayal as the dynamic party of youth and change, while blasting the German Nationalists as the party of out-and-out reaction. Hoping to stem the dramatic exodus of its middle-class and peasant support, the DNVP stressed the Nazis' economic and social radicalism.[30]

While it was clear, then, that Hugenberg had his doubts about a Hitler chancellorship, the logic of his own political course since 1928 dictated that he continue to look to the Nazi leader as the best means of forming a government of 'national concentration'. Certainly the transfer of those previous DNVP supporters, imbued for years with a radical nationalist image of Bismarck, to the Nazis around this time appears to point to the fact that at least some others had seen the logic of Bismarckian political rhetoric and where it ultimately led. Throughout the remainder of 1932 the non-Nazi right-wing press grew increasingly favorable to Hitler. If, as Ian Kershaw points out, they were "disinclined to further the Hitler personality cult or provide shows of open enthusiasm, and if publicly voicing some concern about the prospect of a Hitler-led government, conservative German-National oriented newspapers like the Berlin *Deutsche Tageszeitung* were by the end of 1932 coming to 'see no other solution now than to charge Hitler with the solution of the crisis'."[31]

Added to all this was the fact that the Right's remarkably fractured condition made it impossible for any single vision of the best future system to gain a predominant position. Likewise, no single leadership image could emerge as the ideal. In such a political culture, in which hatred of the system served as one unifying pole, while an image of Bismarck, acting as personification of that hatred, as well as the leadership ideal (variously defined), served as the other, Hitler could maneuver his way into a position close enough to be considered a viable candidate. So, while one should not claim that all Bismarckians saw in Hitler the reincarnation of their hero, it can be said, nevertheless, that the prevalence of Bismarckian rhetoric in the nationalist political culture of Weimar generally, continuing into the early 1930s, made such an option a serious possibility.

From Bismarck to Hitler: The Iron Chancellor in the Wake of the Nazi Seizure of Power

Upon hearing of Hitler's appointment as chancellor on January 30, 1933, retired Lieutenant General Richard Kaden rejoiced at how the "right man, the personality, still always asserts himself. We saw that in Bismarck, now we see it again in Hitler, whose flaming battle cries, in combination with national sentiment and social understanding, have stirred up and united the masses."[32] The ease with which the Bismarck Cult could adapt itself to the Hitler Myth serves as a strong indicator of just how much the former had helped prepare the ground for the latter. In the early years of the Third Reich, the rituals of Bismarck worship continued as they had for decades. From the very beginning of the new regime, such rituals connected the Bismarck image with Hitler. That these connections emerged immediately following Hitler's appointment, before the public sphere had been fully coordinated, indicates the spontaneous, voluntary nature of the Bismarck-to-Hitler theme. Some of the participants truly believed that they had gone 'back to Bismarck'. For many others, the rise of the Third Reich appears to have been a not unwelcome outcome of years of devotion to the Cult of the Iron Chancellor.

When President Hindenburg appointed Adolf Hitler as chancellor, the new leadership immediately embarked upon a process of establishing its legitimacy. The first move which won Hitler widespread approval was his brutal assault on the Left, banning the Communist Party and arresting countless supporters of the Marxist parties. In addition to this violent anti-Marxist policy, the Nazis took even more concrete steps to embed their revolution firmly in the ground of German nationalist symbols and myths. They made their first such move on March 21, 1933 at the Garrison Church in Potsdam.

The 'Day of Potsdam' marked the conscious effort to connect the old and new Germany. All aspects of the event were staged deliberately with an eye to reaping as much symbolic power as possible from the glory of the Prusso-German past. Certainly the location, evoking the 'spirit of Potsdam', was critical, giving Hitler the opportunity to honor the Prussian kings buried there while at the same time bowing humbly before that last living symbol of the Second Reich, President

Hindenburg. Even the date, March 21, beyond the symbolism of life and rebirth connected with the first day of spring, was chosen as the anniversary of Bismarck's opening of the first Reichstag of the new German Empire in 1871.

Hitler played to this intended historical anchoring of his regime perfectly. Temporarily giving up his paramilitary uniform, he appeared in the guise of the respectable bourgeois politician, in top hat and morning coat. After the initial ceremony during which he deferentially shook the hand of the President, Hitler delivered a speech which sounded as if it were inspired much less by the spirit of National Socialist revolution and much more by that of Prussian conservatism. He praised Bismarck, who "allowed the cultural aspirations of the German nation to be followed by political unification," but noted that although many felt that to have marked the end of internal discord, it did not prevent the ultimate "dissolution of the *Weltanschauung* of the German *Volksgemeinschaft*" from which they were still suffering to that day.[33] From that initial Bismarckian accomplishment, Hitler took it as the task of the Nazi revolution to "restore the unity of spirit and will to the German nation" by including "all of the truly living powers of the Volk as the supporting elements of the German future" while making a "sincere effort to unite those with good intentions and ensure that those who attempt to damage the German Volk receive their due."[34] It was an ominous portent of the coming *Volksgemeinschaft* – of the intention to go 'beyond Bismarck' – though depicted in such a way as to conflict with the desires of very few in the Protestant-bourgeois camp.

Through the 'Day of Potsdam', the Nazis hoped to instill a sense of excitement, of rebirth, of the awakening of German national pride. After what many middle-class Germans considered fourteen years of degradation and shame, the spectacle must have gone a long way to doing just that. In some sense similar to the rush to honor Bismarck after his dramatic successes in the wars of unification, towns and cities across Germany honored the new leader, planting 'Hitler-Oaks' and 'Hitler-Lindens' and making him honorary citizen. The connection between old and new which the Nazis hoped to foster was not lost in most cases, as, for example, in Bochum, where they granted him honorary citizenship. The petition there declared that "a Prince Bismarck forged together the Reich, an Adolf Hitler is forging together the nation into a united people."[35]

Historians added to the effect by once again granting intellectual legitimacy to the Nazi claims, as they had done for years with the Bismarckians. One example of a scholar in the service of the National Socialist cause was Professor Johannes Haller. In an article in the *Süddeutsche Zeitung* on the occasion of Bismarck's birthday, he praised the 'Day of Potsdam', declaring that the country had now found its way back to the proper, that is the Bismarckian, path. For Haller, the event affirmed the connection between past Prusso-German glory and the promise of the newly awakened Reich. It was on that day that "all of Germany honored once again the thought that was Bismarck's guiding star: that the German Reich is the continuation and completion of Prussian history, and that therefore in it, if it shall survive and thrive, the forces must also further live and work which made Prussia great."[36] Germans should not worry if the new Germany does not exactly resemble the old, since it was the 'spirit', and not the 'form', that mattered most. "Bismarck himself would be different today and deal differently than seventy years ago, and would still set himself no other task than the one from that time."[37] Hitler, he wrote, "stands on the place where Bismarck stood, his heir, his continuer, yes, God willing, the one who completes his work."[38] In connecting the old with the new, Bismarck with Hitler, Haller stressed that the Iron Chancellor's goal of a free, strong Germany remained the same goal for which the Nazi leader was fighting. The difference was not the goals, but rather the way to achieve them. In the end, Haller made it clear that one must never forget that it was Bismarck – or, more accurately, his spirit – which, kept alive in the hearts of German nationalists for so long, made such an effort possible so soon after defeat.[39]

Haller's connection of Bismarck with Hitler marked a further step in the legitimization of the new regime – a step that was heightened in its effectiveness by the proximity of the Iron Chancellor's birthday to the already successful 'Day of Potsdam'. Around April 1, 1933, Germans came out to celebrate Bismarck in ceremonies nearly as large and as numerous as during that greatest of all Bismarck years, 1915. Across the country Germans honored him under the influence of the excitement that continued to grow following the Nazi takeover. In such a situation, thoughts of the Iron Chancellor and the 'People's Chancellor' could not help but become intertwined. Before a crowd of Bismarckians at the Rottmanshöhe, the head of Munich's Bismarck Society, Herr Meyer, linked the two figures through their historical mission while taking note of their outer differences. "Otto von Bismarck, the earth-bound aristocratic man from Mark-Prussian land, founded the Reich; Adolf Hitler, the earth-bound man of the people from Bavarian land renewed the Reich."[40] Again, it was not the outer differences that counted but the continuity of their spirit. Hitler "found the way to the soul of the German Volk and Bismarck would say today that without Adolf Hitler and the National Socialist people's movement all of this in Germany would not have been possible!"[41]

The theme of continuity ran through many of the speeches and articles on Bismarck's birthday, though already new characteristics were emerging. At that same celebration on the Rottmanshöhe, NSDAP Landtag Fraktion leader Dr. Buttman declared that "Adolf Hitler began to shape the Reich out of the same thoughts as Prince Bismarck, out of the feeling of responsibility before history, before the Volk."[42] With the goal of establishing the absolute unity of the German tribes, confessions, occupations, and classes, he would be able to establish "what Bismarck had failed to shape."[43] Implicit here was a criticism held to varying degrees by individual Nazis – a criticism, though, that at this stage remained mild.

Bismarck, according to this view, did what he could at the time. Now it was up to Hitler to finish the job. "We now have a People's Chancellor who, from providence, has received the historical task of completing the work of Otto von Bismarck."[44] The goals and achievements of the Iron Chancellor's earlier work were to inspire the current generation under its new leader. "When we have overcome Marxism, when we have also shaped the narrow-minded German middle-class mentality in the service of the entire Volk, then there will be no more obstacles to making Germany once again free and great and strong. In this spirit of Bismarck we want to live and die, in the service of Adolf Hitler we want to work."[45]

The ceremonies of 1933, including Hitler's birthday, helped significantly in establishing the regime's legitimacy. In a relatively short time Hitler was moving from being leader of the Nazi Party to leader of the nation. The next several years would see the continued fostering of the ties between Bismarck and Hitler until eventually such connections would no longer be necessary. At a *Reichs-gründungstag* celebration at the Friedrich-Wilhelm University in Berlin in 1934, Alfred Baeumler declared that "on to the position of Bismarck has stepped Hitler, himself as well a realizer of a dream of unity, which all have dreamed. Like the Chancellor of the Second Reich, so one believes that the Chancellor of the Third Reich will realize what all, or at least many, have thought and wanted."[46]

After 1933 Germans continued to portray Bismarck as a forerunner of Hitler, his development similar to that of the Nazi leader, his achievements an inspiration for the current generation. Of course, to establish such an image one must take certain liberties with the historical record. The Stahlhelm did just that, depicting two figures so close in their historical experiences, goals, and accomplishments as to leave little doubt about their inherent similarities. Bismarck was Hitler's fore-runner, having "directly prepared the great revolution of the 20th century, the rev-olution of National Socialism."[47] Both men were revolutionaries acting under similar circumstances.[48] The pre-unification German Bund, for example, was "an interim-Reich, nothing better than that of the Weimar Republic," and so, in deciding to move from Prussia to the German Reich, "he made . . . precisely such a revolutionary decision as Adolf Hitler, as he began the attack on Weimar."[49] They also made similar choices in their political alliances, the revolutionary Bismarck with the conservative King Wilhelm I, and the revolutionary Hitler with the old conservative Hindenburg.[50] With the legitimacy thus acquired, each could move forward for the unity of the Reich.[51] And as with Hitler, the path to national unity led Bismarck through a series of revolutionary acts. In the age of parliament, for example, he put through the army reform in defiance of the constitution. In the age of legitimacy and private property he toppled thrones and confiscated property. In an age of capitalism he socialized the railroads and postal system. In the age of democracy and mass parties Bismarck considered a coup "that was supposed to abolish the errors of the parliamentary constitution" and "smash the Marxist and class struggle-based parties."[52] The Iron Chancellor never shrank from blood, nor did he worry about popularity. In the end, Bismarck, like Hitler, was justified in the steps that he had taken, no matter what the people thought of them at the time.[53] With his career over, Bismarck went into exile knowing his creation was threatened, and though he was aware of the ultimate outcome, he also believed in its resurrection. "He felt himself as ancestor of a revolutionary generation, he was the first conscious National Socialist in the historical expanse of the Reich, and therefore every confession to Bismarckian humanity and the basic laws of the Bismarckian art of state is at the same time also a confession to the National Socialist Reich, to which the future belongs."[54]

The importance of the Bismarck image in legitimizing the Nazi regime is testimony to its power and endurance as the dominant national symbol over more than seventy years. Ironically though, in helping to establish the stability of the Third Reich, it turned out to be sowing the seeds of its own demise. For if the Bismarck image could find a place in this initial phase of the regime, it would soon find itself squeezed to the margins as Hitler's desire to be the sole dominant national symbol grew increasingly boundless and as the regime's policies expanded to areas beyond those of the Bismarckian era. In the increasingly limited public sphere of post-*Gleichschaltung* Nazi Germany, Bismarck's name continued to be used to support various issues. From the 1934 plebiscite to approve Hitler's new position of *Führer*, to the 1935 Saar vote, to defense policy issues, the Iron Chancellor's image continued to find a place.[55] But it was, to be sure, growing increasingly confined. With the Anschluss – Germany's 1938 annexation of Austria – the process was just about complete. Hitler had now accomplished the 'Greater Germany' project that his illustrious predecessor had been unable (and actually unwilling) to achieve. From this time forward, the Iron Chancellor would move into the background as Hitler's seemingly limitless desire for expansion, and the racist overtones that went with it, left little doubt that he was truly moving 'beyond Bismarck'.

In Hitler's Shadow: The Decline of Bismarck in the Third Reich

On March 12, 1938, German troops entered Austria, annexing it to the Third Reich. The dream of Greater Germany had become a reality. If Bismarck's founding of the smaller German Reich in 1871 had been one step in the nation's historical development, Hitler's dramatic coup of 1938 marked the next stage. Comparisons were unavoidable, but with the full power of the state in Nazi hands it was not difficult to guess just who would come out on top. The humor magazine *Kladderadatsch* provided a fitting depiction on the cover of its April 10 issue. An armor-clad Bismarck with massive broad-sword stood before a ballot box dedicated to the 'Creator of Greater Germany' and marked with Nazi insignia. As he dropped his vote into the box, the symbolic transfer was complete. Bismarck, the ultimate hero and leader of Germany for the past seventy-six years, was now handing over the reigns to the nation's newest and, by implication, even greater leader, Adolf Hitler. If the strength of his symbolic power as late as 1933 demonstrated the Iron Chancellor's mighty stature, his decline and ultimate marginalization during the latter years of the Third Reich testified to the god-like stature Hitler had acquired. The Cult of Bismarck, so impressive and powerful for so long, now gave way before the mighty Cult of the *Führer*.

Following the Anschluss, Hitler honored his predecessor for the achievement of national unity, even if it was only the smaller Prusso-German state. In a speech in late March 1938, he praised Bismarck as "one of the greatest statesmen, not only of our people, but rather of all times," noting that "he distinguished himself through the clear, realistic look into the possible. And out of the possible he created a Reich in three wars. Not all Germany did it encompass, but a kernel of our Volk."[56] While Hitler's praise was certainly consistent with his long-standing view of Bismarck, he did make clear his own vital contribution to the German national cause. One week later in Linz, Austria, he spoke no longer of simply a "core," but rather now of a "north German" core. "A north German, mighty statesman once fitted and forced together the reluctant north German tribes and the other states of the old Reich. His name became for us German young people in my youth a holy one."[57] To complete the project, a new element was needed – a south German element. "In all likelihood," he proclaimed, "only a German from the South could have brought about this second unification. After all, he had to return a large parcel of territory to the Reich, a parcel which had been lost to the Reich in the course of our history."[58]

The Anschluss dramatically increased Hitler's stature as a statesman of the highest rank. A report from Saxony by the Social Democratic resistance noted that even those parts of the population that had been less than enthusiastic towards him or who had rejected him completely now admitted "that Hitler is a great and clever statesman who will raise up Germany from the defeat of 1918 to greatness and standing again."[59] This rise in the *Führer's* stature sped Bismarck's decline. Already the Hitler myth had been growing markedly before 1938. When the *Führer* achieved what his illustrious predecessor could not, the shadow Hitler cast began to engulf even the image of the mighty Iron Chancellor. Bismarck's daughter-in-law sensed this trend. In October 1938 she confided to Ulrich von Hassel that her father-in-law "is already today worth absolutely nothing more, is becoming, in contrast, ever smaller."[60] Von Hassel agreed that the assessment was correct "and natural in view not only of the mentality of our people but also of the fact of the successful Anschluss."[61] In trying to reassure the Princess, though, he told her "out of complete conviction that Bismarck would survive this storm victorious."[62]

Whether von Hassel's prediction would come true, however, no one could tell. In fact, indications pointed to a continuing slide. In the spring of 1938 the authorities moved the Berlin Bismarck monument from its place in front of the Reichstag to a position "without historical significance" in the Tiergarten.[63] Valentin von Bismarck noted how the monument and its position before the Reichstag "in its arrangement represented a high point of German history," and warned that "the respect for tradition is one of the best means of education for the developing generation."[64] Perhaps expressing some disillusionment with the regime, he asked, "is this then so completely forgotten? The deepest sadness moves all those who honor the greatest Chancellor and statesman of all times as a result of these measures."[65]

Around the same time that the Nazis removed the Iron Chancellor from his spot in front of the Reichstag, the Bismarck Cult suffered another blow. On May 10, 1938, the Society for the Building of a Bismarck National Monument dissolved itself. Its leader, Karl Jarres, explained the decision and in doing so provided testimony to Bismarck's diminished status. At the heart of this decision "was the conviction, that under the present times, the original plan for the monument is no longer able to be put through, and that also the idea of the Society for the building of a 'German Place of Freedom on the Rhine' cannot be put through by the Society itself, but rather requires the initiative of the heads of the Reich and the Party."[66] It was becoming increasingly clear to Bismarckians that such an initiative would not be forthcoming any time soon.

If most indications pointed to a serious decline in Bismarck's role in German political culture, that did not mean he would vanish altogether. In February 1939 Hitler travelled to Friedrichsruh as a guest of the Bismarck family. After laying a wreath at the sarcophagus, he went on to Hamburg to dedicate the Reich's newest and largest battleship. Christening the ship 'Bismarck' gave Hitler one more opportunity to pay homage, rooting his own legitimacy once again with that of the Iron Chancellor, while at the same time providing his last comprehensive assessment of his historical significance. The speech marked the last serious recognition of Bismarck in the Third Reich, as the onset of the war – a new kind of war – would leave him little room.

Standing before the battleship, Hitler spoke of his predecessor in glowing terms, returning to a number of his favorite themes. The speech, in fact, demonstrated a remarkable continuity of thought on his part. As such, we can see the dedication of the 'Bismarck' as the culmination of nearly two decades of Hitler's thought on the Iron Chancellor. He opened by justifying his decision for the name of the ship. "Among all the men," he began, "who can claim to have been a pioneer of the new Reich, one towers in mighty solitude above all: Bismarck."[67]

If the speech represents the last significant recognition of Bismarck in the Third Reich, it also symbolizes the fusion of the Bismarck Cult with that of the *Führer*. Over time, the gospel of the earlier political religion increasingly meshed with that of its post-war offspring, until by this point the Nazi religion has subsumed it within itself. At the shipyard Hitler praised the founding of the Second Empire as not simply a step in the historical development of the times, but rather "the result of the work of a heavenly inspired one-time appearance."[68] With this he then implicitly tied his own struggle to that of the Iron Chancellor. Bismarck had to fight resistance from all sides. "At every turn the zeros raised themselves up before the singular genius of the time."[69] Hitler, however, could understand what it meant to face such resistance and ultimately triumph. "It is a titanic struggle," he declared, "which perhaps only those can appreciate who themselves were forced to confront such a world of resistance."[70] The strength to overcome such opposition and put through a program clearly struck a chord in Hitler's thinking. What made Bismarck so worthy of wonderment was the "great understanding and wisdom as well as the mighty determination, which kept him from every weak evasion. Three times the consciousness of duty pressed him to take the sword in hand for the solution of problems which, according to his holiest conviction, could not be solved by majority decisions."[71] The characteristics that Hitler praised in his predecessor were clearly among the ones he saw in himself and desired of those in his movement. Bismarck's transformation into proto-Nazi was now complete. Hitler spoke of Bismarck's career-long transformation from Prussian politician to German founder of the Reich. In undergoing this change, he not only created the Reich, "but rather gave the prerequisites for the establishment of the current Greater Germany."[72]

Criticism – what there was of it – remained limited and based on a recognition of the changed times. As Hitler saw it, where Bismarck's struggles ended in failure, "he had to fail, because he lacked the instruments in order to lead through such a struggle."[73] One problem in particular that he focused on was his attempt "to exterminate Marxism from the German people with all means."[74] Though Bismarck recognized the necessity, he lacked the tools that Hitler would ultimately have at his disposal. Failure, therefore, was inevitable. In the end, the task fell to the Nazis, and in fighting their struggle to a successful conclusion, they ended up defeating all of Bismarck's enemies. Hitler was, in fact, carrying Bismarck's mission further, ultimately to completion. It represented much more his admiration for him than any fundamental criticism. His admiration for Bismarck remained strong well into the Third Reich.[75]

Broadcast on radio and printed in newspapers across the country, Hitler's dedication of the 'Bismarck' reached a broad audience. Not all who received the message, however, came away with a renewed optimism in the connection between the *Führer* and the Iron Chancellor. Ulrich von Hassel described the speech as "mere show," though he commented pessimistically that "many will see the praise of the Iron Chancellor as a sign of his understanding for tradition."[76] Von Hassel's observation indicates a process of disillusionment with the Nazi regime that would also affect others and which would grow stronger with the war.

With the commencement of hostilities in 1939, Bismarck's decline gathered momentum. If the 'Hitler Myth' had already reached immense proportions thanks to his peacetime successes, the added stature gained through military achievement left no room for challengers. Bismarck appeared occasionally, when circumstances made it appropriate.[77] The Chancellor of Blood and Iron, for example, could also play a role in the war effort. Some of the Nazi *Wochensprüche*, or 'weekly messages', carried his image with an appropriately stern, inspiring message. In October 1941, for example, a determined-looking Bismarck was positioned above his saying "Struggle is everywhere. Without struggle there is no life and if we want to live further we must also be prepared for further struggles."[78]

Other features of the war, however, would not lend themselves so easily to such connections. In particular, the war's racial aspect made appropriation more difficult. This is not to say, however, that a racist, anti-Semitic Bismarck did not make any appearances during the Third Reich. From the very beginning of the Cult in the 1890s, anti-Semites had tried to invoke his name for their own program. While such connections continued to be made during the Nazi period, they were never particularly strong. They also tended to include an element of criticism, reflecting the Nazis' radicalization far in excess of Bismarck's own day. Thus, while Julius Streicher could quote anti-Semitic statements by Bismarck or write about how the Iron Chancellor had warned of the Jewish danger, and begrudge the fact that Jews were responsible for his fall in 1890, he could also point out that, since "Bismarck had not recognized the Jewish danger," his accomplishment could only be of short duration.[79] Hitler himself was reported to have commented that "the good old Bismarck did not have the slightest idea about the Jewish problem."[80] Beyond the increasingly troublesome fit between Bismarck and the Nazis' racial war, Hitler himself contributed to the decline of Bismarck imagery during the war years as he faded from the scene, making fewer and fewer public appearances, and thus giving himself fewer opportunities to praise his predecessor if he were, in fact, so inclined.

If the Nazis' use of Bismarck declined during the war, for others it appears to have grown or, more accurately, shifted in emphasis. Resistance to the regime, whether it was the conservative 20th of July plotters or the Soviet-inspired National Committee for a Free Germany, involved the Bismarck image to some degree. For the conservative resistance, recognition of Bismarck as a counter to Hitler meant that, to some degree at least, they now realized where their previous Bismarck idolatry had led Germany. There can be no doubt that their agitation against the democratic Weimar Republic played an important role in its destruction and there should equally be little doubt that the Bismarck image served as a significant inspiration for such agitation. In addition, their often hearty welcome of the Nazi takeover in 1933 made their sympathies even more clear. For most within this group it took the war, and usually only the realization that it was a lost cause, to lead them from support to opposition, and in this transition Bismarck once again served as inspiration.

One such member of the conservative resistance who was guided by an image of Bismarck was Ulrich von Hassel. At one point Ambassador to Rome for both Weimar and the Nazis, von Hassel had been an admirer of the Iron Chancellor for years. He had also, however, been an enthusiastic supporter of Hitler in 1933.[81] By 1940 he had noted distinctions between Bismarck and Hitler. In March of that year he read the elder Moltke's description of a conversation with Bismarck and Roon after 1870 in which the Chancellor asked what more they could expect to experience that was as worthy as what they had just gone through, to which Moltke calmly replied, "to see a tree growing."[82] This, according to von Hassel, was what separated these men from Hitler. "Bismarck, Moltke and Roon felt themselves as a part of nature, saw in the growing of a tree the highest form of development and observed themselves as the helpers of God. Hitler has the characteristic building passion of the tyrants (in the Greek sense) and dictators; that is, the drive to immortalize themselves, to immortalize through detached human power, not as a part of divine action."[83] Von Hassel at that point knew to which group he belonged.

Like others in the conservative resistance, von Hassel sought to replace the Nazi dictatorship with another system, by no means necessarily democratic, and more often reflecting a desire to return in some way to the Bismarckian Reich. How easily that could be achieved, nobody knew, but "nevertheless all must be done so that a change comes in order to at least save the rudiments of the Bismarckian Empire."[84] In terms of foreign policy, von Hassel made it clear what he meant by a return to Bismarck. Walking through the estate at Friedrichsruh only weeks before the plot to kill Hitler would actually be carried out, the Prussian aristocrat regretted the cuirassier-booted image of Bismarck Germans had created.[85] The true Bismarck was something quite different. "In reality, the highest diplomacy and moderation were his greatest gifts. He understood how to outmaneuver the opponent and *despite that* in singular fashion to awaken trust in the world, precisely the reverse of today."[86] Inside the Bismarck house, von Hassel noticed a painting of Bismarck by Anton von Werner which depicted him "powerful and violent" next to the two sunken frames of the French politicians Thiers and Favre. This he saw as a "correct example of the foolish interpretation which we ourselves have spread."[87] Von Hassel recommended that the painting with its falsely represented scene be thrown away. "Much else," he noted with resignation, "deserves the same fate."[88]

If it was understandable that the 20th of July plotters would draw inspiration from Bismarck, it might come as a surprise that he actually served a similar role in the Soviet-inspired National Committee for a Free Germany (NKFD). The fact that the organization consisted in part of German officers, though, makes it somewhat more understandable.[89] In fact, part of the impetus for the organization's founding came from Lieutenant Heinrich Graf von Einsiedel, a great-grandson of Bismarck. After having been shot down over Stalingrad, Einsiedel put out a flyer in September 1942, in which he sought to demonstrate that Bismarck had warned against war with Russia, that this warning was correct, and that Germany would lose the war. After Stalingrad, other officers began to shift to Einsiedel's conclusion, thus facilitating the formation of the NKFD under the leadership of Erich Weinert and Wilhelm Pieck, the future Communist leader of East Germany, on July 13, 1943.[90]

At the founding meeting of the NKFD, Graf von Einsiedel spoke about the lessons of Bismarck's foreign policy. According to Einsiedel, Bismarck had recognized that Germany could only be secure through cooperation with Russia.[91] This mix of pro-Soviet, pro-Bismarck propaganda would continue for the remainder of the war as the NKFD utilized a variety of media, including their newspaper *Free Germany*, flyers, radio programs over their own station, and political meetings of prisoners of war, all in order to get its message out. When dealing with Bismarck, that message generally involved his attitude towards preventive war or his moderation in pursuit of political goals.[92] From such a perspective, Hitler fared poorly. In a *Reichsgründungstag* speech delivered over the radio in January 1944, Major General Otto Korfes passed judgment on the two. Bismarck, he declared, "was inspired by a deep feeling for his responsibility before the Volk and the Reich; he possessed the sense for the reality of political life; he knew of the set limits of Germany's powers and held them in wise unpretentiousness with inexorable rigor."[93] Hitler, on the other hand, "risks Reich and Volk for never-to-be-realized feverish dreams ... his thoughts scorn the limits of reality, his character is immoderation."[94] Such an image clearly evokes memories of the Bismarck image put forward so desperately by Stresemann and Bethmann Hollweg and for which they received mostly scorn, in part from many of these same individuals. Perhaps they had finally learned the lesson. If so, it was clearly too late.

The once mighty Bismarck had, by this time, sunk deep within the immense shadow cast by Germany's newest idol, Adolf Hitler. Those who now preached of a moderate Bismarck and sought in his name the inspiration to overthrow the corrupter of that name found themselves branded as traitors. Decades of devotion to the Cult of the Iron Chancellor had evolved into a certain understanding of politics and to expectations which were finally fulfilled on January 30, 1933. That it was the bold and daring blood-and-iron Bismarck that caught the imagination of more Germans than the reasonable, moderate Bismarck made it much more likely that the path of German nationalist political culture would lead in such ominous directions. The ease with which the political culture of Bismarckians could mesh with that of the Hitler movement, at least in its initial phase, points to the conclusion that the Nazi triumph, while certainly not inevitable, should be seen as one logical outcome of the Bismarck Cult.

Notes

1. Aldous Huxley, *Ends and Means: An Inquiry into the Nature of Ideals and into the Methods Employed for Their Realization* (New York: Harper & Brothers Publishers, 1937), 99.

2. Ulrich von Hassel, *Die Hassel-Tagebücher, 1938–1944. Aufzeichnungen vom Andern Deutschland* (Berlin: Wolf Jobst Siedler Verlag, 1988), 436 (entry from July 10, 1944).

3. For Hassel's initial enthusiasm, see Theodore S. Hamerow, *On the Road to the Wolf's Lair: German Resistance to Hitler* (Cambridge, Mass: Harvard University Press, 1997), 187–191.

4. For Hitler's growing acceptance by the bourgeois nationalist Right, see Kershaw, *'Hitler Myth'*, 37–38.

5. Rudy Koshar, "Contentious Citadel: Bourgeois Crisis and Nazism in Marburg/Lahn, 1880–1933," in Thomas Childers, ed., *The Formation of the Nazi Constituency 1919–1933* (London: Croom Helm, 1986), 28.

6. "Der Weg zu Freiheit und Brot," speech to the National Socialist Student Bund, November 21, 1927, in Institut für Zeitgeschichte, eds., *Hitler: Reden, Schriften, Anordnungen*, Volume II, *Vom Weimarer Parteitag bis zur Reichstagswahl. Juli 1926–Mai 1928. Part 2: August 1927–May 1928*, 556.

7. Kershaw, *Hitler: 1889–1936: Hubris*, 250–253.

8. "10 Jahre ungesühnter Verrat," speech to NSDAP Versammlung in Munich, November 9, 1928, in op. cit., Volume III, *Zwischen den Reichstagswahlen, Juli 1928–Februar 1929, Part 1: Juli 1928–Februar 1929*, 207.

9. "Bismarck-Gedenken. Vaterländische Betrachtungen an Bismarcks Todestage, 30. Juli" by W. S. Eckewart, in BAL, RlbPa, R8034 II, 7100, #125: *Deutsche Schnelldienst*, July 30, 1930.

10. Ibid.

11. Dr. Rudolf Beinert, "Bismarck und die Deutsche Republik. Rede zur Bismarckfeier auf dem Brocken am 5. April 1930," in Dr. Rudolf Beinert, *Von Bismarck zu Hitler. Neun Bismarckreden* (Berlin: Brunnen-Verlag, 1934), 89.

12. "Deutsche!" in *Bismarck-Blatt. Zeitschrift des Vereins zur Errichtung eines Bismarck-National-Denkmals E.V.*, nr. 3, May 1930.

13. Lothar Albertin describes this progression in "Die Auflösung der bürgerlichen Mitte und die Krise des parlamentarischen Systems von Weimar," 90. For the Nazi electorate, see Thomas Childers, *The Nazi Voter: The Social Foundations of Fascism in Germany, 1919–1933* (Chapel Hill: The University of North Carolina Press, 1983).

14. "Zeitgemäße Bismarck-Gedanken" by Generalleutnant a. D. von Metzsch, in BAL, RlbPa, R8034 II, 7100, #129: *Berliner Lokal-Anzeiger*, nr. 154, April 1, 1931.

15. "Vom neuen Reich. Zum 18. Januar" in *Völkischer Beobachter*, nr. 18/19, January 18/19, 1931.
16. Ibid.
17. Vögler was a leading industrialist in the DVP. He eventually joined the DNVP and supported the naming of Hitler as chancellor.
18. "Der Bismarcktag der Westfalen auf der Hohensyburg" in *Bismarck-Blatt*, nr. 5, September 1931.
19. Ibid.
20. Ibid.
21. Report on 11th annual Stiftungsfest of the Landsmannschaft "Berlin" of the Bismarckbund, November 12, 1930, from Berlin Police President (prepared by Polizeirat Mittasch) to Prussian Minister of the Interior, November 18, 1930 (received Nov 24) (Nr. 546 IA. 6/1930): GStA PK, I. HA Rep. 77, Ministerium des Innern, Tit. 4043 Nr. 411 Bd. 1 Bl. 143–144 (M); Bismarckjugend der DNVP.
22. Adolf Hitler, speech to NSDAP Versammlung in Coburg, January 18, 1931, in Institut für Zeitgeschichte, eds., *Hitler: Reden, Schriften, Anordnungen*, Volume IV, *Von der Reichstagswahl bis zur Reichspräsidentenwahl Oktober 1930–März 1932, Part 1: Oktober 1930–Juni 1931*, 175–176.
23. See also Adolf Hitler, Speech to Gautag der Thüringer NSDAP in Gera, September 6, 1931, in ibid., Volume IV, *Von der Reichstagswahl bis zur Reichspräsidentenwahl Oktober 1930–März 1932, Part 2: Juli 1931–Dezember 1931*, 79.
24. Jürgen W. Falter, "The Two Hindenburg Elections of 1925 and 1932: a Total Reversal of Voter Coalitions," *Central European History* 23 (June/September 1990): 225–241.
25. Mommsen, *Rise and Fall*, 407. For the campaign, see also Andreas Dorpalen, *Hindenburg and the Weimar Republic* (Princeton: Princeton University Press, 1964), 254–300.
26. Ibid., 407.
27. Adolf Hitler, Speech to NSDAP Versammlung in Dortmund, March 10, 1932, in op. cit., Volume IV, *Von der Reichstagswahl bis zur Reichspräsidentenwahl Oktober 1930–März 1932, Part 3: Januar 1932–März 1932*, 202.
28. BAL: 60 Vo 1 – Deutsche Volkspartei Archive Film #53170, Akten #234, #112–113, "Hindenburg und der Young-Plan. Damals und heute," *Nationalliberale Correspondenz*, nr. 51, March 11, 1932.
29. BAL: 60 Vo 1 – Deutsche Volkspartei Archive Film #53170, Akten #234, #469–470, "Bismarck-Hindenburg," *Nationalliberale Correspondenz*, nr. 64, April 1, 1932; for another equation of Bismarck's dismissal with a possible Hindenburg defeat, see DVP flyer from the same campaign: "Deine Stimme gehört Hindenburg!" in BAL, NS 5 VI, 478, #112: DVP Flyer, 1932.

30. See Kershaw, *'Hitler Myth'*, 37–38. For the Hugenberg–Hitler relationship, and the exodus of the DNVP's middle-class support to the Nazis, see Larry Eugene Jones, " 'The Greatest Stupidity of My Life': Alfred Hugenberg and the Formation of the Hitler Cabinet, January 1933," *Journal of Contemporary History* 27 (1992): 88; see also John A. Leopold, *Alfred Hugenberg: The Radical Nationalist and the Campaign against the Weimar Republic* (New Haven: Yale University Press, 1977), 107–138.

31. Kershaw, *'Hitler Myth'*, 38.

32. Kaden quoted in Pflanze, *Bismarck*, III, 455.

33. Hitler at the 'Day of Potsdam' quoted in Max Domarus, ed., *Hitler: Speeches and Proclamations, 1932–1945. The Chronicle of a Dictatorship, I, 1932–1934* (Illinois: Bolchazy-Carducci Publishers, 1990), 272–273.

34. Ibid.

35. For the 'Hitler-Oaks' and 'Hitler-Lindens', the honorary citizenships, and the Bochum petition quoted above, see Kershaw, *'Hitler-Myth'*, 55.

36. Johannes Haller, "Zum 1. April 1933," in Johannes Haller, *Reden und Aufsätze zur Geschichte und Politik* (Stuttgart: J. G. Cotta'sche Buchhandlung Nachfolger, 1934): 380.

37. Ibid., 380–381.

38. Ibid., 381.

39. Ibid.

40. "Die Bismarckfeier auf der Rottmanshöhe. Adolf Hitler hat das Erbe des Altreichskanzlers übernommen" in *Völkischer Beobachter*, nr. 93, April 3, 1933 (Munich).

41. Ibid.; in another ceremony at the Bismarck tower on the Müggelberg outside Berlin, Goebbels declared that "Bismarck was the great state-political revolutionary of the 19th century, Hitler is the great state-political revolutionary of the 20th century." Goebbels quoted in ibid., 49; for a report of the celebration, see "Bismarckhuldigung" in *Der Angriff*, nr. 79, April 3, 1933.

42. "Die Bismarckfeier auf der Rottmanshöhe. Adolf Hitler hat das Erbe des Altreichskanzlers übernommen" in *Völkischer Beobachter*, nr. 93, April 3, 1933 (Munich).

43. Ibid.

44. Ibid.

45. Ibid.

46. Alfred Baeumler, "Das Reich als Tat," in Alfred Baeumler, *Politik und Erziehung. Reden und Aufsätze* (Berlin: Junker und Dünnhaupt Verlag, 1937), 9.

47. "Der Revolutionär Otto von Bismarck. Das politische Erbe des Großen Kanzlers," *Der Stahlhelm*, April 1, 1934.

48. "Von Bismarck zu Hitler," in *Der Stahlhelm*, nr. 3, January 21, 1934.

49. Ibid.
50. Ibid.
51. Ibid.
52. "Der Revolutionär Otto von Bismarck. Das politische Erbe des Großen Kanzlers," *Der Stahlhelm*, April 1, 1934.
53. "Von Bismarck zu Hitler."
54. Ibid.
55. Political placard collection, BA Koblenz; for the Saar, see "Bismarck, des Reiches Gründer – Hitler, des Reiches Vollender! Zum Gedenken des Tages der Reichsgründung," in *Der Stahlhelm*, January 20, 1935; "Bismarcks erste Tat: Heeresvermehrung. Zum 120. Geburtstag des 'eisernen Kanzlers'," in *Der Stahlhelm*, nr. 13, March 31, 1935; see also "Wir Deutsche fürchten Gott," in BAL, RlbPa, R8034 II, 7101, #28: *Märkische Volkszeitung*, nr. 36, February 6, 1938.
56. Hitler quoted in Andrews, "Hitler, Bismarck, and History," 517–518.
57. Hitler quoted in ibid., 518.
58. Hitler speech from Linz, Austria, April 7, 1938, quoted in Max Domarus, ed., *Hitler: Speeches and Proclamations, 1932–1945. The Chronicle of a Dictatorship II, the Years 1935 to 1938* (Illinois: Bolchazy-Carducci Publishers, 1992), 1086.
59. Social Democratic Party in Exile (Sopade) Report quoted in Kershaw, *'Hitler Myth'*, 132. For general post-Anschluss reaction toward Hitler, see Kershaw, 130–132.
60. Ulrich von Hassel, *Die Hassel-Tagebücher*, 55.
61. Ibid.
62. Ibid.
63. *Nachrichtenblatt für das von Bismarck'sche Geschlecht*, nr. 21, June 1938.
64. Ibid.
65. Ibid.
66. "Auflösung des Vereins zur Errichtung eines Bismarck-National-Denkmals, E.V., Düsseldorf", in *Nachrichtenblatt für das von Bismarck'sche Geschlecht*, nr. 21, June 1938.
67. "Stapellauf Schlachtschiff 'Bismarck' " in *Völkischer Beobachter*, nr. 46, February 15, 1939 (North Germany).
68. Ibid.
69. Ibid.
70. Ibid.
71. Ibid.
72. Ibid.
73. Ibid.
74. Ibid.

75. Ibid.

76. Ulrich von Hassel, *Die Hassel-Tagebücher*, 83.

77. The Nazi–Soviet Non-Aggression Pact of 1939, for example: "Der Russenpakt des Dritten Reiches," in *Der Stürmer*, nr. 7, February 1940.

78. Wochenspruch der NSDAP, Series 42, October 12–18, 1941. See also the Wochenspruch from April 23–29, 1939 as war-clouds were gathering. From collection of the Otto-von-Bismarck Stiftung.

79. Julius Streicher quoted in "Warner und Propheten," in *Der Stürmer*, nr. 2, January 1939; see also, "Bismarck und die Juden," in *Der Stürmer*, nr. 33, August 1933, and "Die Juden haben Bismarck gestürzt," in *Der Stürmer*, nr. 4, January 22, 1942.

80. Hitler quoted in Andrews, "Hitler, Bismarck, and History," 521.

81. Hamerow, *On the Road to the Wolf's Lair*, 187–191.

82. Ulrich von Hassel, *Die Hassel-Tagebücher*, 183 (entry from March 24, 1940).

83. Ibid.

84. Ibid., 385 (entry from August 19, 1943). See also September 4, 1943, 386.

85. Ibid., 436 (entry from July 10, 1944).

86. Ibid.

87. Ibid.

88. Ibid.

89. Interestingly, a group of working-class youth in Hamburg calling themselves the "Bismarck Band" enjoyed beating up Hitler Youth. Detlev Peukert, *Die Edelweißpiraten. Protestbewegungen jugendlicher Arbeiter im Dritten Reich. Eine Dokumentation* (Cologne: Bund Verlag, 1980), 188.

90. Sigrid Wegner-Korfes, *Otto von Bismarck und Rußland. Des Reichskanzlers Rußlandpolitik und sein realpolitisches Erbe in der Interpretation bürgerlicher Politiker (1918–1945)* (Berlin: Dietz Verlag, 1990), 227–228.

91. Ibid., 229.

92. See, for example, speech by General Walther von Seydlitz, founder of the League of German Officers, related to the NKFD, September 1943, related in ibid., 228.

93. Korfes, who was also an historian, quoted in ibid., 231.

94. Ibid.

Conclusion

Fortunate is the land that has heroes.
No. Unfortunate is the land that has need of heroes.
Bertolt Brecht, *Life of Galileo*[1]

Following the Second World War, West Germany's first chancellor, Konrad Adenauer, reflected upon the problems of the nation's past and the necessities of its future. "When you fall from the heights as we Germans have done," he said, "you realize that it is necessary to break with what has been. We cannot live fruitfully with false illusions."[2] The image of Bismarck that had developed over the previous seventy-five years – of the superhuman figure, the ideal leader, the savior, the chancellor of blood and iron – was precisely one such false illusion with which the Germans could no longer live. The effects of the nearly boundless hero-worship of Germany's Protestant middle classes could now be seen in all their finality. Surrender to a leader/savior had helped lead the nation down the path of tyranny, war, genocide, and ultimately complete destruction. Something new was needed.

In the Germany that was emerging from the rubble, it was quickly becoming clear that the old ways would no longer suffice. Germans everywhere experienced the reality of war's destructiveness first hand as Hitler's strategy of fighting until the bitter end meant that few areas of the country were spared the ravages of combat. The effect of such an experience could not fail to seriously diminish the once prevalent militarist coloring of German political culture. Where, in this newly emerging political culture, could the Bismarckian view of war as being but a legitimate extension of international politics find a home? In an age of nuclear weapons such a view was now irresponsible at best, suicidal at worst. This fact of a radically different post-war world had other implications for German politics as well. The division of Germany into two states, each within the orbit of a superpower, meant that its role as a Great Power in the center of European and world politics was at an end, at least for the foreseeable future. Bismarck's tactics clearly belonged to the past. German unification could no longer be achieved by his methods. Not through blood and iron could this problem of the day be solved, but rather through peaceful internal development and the consent of the other major powers. Here we want to take a brief look at the fate of the Bismarck image in post-war Germany and then make a final assessment of the Cult and its impact on German political culture.

From Politics to History: The Decline of Bismarck in German Political Culture after the Second World War

Addressing a crowd of German nationalists as he stood before the Bismarck mausoleum at Friedrichsruh, a speaker declared it a "perfidious lie" that a nation's youth cannot live without models. Bismarck, he asserted, was just one such great model and it was Bismarck they were celebrating "in the hope that we will have a leadership that will learn from the errors and mistakes of the past, learn to overcome the ideological antagonisms of right and left and to come together again in that selfless commitment for which Bismarck set us the example."[3] Such a statement should raise few eyebrows, containing as it does little to distinguish it from the countless other declarations of faith made to Bismarck over the past decades. That is, of course, until one realizes that this pronouncement was made not in 1902, 1922, or even 1932, but rather in 1982! On June 17 of that year Hugo Wellems, editor of the *Ostpreußenblatt* and leader of the right-wing Bismarckbund, made the declaration during a speech marking the "Day of German Unity" which commemorated the failed uprising in East Berlin in 1953.

If the destruction that the Second World War brought home to the German people helped lessen the appeal of radical nationalist politics, it did not completely erase it. While Hitler himself retained a surprising degree of popularity in the ten years after his suicide, a number of radical nationalists sought to revive after the war a German nationalism that would be cleansed of its Nazi connections.[4] One can see this in the case of Reinhold Wulle, former DNVP member who had broken away in 1922 to form the German Racial Freedom Party.[5] He now sought a third path between the two foreign impositions of Soviet communism in East Germany and Western democracy in the Federal Republic, wondering "whether we will come to a genuine idea of the state, or whether we, like after 1918, want to make a new experiment, which from the start is doomed to fail."[6]

Wulle's inspiration for this alternative Germany was none other than Bismarck. This incarnation differed markedly, however, from the image that he and those around him were circulating before the war. His Bismarck was not the one whom the German people imagined "strangely," in cuirassier uniform, as the Iron Chancellor "who achieved his successes by being sure to bang the table with the fist." "In reality," he wrote, "Bismarck was the precise opposite of the Iron Chancellor. He was a highly sensible and sensitive statesman." He was a statesman who rejected all ideology, who felt a responsibility before God, and who realized that man could not make history. Such a figure contrasted sharply with the 'loose cannon' Hitler. The question facing Germany was once again: Russian or Western?

The answer had to be just as Bismarck had answered so many years before: "neither the one nor the other, rather German." The coming Germany should not be an appendage of either Moscow or London, he wrote. It had the opportunity to think about the idea of the state and what the guiding principle of the future Germany should be. This idea, he wrote, "must join where Bismarck ended. When the thinking Germans again have the courage to acknowledge Bismarck and his state and to free themselves of all romantic dreams," then, according to Wulle, a 'new day' will dawn in Germany.[7] Considering the reality of Germany's situation at the time, it would seem that Wulle was the one still harboring unrealistic 'romantic' dreams. Still, if Bismarck could serve as the inspiration for someone like Wulle for a kind of non-democratic, non-Nazi Germany, this was growing increasingly less common after 1945.

The years during which Bismarck served as the central icon of German political culture were coming to an end.[8] While he certainly remained within the pantheon of national heroes, the immediate impact that his name once had, and the passions that it once aroused, were on the decline since the catastrophe of defeat and destruction had brought home to millions of Germans the price they had paid for such uncritical hero-worship. In part, this was also due to the fact that the Bismarckians after the war found themselves in a significantly different position than before. Essentially, they were unsure of where they belonged. Some sought to revive a DNVP-style party or something even more radical. Such groups, however, while worrisome at times, never achieved the level of importance of their Weimar-era predecessors. Others, believing themselves to be following true Bismarckian principles, sought to align themselves with the Soviet Union and thus leaned towards East Germany. Beyond this, the particular style of leadership which the Federal Republic's first chancellor, Konrad Adenauer, provided also served to lessen the perceived need for a return to Bismarck. At a critical time in the development of the new nation, "he provided what Germany desperately needed – clear, firm, imaginative, and realistic leadership."[9] Along with the prosperity that soon followed, Adenauer helped smooth Bismarck's transition from the immediacy of the Weimar years to a more distant past.

Still, the revival of older political values remains a possibility, particularly in times of crisis. The end of the economic miracle in the 1970s, for instance, was accompanied by a rise in right-wing political activity. Likewise, the years after German reunification in the 1990s also witnessed a resurgence of extreme nationalist sentiment. Right-wing parties like the German People's Union and neo-Nazi skinhead groups have taken advantage of the difficulties involved in the unification process to appeal to the less savory features of German political culture. Despite the distance in time, the Bismarck image has appeared in the rhetoric of a number of these groups. The one hundredth anniversary of his death in July 1998 brought out right-wingers and neo-Nazis to celebrate Bismarck's memory. Michael

Swierczek, Vice-General Secretary of the banned Free German Workers' Party (*Freiheitliche Deutsche Arbeiterpartei* (FAP)) and founder of the *Nationale Offensive*, spoke at a ceremony in Aumühle by Friedrichsruh where he called Bismarck "one of ours" and claimed that "if he lived in the present time, he would march in our ranks."[10] Such eerie reminders of an ominous chapter in German history should be enough to give anyone pause. Political culture changes, but not overnight. Still, the crisis situation that exists primarily in the east has not yet risen to Weimar-era proportions and thus the danger, while ever present, remains relatively low. For most of post-war Germany's history, the Iron Chancellor has occupied a position somewhere below the level of immediate political concern. To a large degree, the arena of debate over Bismarck shifted from that of the politicians to that of the historians. In doing so, it moved beyond the scope of this study and thus provides an opportunity to step back and assess the role of the Bismarck Cult in German political culture and, in particular, its role in the transformation of the German Right.

Analyzing the Shadow: Bismarck's Role in the Crisis of German Leadership and the Transformation of the German Right

This study has traced the development of the Bismarck image in Germany from its earliest forms to its ultimate appropriation by and subordination to that of Hitler in the Third Reich. In doing so, it has examined the ways in which it was expressed and propagated, the uses to which it was put, and the effects that it had on German politics and political culture. It is thus appropriate at this point to discuss both the Bismarck Cult and Germany's crisis of leadership together and thereby come to some clearer understanding of their significance with regard to the German Right and to German history more generally.

Bismarck's direct legacy – the lessons and precedents drawn from his words and actions as Minister-President and Chancellor – is an ambivalent one. In many ways he himself contributed significantly to the crisis of leadership that was to plague Germany for the first half of the twentieth century. Crowned by success, his methods and style came to be the model to which most others who followed him aspired. In becoming the standard by which all future leaders were to be judged, however, Bismarck set the bar way above the level which most politicians could hope to reach. The style with which he attained his greatest victories – through three spectacularly successful wars, for example – left a lasting impression on many Germans in terms of how a leader should look and act. Yet such a negative judgment should be tempered by the recognition of more positive achievements during his twenty-eight years in office.

For someone like Bernhard von Bülow, the appearance and style of the statesman seemed to count for more than the substance of his policies. Such an approach to politics meant extensive rehearsals before Reichstag speeches, in which the gestures and intonation carried more weight than the message. It also meant daring and provocative policies on the international stage. From the naval and colonial policies that marked the introduction of *Weltpolitik* to the dramatic and highly charged arrival of the Kaiser at Tangier during the Moroccan Crisis of 1905, international politics for Bülow meant show over substance so long as he stood at center stage. When the bankruptcy of his policies revealed itself, as in the case of Morocco, he merely packed up and moved on, leaving Germany in a far worse situation. In this sense he earned his nickname of 'the eel', for he steadfastly avoided responsibility for his bombastic politics, even going so far as to leave the Kaiser in the lurch following the *Daily Telegraph* Affair in 1908. All of these instances reflect the problems of a particular reading of Bismarck which sees his greatness in success itself rather than the process that went into achieving that success – all this despite Bülow's own dramatic protests against the 'misunderstood Bismarck' of the Pan-German League.[11]

The connection between Bismarck and German militarism remained strong throughout the Empire (militarism having had a positive connotation). The solution of crisis situations through war had gained the ultimate seal of approval and took its place as a perfectly legitimate option for subsequent leaders. Alfred von Kiderlen-Wächter, the 'Swabian Bismarck', certainly utilized the threat of war in his diplomacy, using the Pan-Germans to stir up nationalist passions – "letting all the dogs bark," as he put it – until the reality of his predicament set in. Then, like Bülow, the hollow nature of his politics required an ignominious retreat, leaving Germany with no tangible gains but only increased mistrust and suspicion among the European powers. This conception of a forceful policy backed by a less than subtle brandishing of the saber extended beyond government circles, as it also became a staple of right-wing politics in both the Empire and Weimar. Bismarckian attacks on both Bethmann Hollweg and Stresemann reflected this, ruthlessly condemning them for their timid, 'un-Bismarcklike' approach to diplomacy. Hitler, of course, took this interpretation to its extreme, though logical, conclusion.

This is not to say that the militarist Bismarck was completely a figment of his successors' imaginations. Again, the wars of unification and the war scares of 1875 and 1887 set precedents that were picked up on by those who followed. And despite the protests of some Germans that the militarist image of Bismarck – the Iron Chancellor in cuirassier boots and steel helmet – was a false one, it must be noted that the public outfit he himself preferred was, indeed, the military uniform. After him, even the mild-mannered and relatively moderate Bethmann Hollweg felt the need to don the uniform of a Prussian officer when addressing the Reichstag in order to garner at least some of the respect bestowed upon his glorious predecessor.

If many of his followers chose the bold, daring, blood-and-iron chancellor from which to draw their lessons, there were undoubtedly more positive aspects of the man and his policies that too often had been sadly underestimated. Following the years of war and nation-building, Bismarck embarked upon a policy the overriding purpose of which was the maintenance of peace. Certainly there was an inherently conservative motivation behind this policy, and it is true that it was not always fully consistent, as again the war scares of 1875 and 1887 demonstrate. On the whole, however, the legacy of one who for the most part avoided the temptation of war and conquest was lost on far too many Germans until it was too late.

The standard that Bismarck established in terms of the proper approach to politics was not limited to the international arena, but also extended to domestic affairs. For the Iron Chancellor, politics often took the form of an all-or-nothing struggle in which no opposition would be permitted to go unchallenged – ideally, it would be destroyed. To oppose Bismarck meant opposing the nation. His enemies were the enemies of Germany, the *Reichsfeinde*. The practical results of such a view of politics were the campaigns against the Catholics in the 1870s and the Social Democrats in the 1880s. Despite the utter failure of both efforts, the division of the population into friend and foe, German and non-German, left a deep imprint on the nation's political culture, finding its ultimate expression in the Nazi policies of exclusion and ultimately extermination.

Partly the result of his desire to integrate some Germans through the exclusion of others, Bismarck's friend–foe political style also derived from his desire to be the sole driver and shaper of German politics – a desire which left terrible scars on the nation's political landscape. At a crossroads in his life, a young Bismarck once asserted that he could never be a member of the orchestra – he would have to play *his* music or none at all. Such an attitude meant that he had to eliminate the appearance of other potential 'conductors'. If, in the early years of the Second Reich, there existed an impressive pool of political talent, their role as independent power factors remained either limited or non-existent. As soon as a potential challenger arose, Bismarck acted in an often ruthless manner to eliminate him. His response to Harry Arnim's aspirations left the diplomat destroyed and the diplomatic corps a pliant tool of the master back in Berlin. By the time of his departure, the country was left with no political figures of a stature that came close to his. After twenty-eight years in Bismarck's shadow, almost all political talents of an independent mind had wilted and died. Left behind was a pool of politicians, and a nation in general, grown accustomed to leaving the decision-making in the hands of a towering figure.

Upon their emergence from the shadow, most Germans were unprepared for the task of political leadership. This situation had its roots not only in Bismarck's desire to stand alone at the top, but also in the actual institutional system which he had established. Gerhard Weinberg has pointed to a critical, fundamental flaw in the Bismarckian system that distinguished it from almost every other state in Europe.[12] This was the fact that, despite the democratic suffrage, no degree of success at the polls would bring any party or individual any closer to exercising political power or responsibility. The figures who would come to lead Weimar, whether Ebert, Erzberger, or Stresemann, not only spent their early years out of power, but also spent them *without any expectation of ever attaining power*. They were used to a system in which, assured of the impossibility of ever having to put their program into practice, they could eschew responsible politics for the vocal promotion of extreme positions or intensely narrow interest politics. When the Empire collapsed, they found themselves suddenly in the position in which they had previously never had any reason to expect to be. The realization of their predicament left many wishing for the emergence of a new figure of Bismarckian stature to save them from the responsibility of running a modern nation-state.

In the First World War Bethmann Hollweg's relatively moderate position elicited a virulent response from those Germans imbued with a different conception of proper national leadership. Looking back to the Bismarck of the wars of unification, annexationists used a selective reading of history to posit a ruthless and determined chancellor of blood and iron who would not accept compromise with the enemy but would demand extravagant territorial compensation. As those on the right feared the possibility of democratic reform at home and the resulting threat to the war effort, not to mention their social and political positions, the Bismarck of the 1860s – the dictator – inspired calls for the strong man, calls which were ultimately answered with the Hindenburg–Ludendorff dictatorship of 1917. Such an image of Bismarck as the strong man who would sweep away a weak government persisted on in much stronger form in Weimar, as an intense crisis of leadership – at least in the minds of those on the right – plagued post-war Germany.

If, however, Bismarck himself destroyed or stunted the development of potential political talents who might have challenged him, thus leaving a political vacuum upon his dismissal, and if the image that developed of him was that of the ultimate genius to which few if any could hope to aspire, this does not mean that the crisis of leadership that followed was not at least in part a matter of perception. It is important to remember, however, that the perception of a crisis can often be just as significant as its reality. The fact that much of the Right felt there to have been a crisis of leadership meant that the political decisions they made were often shaped in some way by this perception. While they were correct at times, their view of the leadership situation cannot be said to have been true for the entire period.

If Germany did, in fact, produce political talents capable of effectively running the state, one must be careful about making any over-arching judgment regarding the crisis of leadership. Certainly no new Bismarck ever emerged, and, for many, the lack of a leader of Bismarckian stature and ability by definition left the country with a continual crisis of leadership. But that speaks more to the particular nature of the German Right's political culture than it does to the question of a true leadership crisis, for a properly functioning modern political system should be able to operate effectively without the continual presence of a single, overwhelmingly dominant figure. In the post-Bismarck Second Reich one might very well say that there was a genuine dearth of talented political leadership – or, perhaps better put, that there was a genuine dearth of political talent that would have been able to take up positions of leadership under the particular constitutional constraints then in force. After all, many of those same men who would indeed prove to be capable leaders in Weimar were already there in Wilhelmine Germany. Stresemann, Ebert, and Rathenau all began their careers before 1918. This problem would continue as the war clearly did not provide the necessary leadership – despite Bethmann Hollweg's efforts – for the illusions that the men at the top fostered, and the model for dictatorship that they implanted in the political culture proved to have had devastating results when the defeat and revolution finally came.

Weimar, however, should not be seen as the wasteland of political talent that many on the right would have liked us to believe it was. After all, Friedrich Ebert proved himself a dignified and capable leader who used the immense powers of the presidency with impressive moderation in order to ensure the survival of the republic. Gustav Stresemann, too, deserves credit as a more than worthy successor to the Iron Chancellor in the realm of foreign policy. They were certainly no Bismarcks, but outside the world-view of the Right such a figure should not necessarily stand as the sole measure of ability. If, in the end, these men could not save the republic, that should not take anything away from their talents as political leaders. Unfortunately they found themselves in a situation that would have taxed the most talented minds anywhere – a political system born of military defeat, a political culture attuned more towards authoritarianism and stamped with the massive imprint of a political icon like Bismarck, a bureaucracy imbued with that very same anti-democratic political culture left untouched by the changes of the revolution, and a pair of economic crises that would have felled many a government. That they survived one of those crises with democracy intact speaks well indeed of those very same leaders on whom the Right never failed to heap scorn. That the last crisis should have ended with the horribly unnecessary naming of Hitler to the chancellorship speaks more to the *lack* of political ability of the German *Right*, which, in following the logic of its Bismarckian conception of politics, squeezed out the voices of moderation and made a decision it hoped would save Germany but ultimately destroyed it.

The decisions of these radical nationalists were based on a world-view that had developed over decades and was shaped to a large degree by their image of Bismarck and the style and content of politics they associated with it. As we have seen, the Bismarck image grew to massive proportions even before he died. In his mythologized role as the 'old man in the Saxon Forest', his words and image gained the power to galvanize and legitimize a new-style populist politics of 'national opposition' along with the new men and organizations that espoused it and to keep the government leaders in a constant state of fear. Upon his death, the process turned into one of deification as Bismarck grew in stature beyond any other national hero. As the political religion of the Bismarck Cult developed, his life was recast into a new nationalist gospel in which he became the ultimate, all-powerful leader sent by God to lead the people from the wilderness of national division and fulfill the dream of German unification, who acted as protector of the nation and its position at the center of European power politics, and who was ultimately betrayed and cast off by a brash young Kaiser and abandoned by an uncaring populace. Just what kinds of lessons that gospel contained, however, would be determined through a process of contestation between two divergent groups of Bismarckians, each with their own particular reading of the Iron Chancellor's history, and each with their own competing visions of Germany's future.

When Bernhard von Bülow complained about the 'misunderstood Bismarck' in 1906, he was pointing to a fundamental feature of the Bismarck Cult. At no time did there exist a unified vision of the 'true' Iron Chancellor. Instead, a number of differing conceptions competed with each other for primacy. The Right's fractured nature translated into a multitude of images, each corresponding to the peculiarities of the group or individual in question. Overall, though, a general image does emerge from the cauldron of right-wing politics – an image imbued with the politics of extremism: anti-democracy, anti-liberalism, anti-Marxism, militarism, expansionism, and racism. In addition to the traditional enemies against which this radical Bismarck had to fight, namely Social Democrats, Catholics, and Democrats, there also existed another Bismarck which denied the legitimacy of the radical Right's icon. This figure was a man of moderation, a political realist who sought to attain only what could be attained within the confines of the existing power relationships. A passionate nationalist who shared a number of characteristics with his more radical incarnation, he nevertheless served as an important counter to that extreme Bismarck and, so long as he remained vital, held out the possibility of an alternative path for German politics.

In the Empire, the conflict took the form of two competing visions of the proper direction of German nationalist politics within the context of the existing Second Reich. The radical Bismarck began as a product of those newly emerging organizations of the national opposition, in particular the Pan-German League, the Agrarian League, the Hakatisten, and the Army League. Their Bismarck was forceful, advocating a politics of expansion, racial affinity, and opposition to democratic reform. When it criticized the leadership, it did so in the hopes of pushing it in the direction of more national, more 'German' policies. It squared off against a government that was, itself, pursuing a dynamic policy of expansion which, in many respects, differed more in degree than in substance from that of the national opposition. This relative congruity of interest made it difficult for the government to effectively combat the radical Bismarck with its more moderate incarnation. For Bülow, his own flair for the spectacular undermined the sincerity of his periodic pleas for restraint. A more genuine advocate of the moderate Bismarck, at least within the context of Wilhelmine political culture, was Bethmann Hollweg. Like Bülow, his vision of a future Germany differed more in degree than in substance from that of the radical Right. Nevertheless, he was able to combine within his own mind his conception of a moderate Bismarck with a moderate approach to the problem of German expansion. His reserved demeanor reflected this moderation, but like Bülow (only from the other extreme) Bethmann's public style would prevent him from effectively countering his radical opposition. As he discovered both before and during the war, moderate, reasoned argument fared poorly against dazzling visions of salvation through dynamic action and glorious triumphs that the Bismarckian political religion provided.

In the war the two Bismarcks faced off over the issues of annexations and democratic reform. The crisis situation of the war years led to a radicalization of the Right's Bismarck as it inspired the new incarnation of right-wing politics: the Fatherland Party. Four years of extraordinarily bloody fighting, however, led to a war-weariness that sapped even the power of the Iron Chancellor to motivate the nation, and in the end the Fatherland Party proved unable to assure victory and avert collapse. In the democratic Weimar Republic which then emerged, many Bismarckians would carry before them an even more extreme incarnation of their idol in what became an all-or-nothing struggle for control of the nation. The multiplicity of radical Bismarckians that emerged from the crisis of defeat and revolution found themselves faced with an imposing figure who claimed for himself the title of true disciple of Germany's first chancellor. For the remainder of his life, Gustav Stresemann would fight a long, difficult struggle to promote his moderate, reasonable Bismarck in the face of blistering attacks from his right. Both sides were well aware of the stakes involved, for, unlike in the Empire, where victory meant a faster or slower tempo of expansion, it now meant literally the survival or destruction of the new democratic system. Such an increase in the intensity of the struggle reflected the radicalization of politics in general as a result of the war and revolution. It also reflected an important change in the nature of the Bismarck image itself and therefore its significance for German political culture. Over the years since his death, and in particular thanks to the experiences of the years from 1914 to 1923, the Iron Chancellor was being transformed into a charismatic leader.

As one of Max Weber's three forms of legitimate authority, charisma recently has come to play an important role in understanding the rule of Hitler, first on the level of the Nazi Party itself, and then on the level of the nation.[13] Here we want to look at it in another sense – not that of a tangible, living figure, but rather in the sense of the impact that the *image* of a charismatic figure, a dead charismatic figure, can have on a country's politics. While the living Bismarck resembled a charismatic figure in some ways, he did not completely fit the definition, and any features he did have were gone by the time of his dismissal in 1890. His abandonment by both Kaiser and people illustrates the critical role of the following in the successful maintenance of power by the charismatic leader.[14] Not only his own sense of mission, but also the belief in his special abilities among the people must be present. When that goes, his mission ends "and hope expects and searches for a new bearer."[15] In the years after Bismarck's dismissal, however, that search for the new bearer turned out to be fruitless. The successors could never live up to the standard that had been set and as the people perceived their situation to be deteriorating, they proceeded to do something quite remarkable – they created their own charismatic leader. Over the years, they ascribed to Bismarck powers that he never possessed while exaggerating the level of those he did. It was thus in these years after his death that he much more closely approached that type of figure which Weber described as the bearer of "specific gifts of body and mind that were considered 'supernatural' (in the sense that not everybody could have access to them)."[16]

To borrow the symbolism of the Bismarckians themselves, then, the Iron Chancellor was, in a sense, reborn. Over the years he developed into a Messiah-like figure longed for by many in the Protestant-bourgeois camp – either in the form of some quasi-mystical resurrection or, more likely, in the emergence of a new leader imbued with the 'spirit of Bismarck' who would save Germany and restore it to its previous greatness. He therefore performed the role of a charismatic leader or, more accurately in this case, a kind of 'charismatic placeholder', inspiring his followers to pursue a particular brand of politics while keeping alive the memory of superior leadership and sowing the ground of German political culture for the ultimate arrival of the true savior. How did this 'charismatic placeholder' function in the years after Bismarck and what kinds of conclusions can we then draw from this phenomenon?

Under the Empire, the conditions for the acceptance of charismatic leadership did not prevail. There did exist a general uneasiness among many on the Right with the national leadership as well as with the process of modernization, but that did not result in any fundamental questioning of the system and corresponding desire for its overthrow. As a response to modernity, the Bismarck Cult can be seen as a renewed longing for myth in an age of spiritual decline as well as a more general desire to return to the 'good ol' days' of the Bismarckian era. Thus in this period the Iron Chancellor should probably best be seen as a guide or inspiration for nationalist politics and, as the years went by, for a politics with an increasingly *radical* nationalist flavor. This played a crucial role in legitimizing that new style of populist radical nationalism and thus enabled previously marginal figures to play new roles and challenge and influence the established power-holders and decision-makers. The desire for a 'return' of Bismarck as a response to the problems of German leadership at the time, though, primarily took the form of calls for a strong chancellor in the image of the Reich's founder – not a revolutionary figure to overthrow the system.

Such a revolutionary figure –a much truer fit for Weber's model of the charismatic leader – would have to await the cataclysm of world war, revolution, and civil war that confronted Germany after 1914. The immense shock of defeat and the revolution that followed, when the *Reichsfeinde* now stood in the main positions of power, helped produce among Bismarckians one of those "unusual, especially political or economic situations," and "extraordinary psychic . . . states . . ." that Weber saw as essential for the rise of charismatic leaders. Early on, the situation was such that no individual on the right could step in and claim the mantle. Thus Bismarck, continuing in his previous role as inspiration for a radical nationalist politics – now even more radical following the events of 1914–1923 – took on the added role of charismatic leader in lieu of a tangible, living option. In this role he, at least in part, fulfilled the wishes of those on the right for someone who embodied the fundamental principles of their politics and who, as such, stood as a powerful force in the fight against Weimar.

In the years that followed, many sought to claim the Bismarckian mantle for themselves and thus gain the symbolic power and legitimacy that the name bestowed, ideally, in the end, becoming the 'new Bismarck' and thereby transforming a latent charismatic situation into a manifest one. With the passage of time such connections became increasingly difficult to make. In the years immediately following the Iron Chancellor's dismissal and even his death, the possibilities for linkage were great. Personal connections conveyed a degree of legitimacy on people like Max Harden or the leaders of the Hakatisten that would be unavailable in later years. His own advocacy of a group, like his honorary membership of the Pan-German League, was something that the new Weimar-era groups could not claim. The time in which he lived and the particular socio-political conditions that prevailed also made certain connections much more viable than they would be after the upheavals of the war and revolution. Stressing one's status as Prussian Junker and loyal monarchist made the linkage with Bismarck self-evident, and in some cases a much stronger one than that of the middle-class upstarts in the Pan-German League. In Weimar the political benefits of such a position were questionable at best. Of course, efforts at linkage continued even as the span of time from Bismarck's death grew ever greater, and if they proved somewhat more difficult, a number of methods were regularly used.

One such method of linking oneself to Bismarck involved the establishment of a correspondence of situations. Choosing a particular period from his career, a

Bismarck-hopeful could demonstrate the inherent connections between himself and his hero by pointing to the remarkable similarities of their predicaments. The increasingly difficult situation during the latter years of the First World War led many nationalists to see in Tirpitz the man who could, like Bismarck in 1862, return to rescue the nation in its hour of need. And we have also seen how his departure not only reminded many of Bismarck's back in 1890, but how it had a similar effect in radicalizing a new generation of Bismarckians. In Weimar, Gustav Stresemann regularly portrayed himself in the Bismarckian situation of standing alone in the face of bitter opposition – his acceptance of the need to be unpopular as he 're-forged' a nation after the upheaval of 1918–1919 placed him squarely in the footsteps of his idol.

One could also establish a relationship through a similar political ideology or through the advocacy of particular policies that could be seen as those of the Iron Chancellor. Both Hugenberg and Seldte fashioned themselves after the founder of the Reich, posing as dedicated nationalists who would forcefully put forward the interests of Germany above all else while they also stood as fierce opponents of democracy, Liberalism and Marxism. This translated into unbending opposition to Weimar and an aggressive foreign policy that aimed to break the chains of Versailles and free Germany from international control just as Bismarck had freed Prussia. These two men were certainly not alone, but if most of the policies advanced in the name of the Iron Chancellor were of the radical nationalist variety, some, like Bethmann Hollweg and Stresemann, sought to add weight to theirs through a connection to the moderate Bismarck. For Stresemann, this applied generally to his entire approach to foreign policy, while he made sure to note the first chancellor as inspiration for specific policies, such as the Treaty of Berlin in 1926 between Germany and the Soviet Union.

Posing as the one who would complete the great man's work also served to link a contemporary figure to Bismarck. Among the first 'new Bismarcks', Hindenburg was depicted during the First World War as the one who would continue what the first chancellor had begun. The Pan-Germans, who played a substantial role in developing the concept of the 'spirit of Bismarck', certainly saw themselves as the successors of the great man, as the ones who clearly understood what it was that Bismarck had wanted and what he would have done. Therefore their policies were the truest interpretation of his spirit. Their Bismarck – that of Hugenberg and Class – the expansionist dictator, was the proper guide for the future. Carrying out their policies would complete the work that he had begun.

Another means of connection to Bismarck was through a similarity in style. With the onset of war and the need for iron hard leadership, Hindenburg emerged as a natural choice for 'new Bismarck'. Clearly, on a purely physical level, his sheer size and demeanor as well as the impression of forcefulness that he gave off had to evoke memories of the Iron Chancellor, while his Prussian Junker background only added to the effect. Such connections to Bismarck, both physical and stylistical, were not lost on the German people as the phenomenon of 'Iron Hindenburgs' would seem to indicate. If Hindenburg as president exhibited only the outer appearance of a new Bismarck, he nevertheless held a conception of how a Bismarckian politician should behave, as he once complained to Stresemann about a candidate for an important diplomatic post as not being a man who could "pound on the table."[17] The bold, aggressive style of Tirpitz in demanding unlimited submarine warfare was also seen to be acting in Bismarckian fashion during the First World War.

In the end, despite all their efforts, neither Tirpitz nor Seeckt, neither Hindenburg, Hugenberg nor Seldte – not one of them could claim the crown. In the changed times of post-war Germany, their image of Bismarck conformed to an older era. While certainly effective in mobilizing opinion against Weimar democracy, when it came to offering the ultimate solution, each of their Bismarcks continued to be outflanked by a new vision further to the right. Even in the 'years of stability' of the mid-1920s, the adherents of the bourgeois-liberal parties followed their idol further rightward, leaving behind the DDP and the DVP first for the splinter parties, but then to groups beyond that, including the DNVP and the Stahlhelm. In the end, it took the conjuncture of an extraordinary crisis in the form of the Great Depression and the emergence of a figure who could travel the path which the Cult of Bismarck had carved into German political culture and thus plausibly claim the Bismarckian mantle for himself.

Hitler's arrival following the dramatic breakthrough in the 1930 Reichstag elections opened the possibility that the Bismarckians' dreams might soon be fulfilled. That the Nazi leader did not initially conform to the popular conception of a new Bismarck is likely. However, he performed a masterful job of developing an image of Bismarck that portrayed the first chancellor as a remarkably pure type of charismatic leader. Hitler's Bismarck, after all, was a revolutionary figure who fought his whole career against unimaginable opposition and, through the sheer force of genius and will, succeeded in forging a nation and leading it to the heights of European and world power.

Utilizing all four methods of linkage discussed above, Hitler made a conscious effort to connect his image with that of the national icon. From the time of his trial in 1924 for the failed Beer Hall Putsch, he portrayed his situation as nearly identical to that of Bismarck during his struggle to unify the country back in the 1860s. In terms of ideology, Bismarck became the purest, most intense German nationalist. The Iron Chancellor's anti-democracy and anti-Marxism also figured prominently in Hitler's speeches. Throughout his quest for power, the Nazi leader positioned himself as a loyal disciple of Bismarck. He noted the old man's shortcomings but forgave them since they were a result of the particular times in which he lived – though he wanted to do more, it was simply not possible at the time.

Hitler, however, was working under different conditions, and, since the two men shared the same ideas, he would now complete the work of Germany's greatest statesman. Indeed, this continued as a theme after the establishment of the Third Reich as Hitler returned the country to a position of power in Europe and completed the project of German unification through the Anschluss with Austria. In terms of political style, Hitler portrayed Bismarck as an unconventional outsider – a lone figure, confident in the justice of his cause – who changed the course of history. His own self-image was remarkably similar as he fought against the notion that it was a popular movement that had made Germany rather than the incomparable brilliance and will of a single man. If Bismarck was that man in the 1860s, Hitler was the new man of the 1930s. In numerous speeches, then, the Nazi leader placed himself in this Bismarckian mold, tying the story of his own development and rise to prominence to that of the Iron Chancellor. The connections between the two stories are unmistakable and must have had some degree of resonance among Bismarckians. In tapping into the mythology of these segments of the population, he was easing the transition from bourgeois-liberal and conservative nationalism to the extreme radical nationalism of the Nazis and thereby accelerated the process of disintegration which the traditional parties of the Right had been experiencing since the middle of the decade.

Here we can see the role Bismarck played as charismatic placeholder and some of its most important effects. As the leader of the national opposition in Weimar he espoused a politics of extreme anti-democracy, anti-Marxism, anti-Liberalism, racism, and expansionism. In the name of such a brand of politics his followers fought tenaciously for the destruction of the democratic system, and with the authority of Bismarck they succeeded in battering a regime that was already less than sure of itself, until it could no longer resist the next crisis situation. The Iron Chancellor's role in the destruction of the Weimar Republic should by now be clear. His role in helping determine what would replace it should also be apparent.

The Bismarck image, as that of the ultimate leader, one who would lead Germany out of darkness and despair into the bright future of the *Volksgemeinschaft*, had been present since the turn of the century. Thanks to the growing political religion of the Bismarck Cult, this image worked its way for decades into the very fabric of German political culture until it became an integral part of radical nationalist discourse to be sure, but would also find acceptance among the less extreme groups in the country. The search for this new leader, this new Bismarck, led Germans on a journey that ended ultimately with Hitler. Was this inevitable? Certainly not. Gustav Stresemann demonstrated the potential of a different kind of Bismarck – a more positive Bismarck that symbolized a politics of moderation and was used in an effort at reconciliation, not confrontation. Unfortunately, the possibilities of this image were lost on too many Germans during the life of its greatest advocate. Only after the path down which the blood-

and-iron Bismarck had led them turned out to be a nightmare did some – and still only some – come to see the value in Stresemann's model. Even other radical Bismarcks were possible. Certainly democracy was out of the question for all of them, but the character of these authoritarian Germanies might very well have been different from that of the Third Reich. After all, many of the Bismarckians discussed here did not share Hitler's psychotic level of anti-Semitism. Although a war was likely under the leadership of most of them, even a Seldte or a Hugenberg, and certainly a Tirpitz, would not have led Germany into the genocidal struggle in which it ultimately found itself. In the end, Hitler was not a natural match – then again, nobody else was either. But the logic of decades of Bismarckian rhetoric, made more radical and more flexible under the changed conditions of war and revolution, made a Hitler dictatorship a serious possibility. The acceptance of Hitler by the followers of Bismarck and the ease with which the Iron Chancellor could be fitted into Nazi propaganda in the early years of the Third Reich would seem to bear this out.

In Bertolt Brecht's play *Life of Galileo* the main character corrects a young girl who asserts: "Fortunate is the land that has heroes." "No," replies Galileo: "Unfortunate is the land that has need of heroes."[18] This study has examined the case of one country's fascination with one of its most dominant political figures and the results of that fascination. Over the last third of the nineteenth century and the first half of the twentieth, the German Right elevated the man who helped found the nation to the level of a political god. He became for this group the symbol of ideal leadership, though this symbol had different meanings even amongst his most devoted followers. On the one hand, he symbolized moderation and a realization of the limitations on the exercise of power. To others he embodied boldness, power, genius and will in a menacing form that recognized few if any limitations on the exercise of that strength. These symbols fought continuous battles in the German public sphere for the right to define the nation's character and guide its destiny according to the vision they embodied. The battles were hard fought, with final victory uncertain until that fateful night of January 30, 1933. The longing for a hero, of which Brecht's Galileo warned so poignantly, and which had become such an important feature of German political culture, was fulfilled in a way which few could have imagined back in August 1898 as Germany's first chancellor was laid to rest. In life, but much more so in death, Otto von Bismarck cast a shadow over Germany that prevented too many from seeing the solution to their crisis of leadership in themselves, and not in the search for some redeeming savior.

Notes

1. Bertolt Brecht, *Leben des Galilei*, H. F. Brookes and C. E. Fraenkel, eds. second edition (London: Heinemann Educational Books, 1981), 118.

2. Adenauer quoted in Gordon Craig, *From Bismarck to Adenauer: Aspects of German Statecraft* (Baltimore: The Johns Hopkins Press, 1958), 137.

3. Hugo Wellems, *Bismarck und unsere Zeit. 17. Juni 1982 in Friedrichsruh* (Hamburg: Staats- und Wirtschaftspolitische Gesellschaft e.V., 1982), 14.

4. Kershaw, *'Hitler Myth'*, 265–266. For German nationalism after the Second World War, see Kurt P. Tauber, *Beyond Eagle and Swastika: German Nationalism since 1945*, 2 vols. (Connecticut: Wesleyan University Press, 1967).

5. For Wulle's post-1945 activity, see Tauber, *Beyond Eagle and Swastika*, 47–56.

6. Reinhold Wulle, *Bismarck als Staatsmann* (Gronau/Westfalen: Selbstverlag Reinhold Wulle, 1950), 5. From the collection of the Otto-von-Bismarck Stiftung.

7. Ibid., 28–31.

8. Still, in 1950, 32 per cent of West Germans polled considered him Germany's greatest statesman. Kershaw, *'Hitler Myth'*, 265.

9. Dennis L. Bark and David R. Gress, *A History of West Germany, Vol. 1, From Shadow to Substance*, second edition (Oxford: Blackwell, 1993), 252.

10. Michael Swierczek, quoted in Andreas Spielt, "Einer von uns. Bismarckbund und Freie Nationalisten huldigten Otto von Bismarck unter fürstlicher und staatlicher Protektion," http://www.nadir.org/nadir/periodika/jungle_world/_98/34/12b.htm, August 18, 1998.

11. Craig, *From Bismarck to Adenauer*, 45–53.

12. Gerhard L. Weinberg, "Reflections on Two Unifications," *German Studies Review* XXI (February 1998): 20–21.

13. Mario Rainer Lepsius, "Charismatic Leadership: Max Weber's Model and Its Applicability to the Rule of Hitler," in Carl F. Graumann and Serge Moscovici, eds., *Changing Conceptions of Leadership* (New York: Springer-Verlag, 1986), 56–57; Luciano Cavalli, "Charismatic Domination, Totalitarian Dictatorship, and Plebiscitary Democracy in the Twentieth Century," in ibid., 67–81; Ian Kershaw, " 'Working towards the Führer.' Reflections on the Nature of the Hitler Dictatorship," *Contemporary European History*, 2(2) (1993): 103–118.

14. Douglas Madsen and Peter G. Snow, *The Charismatic Bond: Political Behavior in Time of Crisis* (Cambridge, Mass: Harvard University Press, 1991), 1–9.

15. Weber, *Economy and Society*, 1114.

16. Ibid., 1112.

17. Turner, *Stresemann*, 201.

18. Brecht, *Leben des Galilei*, 118.

Bibliography

Primary Sources

Archival Sources

Bundesarchiv Koblenz
Nachlässe:
NL 1024, Otto von Bismarck
NL 1231, Alfred Hugenberg
Zeitgeschichtliche Sammlung:
ZSg 1 2/3 (15), Alldeutsche Verband, Flugblätter
ZSg 1 13/6, Bund neues Vaterland, Flugblätter
ZSg 1 252/5, Unabhängiger Ausschuß für einen deutschen Frieden, Satzungen, Veröffentlichungen, Mitteilungen und Flugblätter
ZSg 1 42/7, Deutsche Volkspartei, Flugblätter 1919–1933
ZSg 1 42/8, Deutsche Volkspartei, Flugblätter 1928–1933
ZSg 1 44/9, Deutschnationale Volkspartei, Flugblätter 1932–33
ZSg 1 44/9, Deutschnationale Volkspartei, Flugblätter 1928–1930
ZSg 1 45/18, Deutschvölkische Partei, Veröffentlichungen 1921–1924
ZSg 1 17/570, Hauptarchiv der NSDAP, Bismarck

Bundesarchiv Lichterfelde
R 8034, Reichslandbund Pressearchiv:

R 8034 II, Nr. 1550 – 1553, Politische Karikaturen.
R 8034 II, Nr. 5119, Konservative Reichstagswahlen, 1928–1930.
R 8034 II, Nr. 5132 – 5133, Reichstagswahlen und einzelne Parteien und Organisationen, DVP.
R 8034 II, Nr. 6148, Konservative.
R 8034 II, Nr. 6172 – 6173, Parteileben der Nationalliberalen Partei.
R 8034 II, Nr. 6175, Nationalliberale Partei.
R 8034 II, Nr. 6180, Deutschvölkische Freiheitspartei.
R 8034 II, Nr. 7085 – 7102, Bismarck.

R 8034 II, Nr. 7886, Vaterländische Gedanke.

R 8034 II, Nr. 8541, Deutsches Kaiserhaus.

R 8034 II, Nr. 8743, DNVP.

R 8034 II, Nr. 8752, Nationalliberale Partei. Haltung im I. Weltkrieg. Stellung zur November-Revolution und Friedensfrage, 1917–1918.

R 8034 II, Nr. 8868, Deutsche Vaterlandspartei.

R 8034 II, Nr. 8871 – 8873, Rechtsradikal, militärische, monarchistische Parteien und Verbände.

R 8034 II, Nr. 9107, Parteileben der Deutschen Volkspartei.

R 8034 II, Nr. 9160, Reichspräsidentenwahl.

R 8034 III, Personalia, Nr. 371, Reventlow.

R 8034 III, Personalia, Nr. 449, Spahn.

R 8034 III, Personalia, Nr. 450, Stolberg-Wernigerode.

R 8034 III, Personalia, Nr. 471, Tirpitz.

R 8034 III, Personalia, Nr. 477, Weber.

NS 5 VI, Deutsche Arbeitsfront, Zeitungsausschnittsammlung:

NS 5 VI, Nr. 478: Reichspräsident und Reichskanzler, Wahlaufrufe, Flugblätter- und schriften, Plakate, Karikaturen.

NS 5 VI, A 1023 DNVP, Nr. 695: Flugblätter und Flugschriften.

R 43I: Akten des Reichskanzlei:

R43I/2825 – 2828: Akten betreffend Personalsachen des Reichskanzlers Fürsten von Bismarck.

R 72/407, #225–226 and #397–398: *Stahlhelm*.

60 Vo 1 – Deutsche Volkspartei Archiv:

Film #53170, Akten #234, Nationalliberale Correspondenz.

Film #53172, Akten #237, Nationalliberale Correspondenz.

Film #53173, Akten #241, Archiv der Deutschen Volkspartei.

Geheimes Staatsarchiv Preussischer Kulturbesitz
GStA PK, I. HA Rep. 77, Ministerium des Innern, Tit. 4043 Nr. 411 Bd. 1 Bl. 143–144 (M); Bismarckjugend der DNVP.

Otto-von-Bismarck Stiftung
Collections of published materials: newspaper and magazine articles; political cartoons; visual images, etc.

Landesarchiv Berlin
Rep 240: Zeitgeschichtliche Sammlung.

Newspapers and Contemporary Journals

Alldeutsche Blätter
Der Angriff
Berliner Tageblatt
Bismarck-Blatt. Zeitschrift des Vereins zur Errichtung eines Bismarck-National-Denkmals, E.V.
Bismarck-Bund. Monatschrift herausgegeben vom Deutschen Bismarck-Bunde
Deutsche Allgemeine Zeitung
Deutsche Stimmen
Deutsche Tageszeitung
Deutsche Zeitung
Deutschlands Erneuerung
Frankfurter Zeitung
Der Führer
Germania
Hamburger Nachrichten
Kölnische Zeitung
Münchener Neueste Nachrichten
Nachrichtenblatt für das von Bismarck'sche Geschlecht
Neue Preußische (Kreuz-) Zeitung
Der Stahlhelm
Der Stürmer
Der Tag
Die Tradition
Völkischer Beobachter
Vorwärts

Contemporary Published Materials

Alldeutscher Verband. *Zwanzig Jahre alldeutscher Arbeit und Kämpfe.* Leipzig: Dieterich'sche Verlagsbuchhandlung, 1910.

Baeumler, Alfred. "Das Reich als Tat." Chap. in *Politik und Erziehung. Reden und Aufsätze.* Berlin: Junker und Dünnhaupt Verlag, 1937.

Bernhard, Henry, ed. *Gustav Stresemann. Vermächtnis. Der Nachlass in drei Bänden.* Berlin: Ullstein Verlag, 1932.

Biefang, Andreas, ed. *Der Deutsche Nationalverein 1859–1867. Vorstands- und Ausschußprotokolle.* Düsseldorf: Droste Verlag, 1995.

Bismarck, Otto von. *The Kaiser vs. Bismarck.* Translated by Bernard Miall. New York: Harper & Brothers Publishers, 1921.

Class, Heinrich. *Wider den Strom. Vom Erben und Wachsen der nationalen Opposition im alten Reich.* Leipzig: Verlag von K. F. Koehler, 1932.

Domarus, Max, ed. *Hitler: Speeches and Proclamations, 1932–1945. The Chronicle of a Dictatorship, I and II.* Illinois: Bolchazy-Carducci Publishers, 1990–92.

Eulenburg, Philipp. *Philipp Eulenburgs politische Korrespondenz, Band I, Von der Reichsgründung bis zum Neuen Kurs 1866–1891,* ed. John C. G. Röhl. Boppard am Rhein: Haraldt Boldt Verlag, 1976.

Frymann, Daniel [Heinrich Class]. *Wenn ich der Kaiser wär' – Politische Wahrheiten und Notwendigkeiten.* Leipzig: Dieterich'sche Verlagsbuchhandlung, 1912.

Haller, Johannes. "Zum 1. April 1933." Chap. in *Reden und Aufsätze zur Geschichte und Politik.* Stuttgart: J.G. Cotta'sche Buchhandlung Nachfolger, 1934.

Harden, Maximilian. *Maximilian Harden. Kaiser-Panorama; literarische und politische Publizistik,* ed. Ruth Greuner. Berlin: Buchverlag der Morgen, 1983.

Hassel, Ulrich von. *Die Hassel-Tagebücher, 1938–1944. Aufzeichnungen vom Andern Deutschland.* Berlin: Wolf Jobst Siedler Verlag, 1988.

Holstein, Friedrich von. *The Holstein Papers. Vol. 3, Correspondence 1861–1896,* eds. Norman Rich and M. H. Fischer. Cambridge: Cambridge University Press, 1961.

Hugenberg, Alfred. *Streiflichter aus Vergangenheit und Gegenwart.* second edition. Berlin: August Scherl G.m.b.H., 1927.

Institut für Zeitgeschichte, eds. *Hitler: Reden, Schriften, Anordnungen. Februar 1925 bis Januar 1933.* Munich: K. G. Saur, 1992–1998.

Jäckel, Eberhard, ed. *Hitler. Sämtliche Aufzeichnungen 1905–1924.* Stuttgart: Deutsche Verlags-Anstalt, 1980.

Jäckh, Ernst, ed. *Kiderlen-Wächter. Der Staatsmann und Mensch, Briefwechsel und Nachlaß.* Stuttgart: Deutsche Verlags-Anstadt, 1924.

Lange, Friedrich. *Reines Deutschtum: Grundzüge einer nationalen Weltanschauung.* fifth edition. Berlin: Verlag von Alexander Duncker, 1904.

Lepsius, Johannes, and Albrecht Mendelsson Bartholdy, Friedrich Thimme, eds. *Die Große Politik der Europäischen Kabinette.* Vol. XXIX. Berlin: Deutsche Verlagsgesellschaft für Politik und Geschichte, 1922–1927.

Mann, Heinrich. *Man of Straw* [*Der Untertan*]. New York: Penguin, 1984.

Michaelis, Dr. Herbert and Dr. Ernst Schraepler, eds. *Ursachen und Folgen. Vom deutschen Zusammenbruch 1918 und 1945 bis zur staatlichen Neuordnung Deutschlands in der Gegenwart.* Vol. 4, *Die Weimarer Republik, Vertragserfüllung und innere Bedrohung 1919/1922.* Berlin: Dokumenten-Verlag Dr. Herbert Wendler & Co., 1960.

——— *Ursachen und Folgen.* Vol. 5, *Die Weimarer Republik, das kritische Jahr*

1923. Berlin: Dokumenten-Verlag Dr. Herbert Wendler & Co., 1960.

Spitzemberg, Baroness. *Das Tagebuch der Baronin Spitzemberg*, ed. Rudolf Vierhaus. Göttingen: Vandenhoeck & Ruprecht, 1960.

Stenographische Berichte über die Verhandlungen des Deutschen Reichstages.

Stresemann, Gustav. *Nationale Realpolitik. Flugschriften der Deutschen Volkspartei.* Vol. 56. Berlin: Staatspolitischer Verlag, 1924.

Westarp, Kuno. *Konservative Politik im Übergang vom Kaiserreich zur Weimarer Republik*, ed. Friedrich Freiherr Hiller von Gaertringen with Karl J. Mayer and Reinhold Weber. Düsseldorf: Droste Verlag, 2001.

Contemporary Bismarck Articles, Pamphlets and Special Publications

Aßmann, Julius. *Bismarck – der Erfüller deutscher Sehnsucht und der Wegweiser deutscher Zukunft. Festrede bei d. Feier d. 100. Geburtstages Bismarcks zu Bromberg.* Bromberg: Jahne, 1915.

Beinert, Rudolf. *Von Bismarck zu Hitler. Neun Bismarckreden.* Berlin: Brunnen-Verlag, 1934.

Berliner Bismarck-Ausschuß. *Bismarck-Kommers in der Philharmonie zu Berlin am 31. März 1928.* Berlin: Verlag vom Berliner Bismarck-Ausschuß, 1928.

Birt, Theodor. *Gedenkwort beim Tode des Fürsten Bismarck am 2. August 1898 in der Aula der Marburger Universität.* Marburg: N. G. Elwert'sche Verlagsbuchhandlung, 1898.

Bismarck-Verein. *Mittheilungen des "Bismarck-Vereins" Verein für nationale Politik.* Marburg: N. G. Elwert'sche Verlagsbuchhandlung, 1885.

Buchholz, Gustav. *Bismarck und wir. Betrachtungen an seinem 99. Geburtstage.* Leipzig: Dieterich'sche Verlagsbuchhandlung, 1914.

Bülow, Professor Dr. Georg. *Unser Bismarck. Festrede, gehalten bei der von der Stadt Schweidnitz veranstalteten öffentlichen Bismarckjahrhundertfeier am 1. April 1915.* Schweidnitz: Reisse, 1915.

Evers, M. *Rede auf den Fürsten Bismarck. Gehalten bei der vaterländischen Feier zu Ehren des 70. Geburtstages des Fürsten Reichskanzlers zu Düsseldorf am 31. März 1885.* Düsseldorf: L. Voß & Co., 1885.

Gierke, Otto von. "Krieg und Kultur." In *Deutsche Reden in schwerer Zeit.* Berlin: Carl Heymanns Verlag, 1914.

Göppert, Heinrich. *Bismarck und die deutsche Demokratie. Zum 1. April 1924.* Bonn: Kommissionsverlag von Albert Falkenroth, 1924.

Human, Dr. A. *Gedächtnisrede auf Seine Durchlaucht Fürst Otto von Bismarck. Bei der Trauerfeier am Sonnabend, 6. August 1898, abends 8 Uhr im Kaisersaale von Hildburghausen.* Hildburghausen: F. W. Gadow & Sohn, 1898.

Hunziger, Professor Dr. *Bismarcks Werk und Geist. Gedächtnisrede.* Hamburg: Herold'sche Buchhandlung, 1915.

Kaemmel, Prof. Dr. Otto. *Festrede zur Feier des siebzigjährigen Geburtstages*

Fürst Bismarcks gehalten im Saale des Gewerbehauses zu Dresden am 31. März 1885. Dresden: Carl Höckner, 1885.

Kahl, Wilhelm. *Bismarck lebt. Gedächtnisrede bei der allgemeinen Trauerfeier in Berlin am 7. August 1898*. Freiburg i. B.: Verlag von J. C. B. Mohr, 1898.

Kantorowicz, Hermann. *Bismarcks Schatten*. Freiburg, i. B.: J. Bielefeld, 1921.

Kohl, Horst, ed. *Bismarck-Gedichte des Kladderadatsch*. Berlin: U. Hofmann & Comp., 1894.

—— *Bismarck-Jahrbuch*, 6 vols. Berlin: D. Häring Verlag, 1894.

Lehnard, Paul R. *Festrede zum 80. Geburtstage Sr. Durchlaucht des Fürsten Bismarck*. Mülhausen: G. Danner Verlag, 1895.

Liebert, Eduard von. *Fürst Bismarck und die Armee. Vortrag beim Bismarck-kommers in der Philharmonie am 30. März 1912*. Berlin: Ernst Siegfried Mittler und Sohn, 1912.

Litzmann, Berthold. *Bismarck und wir. Rede bei der Bismarckfeier des liberalen Bürgervereins in Bonn am 31. März 1915*. Bonn: Friedrich Cohen, 1915.

Marcks, Erich. *Vom Erbe Bismarcks. Eine Kriegsrede*. Leipzig: Quelle & Meyer Verlag, 1916.

—— "Gedächtnisrede zu Bismarcks 100. Geburtstag." Chap. in *Männer und Zeiten. Aufsätze und Reden zur neueren Geschichte*. Vol. 2. Leipzig: Quelle & Meyer Verlag, 1922.

—— "Gedenkworte, gesprochen bei der Trauerfeier des Vereins deutscher Studenten zu Leipzig am 2. August 1898." Chap. in *Männer und Zeiten. Aufsätze und Reden zur neueren Geschichte*. Vol. 2. Leipzig: Quelle & Meyer Verlag, 1922.

Martin, Julius. *Die Wahrheit über den Fürsten Bismarck. Vortrag gehalten in der Versammlung der Hessischen Rechtspartei zu Kassel am 28. März 1895*. Second edition. Melsungen: W. Hopf Verlag, 1899.

Meyer, Dr. A. L. *Fürst Bismarck und seine Verdienste um Wiederaufrichtung des deutschen Reiches. Rede, gehalten am 22. März 1881 im Prüfungssaale der höheren Bürgerschule zu Freiburg i. Schl.*. Freiburg i. Schl.: G. Rieck'schen Buchdruckerei, 1881.

Müller, Karl Alexander von. "Bismarcks Sturz." In Karl Alexander von Müller, *Deutsche Geschichte und deutsche Charakter. Aufsätze und Vorträge*. Stuttgart: Deutsche Verlags-Anstalt, 1926.

Neue Bonner Zeitung. *Die Bismarckfeier in Bonn 1895*. Bonn: Emil Strauß Verlag, 1895.

Reinhold, Dr. Karl Theodor. *Fürst Bismarck als Reformator des deutschen Geistes. Eine Festrede*. 2nd Edition. Barmen: D. B. Wiemann Verlag, 1887.

Roethe, Gustav. *Zu Bismarcks Gedächtnis. Rede gehalten bei der Bismarckfeier des Vereins für das Deutschtum im Ausland am 30. März 1915*. Berlin: Weimannsche Buchhandlung, 1915.

Schiemann, Prof. Theodor. *Fürst Bismarck. Festrede zu seinem achtzigsten Geburtstage. Gesprochen auf dem Commers des Bismarckausschusses zu Berlin.* Berlin: Wilhelm Hertz Verlag, 1895.

Stolberg-Wernigerode, Albrecht Graf zu. *Zurück zu Bismarck.* Berlin: Staatspolitischer Verlag, 1926.

Stresemann, Gustav. *Bismarck und wir. Rede . . . zum 25. Bismarck-Kommers des Berliner Bismarck-Ausschusses, 1. April 1916.* Berlin: Reichsverlag, 1916.

Vorberg, Max. *Zum Gedächtnis des Fürsten Bismarck. Trauerrede.* Berlin: Evangelische Buchdruckerei, 1898.

Wellems, Hugo. *Bismarck und unsere Zeit. 17. Juni 1982 in Friedrichsruh.* Hamburg: Staats- und Wirtschaftspolitische Gesellschaft e.V., 1982.

Wulle, Reinhold. *Bismarck als Staatsmann.* Gronau/Westfalen: Selbstverlag Reinhold Wulle, 1950.

Secondary Works

Albertin, Lothar. "Die Auflösung der bürgerlichen Mitte und die Krise des Parlamentarischen Systems von Weimar." In *Demokratie in der Krise. Parteien im Verfassungssystem der Weimarer Republik*, eds. Eberhard Kolb and Walter Mülhausen. Munich: R. Oldenbourg Verlag, 1997.

Almond, Gabriel and Sydney Verba, *The Civic Culture: Political Attitudes and Democracy in Five Nations.* Princeton: Princeton University Press, 1963.

Anderson, Benedict. *Imagined Communities: Reflections on the Origin and Spread of Nationalism.* London: Verso, 1991.

Andrews, Herbert. "Hitler, Bismarck, and History," *German Studies Review* 14 (3) (1991): 516–517.

Aschheim, Steven. *The Nietzsche Legacy in Germany 1890–1990.* Princeton: Princeton University Press, 1992.

Baehr, Peter. "Max Weber as a Critic of Bismarck." *European Journal of Sociology* 29 (1988): 149–164.

Baeumer, Max. "Imperial Germany as Reflected in Its Mass Festivals." In *Imperial Germany*, eds. Volker Dürr, Kathy Harms, Peter Hayes. Madison: University of Wisconsin Press, 1985.

Bark, Dennis L. and David R. Gress. *A History of West Germany, Vol. 1, From Shadow to Substance.* Second edition. Oxford: Blackwell, 1993.

Bayerisches Hauptstaatsarchiv. *Plakate als Spiegel der politischen Parteien in der Weimarer Republik. Eine Ausstellung des Bayerischen Hauptstaatsarchives.* Munich: Verlagsdruckerei Schmidt, GmbH, 1996.

Bellah, Robert N. and Phillip E. Hammond. *Varieties of Civil Religion.* San Francisco: Harper & Row Publishers, 1980.

Berg, Manfred. *Gustav Stresemann. Eine politische Karriere zwischen Reich und*

Republik. Göttingen: Muster-Schmidt Verlag, 1992.

Berg-Schlosser, Dirk and Ralf Rytlewski. "Political Culture in Germany: a Paradigmatic Case." In *Political Culture in Germany*, eds. Dirk Berg-Schlosser and Ralf Rytlewski. New York: St. Martin's Press, 1993.

Berghahn, Volker R. *Der Stahlhelm. Bund der Frontsoldaten 1918–1935.* Düsseldorf: Droste Verlag, 1966.

—— *Germany and the Approach of War in 1914*. New York: St. Martin's Press, 1973.

—— *Imperial Germany, 1871–1914. Economy, Society, Culture, and Politics.* Providence: Berghahn Books, 1994.

Born, Karl Erich, ed. *Bismarck-Bibliographie. Quellen und Literatur zur Geschichte Bismarcks und seiner Zeit.* Cologne: Grote, 1966.

Breitenborn, Konrad. *Bismarck. Kult und Kitsch um den Reichsgründer.* Leipzig: Reprintverlag im Zentralantiquariat der DDR.

Brenner, Arthur D. *Emil J. Gumbel: Weimar German Pacifist and Professor.* Boston: Humanities Press, 2001.

Cavalli, Luciano. "Charismatic Domination, Totalitarian Dictatorship, and Plebiscitary Democracy in the Twentieth Century." In *Changing Conceptions of Leadership*, eds. Carl F. Graumann and Serge Moscovici. New York: Springer-Verlag, 1986.

Cecil, Lamar. *Wilhelm II: Prince and Emperor, 1859–1900.* Chapel Hill: UNC Press, 1989.

Chickering, Roger. *We Men Who Feel Most German: A Cultural Study of the Pan-German League, 1886–1914.* Boston: George Allen & Unwin, 1984.

Childers, Thomas. *The Nazi Voter: The Social Foundations of Fascism in Germany, 1919–1933.* Chapel Hill: The University of North Carolina Press, 1983.

—— "Languages of Liberalism: Liberal Political Discourse in the Weimar Republic." In *In Search of a Liberal Germany: Studies in the History of German Liberalism from 1789 to the Present*, eds. Konrad H. Jarausch and Larry Eugene Jones. New York: Berg Publishers, 1990.

Clark, Christopher. *Kaiser Wilhelm II.* London: Longman, 2000.

Cole, Terence F. "The *Daily Telegraph* Affair and Its Aftermath: the Kaiser, Bülow and the Reichstag, 1908–1909." In *Kaiser Wilhelm II: New Interpretations*, eds. John C. G. Röhl and Nicolaus Sombart. Cambridge: Cambridge University Press, 1982.

Craig, Gordon. *The Politics of the Prussian Army, 1640–1945.* Oxford: The Clarendon Press, 1955.

—— *From Bismarck to Adenauer: Aspects of German Statecraft.* Baltimore: The Johns Hopkins Press, 1958.

Deutsches Historisches Museum. *Bismarck – Preussen, Deutschland und Europa.* Berlin: Nicolaische Verlagsbuchhandlung, 1990.

Diehl, James M. *Paramilitary Politics in Weimar Germany*. Bloomington: Indiana University Press, 1977.

Doerry, Martin. *Übergangsmenschen. Die Mentalität der Wilhelminer und die Krise des Kaiserreichs*. Munich: Juventa Verlag, 1986.

Dorpalen, Andreas. *Hindenburg and the Weimar Republic*. Princeton: Princeton University Press, 1964.

—— *German History in Marxist Perspective: The East German Approach*. Detroit: Wayne State University Press, 1985.

Düding, Dieter, and Peter Friedemann and Paul Münch, eds., *Öffentliche Festkultur: Politische Feste in Deutschland von der Aufklärung bis zum Ersten Weltkrieg*. Hamburg: Rowohlt, 1988.

Durkheim, Emile. *The Elementary Forms of Religious Life*. Translated by Karen Fields. New York: The Free Press, 1995.

Eley, Geoff. *Reshaping the German Right: Radical Nationalism and Political Change after Bismarck*. Ann Arbor: University of Michigan Press, 1980.

—— *From Unification to Nazism: Reinterpreting the German Past*. Boston: Allen & Unwin, 1980.

—— "Conservatives and Radical Nationalists in Germany: the Production of Fascist Potentials, 1912–28." In *Fascists and Conservatives: The Radical Right and the Establishment in Twentieth-century Europe*, ed. Martin Blinkhorn. London: Unwin Hyman, 1990.

—— "Anti-Semitism, Agrarian Mobilization, and the Conservative Party: Radicalism and Containment in the Founding of the Agrarian League, 1890–1893." In *Between Reform, Reaction, and Resistance: Studies in the History of German Conservatism from 1789 to 1945*, eds. Larry Eugene Jones and James Retallack, 187–228. Providence: Berg, 1993.

Elias, Norbert. "On the State Monopoly of Physical Violence and Its Transgression." Chap. in *The Germans: Power Struggles and the Development of Habitus in the Nineteenth and Twentieth Centuries*. New York: Columbia University Press, 1996.

Engelberg, Ernst. *Bismarck. Das Reich in der Mitte Europas*. Berlin: Siedler Verlag, 1990.

Erger, Johannes. *Der Kapp-Lüttwitz-Putsch. Ein Beitrag zur deutschen Innenpolitik 1919/20*. Düsseldorf: Droste Verlag, 1967.

Eyck, Erich. *Bismarck after Fifty Years*. London: George Philip and Son, Ltd., 1948.

—— *Bismarck and the German Empire*. New York: W. W. Norton & Co., 1950.

Falter, Jürgen W. "The Two Hindenburg Elections of 1925 and 1932: a Total Reversal of Voter Coalitions." *Central European History* 23 (June/September 1990): 225–241.

Fehrenbach, Elisabeth. "Images of Kaiserdom: German Attitudes to Kaiser Wilhelm

II." In *Kaiser Wilhelm II: New Interpretations, the Corfu Papers*, eds. John C. G. Röhl and Nicolaus Sombart. Cambridge: Cambridge University Press, 1982.

Fischer, Fritz. *War of Illusions: German Policies from 1911 to 1914*. Translated by Marian Jackson. New York: W. W. Norton & Company, 1975.

Frankel, Richard E. "Bismarck's Shadow: The Iron Chancellor and the Crisis of German Leadership, 1898–1945." Ph.D. diss., University of North Carolina at Chapel Hill, 1999.

—— "From the Beer Halls to the Halls of Power: the Cult of Bismarck and the Legitimization of a New German Right, 1898–1945." *German Studies Review* 26 (October 2003): 543–560.

Freisel, Ludwig. "Das Bismarckbild der Alldeutschen: Bismarck im Bewußtsein und in der Politik des Alldeutschen Verbandes von 1890 bis 1933; ein Beitrag zum Bismarckverständnis des deutschen Nationalismus." Ph.D. diss., University of Würzburg, 1964.

Fricke, Dieter. "Bund Neues Vaterland." In *Lexicon zur Parteiengeschichte: Die bürgerlichen und kleinbürgerlichen Parteien und Verbände in Deutschland (1789–1945)*. Vol. I, ed. Dieter Fricke, 351–360. Cologne: Pahl-Rugenstein Verlag, 1983.

—— "Deutschbund." In *Lexicon zur Parteiengeschichte: Die bürgerlichen und kleinbürgerlichen Parteien und Verbände in Deutschland (1789–1945)*. Vol. I, ed. Dieter Fricke, 517–525. Cologne: Pahl-Rugenstein Verlag, 1983.

—— "Der 'Deutschbund'." In *Handbuch zur "Völkischen Bewegung" 1871–1918*, eds. Uwe Puschner, Walter Schmitz and Justus H. Ulbricht, 328–340. Munich: K. G. Saur, 1996.

Fricke, Dieter and Edgar Hartwig. "Bund der Landwirte (BdL) 1893–1920." In *Lexicon zur Parteiengeschichte: Die bürgerlichen und kleinbürgerlichen Parteien und Verbände in Deutschland (1789–1945)*. Vol. I, ed. Dieter Fricke, 241–270. Cologne: Pahl-Rugenstein Verlag, 1983.

Fritzsche, Peter. *Rehearsals for Fascism: Populism and Political Mobilization in Weimar Germany*. New York: Oxford University Press, 1990.

—— *Germans into Nazis*. Cambridge: Harvard University Press, 1998.

Gall, Lothar, ed. *Das Bismarck-Problem in der Geschichtsschreibung nach 1945*. Cologne: Kiepenhauer & Witsch, 1971.

—— *Bismarck: The White Revolutionary*. Vol. 1. Translated by J.A. Underwood. London: Allen & Unwin, 1986.

Gatzke, Hans W. *Stresemann and the Rearmament of Germany*. Baltimore: The Johns Hopkins Press, 1954.

Geyer, Michael. "The Stigma of Violence, Nationalism, and War in Twentieth-Century Germany." *German Studies Review* (Winter 1992): 75–110.

Gildea, Robert. *The Past in French History*. New Haven: Yale University Press, 1994.

Grathwol, Robert P. *Stresemann and the DNVP: Reconciliation or Revenge in German Foreign Policy 1924–1928.* Lawrence: The Regents Press of Kansas, 1980.

Habermas, Jürgen. *The Structural Transformation of the Public Sphere: An Inquiry into a Category of Bourgeois Society.* Translated by Thomas Burger with the assistance of Frederick Lawrence. Cambridge, Mass: MIT Press, 1989.

Hagenlücke, Heinz. *Deutsche Vaterlandspartei. Die nationale Rechte am Ende des Kaiserreiches.* Düsseldorf: Droste Verlag, 1997.

Hamel, Iris. *Völkischer Verband und nationale Gewerkschaft: Der Deutschnationale Handlungsgehilfen-Verband, 1893–1933.* Frankfurt: Europäische Verlagsanstalt, 1967.

Hamerow, Theodore S., ed. *Otto von Bismarck and Imperial Germany: A Historical Assessment.* Massachusetts: D.C. Heath and Company, 1994.

—— *On the Road to the Wolf's Lair: German Resistance to Hitler.* Cambridge, Mass: Harvard University Press, 1997.

Hank, Manfred. *Kanzler ohne Amt. Fürst Bismarck nach seiner Entlassung 1890–1898.* Munich: Tuduv-Verlagsgesellschaft, 1977.

Hartwig, Edgar. "Alldeutscher Verband (ADV) 1891–1939." In *Lexicon zur Parteiengeschichte: Die bürgerlichen und kleinbürgerlichen Parteien und Verbände in Deutschland (1789–1945).* Vol. I, ed. Dieter Fricke, 13–47. Cologne: Pahl-Rugenstein Verlag, 1983.

—— "Deutscher Ostmarkenverein (DOV) 1894–1934." In *Lexicon zur Parteiengeschichte: Die bürgerlichen und kleinbürgerlichen Parteien und Verbände in Deutschland (1789–1945).* Vol. II, ed. Dieter Fricke, 225–244. Cologne: Pahl-Rugenstein Verlag, 1983.

Hedinger, Hans-Walter. "Der Bismarck-Kult. Ein Umriß." In *Der Religionswandel unserer Zeit im Spiegel der Religionswissenschaft,* ed. Gunther Stephenson, 201–215. Darmstadt: Wissentschaftliche Buchgesellschaft, 1976.

—— "Bismarck-Denkmäler und Bismarck Verehrung." In *Kunstverwaltung, Bau- und Denkmal-Politik im Kaiserreich,* eds. Ekkehard Mai und Stephan Waetzoldt. Berlin: Gebr. Mann Verlag, 1981.

Hermand, Jost. *Old Dreams of a New Reich: Volkisch Utopias and National Socialism.* Translated by Paul Levesque. Bloomington: Indiana University Press, 1992.

Hessisches Landesmusem, Darmstadt. *Politische Plakate der Weimarer Republic 1918–1933.* Darmstadt: Druckerei H. Anthes, 1980.

Hull, Isabel. *The Entourage of Kaiser Wilhelm II, 1888–1918.* Cambridge: Cambridge University Press, 1982.

Hunt, Lynn. *Politics, Culture, and Class in the French Revolution.* Berkeley: University of California Press, 1984.

Jackisch, Barry. "'Not a Large, but a Strong Right': The Pan-German League,

Radical Nationalism, and Rightist Party Politics in Weimar Germany, 1918–1933." Ph.D. diss., State University of New York at Buffalo, 2000.

Jarausch, Konrad H. *The Enigmatic Chancellor: Bethmann Hollweg and the Hubris of Imperial Germany*. New Haven: Yale University Press, 1973.

—— *Students, Society, and Politics in Imperial Germany: The Rise of Academic Illiberalism*. New Jersey: Princeton University Press, 1982.

Jones, Larry Eugene. *German Liberalism and the Dissolution of the Weimar Party System, 1918–1933*. Chapel Hill: The University of North Carolina Press, 1988.

—— " 'The Greatest Stupidity of My Life': Alfred Hugenberg and the Formation of the Hitler Cabinet, January 1933." *Journal of Contemporary History* (27) (1992).

Kaminski, Ted M. "Bismarck and the Polish Question: the 'Huldigungsfahrten' to Varzin in 1894." *Canadian Journal of History* XXII (August 1988): 235–250.

Kardorff, Siegfried von. *Wilhelm von Kardorff. Ein nationaler Parlamentarier im Zeitalter Bismarcks und Wilhelms II, 1828–1907*. Berlin: E. S. Mittler & Sohn Verlag, 1936.

Kazin, Michael. *The Populist Persuasion: An American History*. Ithaca: Cornell University Press, 1995.

Kent, George O. *Bismarck and His Times*. Carbondale: Southern Illinois University Press, 1978.

Kershaw, Ian. *The 'Hitler Myth': Image and Reality in the Third Reich*. Oxford: Clarendon Press, 1987.

—— "'Working towards the Führer.' Reflections on the Nature of the Hitler Dictatorship." *Contemporary European History* 2(2) (1993): 103–118.

—— *Hitler: 1889–1936: Hubris*. New York: W. W. Norton, 1998.

—— *Hitler: 1936–1945: Nemesis*. New York: W. W. Norton, 2001.

Kertzer, David I. *Ritual, Politics, and Power*. New Haven: Yale University Press, 1988.

Kolb, Eberhard. *The Weimar Republic*. Translated by P. S. Falla. London: Unwin Hyman, 1988.

Koshar, Rudy. "Contentious Citadel: Bourgeois Crisis and Nazism in Marburg/Lahn, 1880–1933." In *The Formation of the Nazi Constituency 1919–1933*, ed. Thomas Childers. London: Croom Helm, 1986.

—— *From Monuments to Traces: Artifacts of German Memory, 1870–1990*. Berkeley: University of California Press, 2000.

Krabbe, Wolfgang. "Die Bismarckjugend der Deutschnationalen Volkspartei." *German Studies Review* XVII (February 1994): 9–32.

Krebs, Willi. "Deutschvölkischer Schutz- und Trutzbund (DSTB) 1919–1922 (1924)." In *Lexicon zur Parteiengeschichte: Die bürgerlichen und kleinbürgerlichen Parteien und Verbände in Deutschland (1789–1945)*. Vol. II, ed. Dieter Fricke, 562–568. Cologne: Pahl-Rugenstein Verlag, 1983.

Lange, Karl. *Bismarcks Sturz und die öffentliche Meinung in Deutschland und im Auslande*. Stuttgart: Deutsche Verlags-Anstalt, 1927.

Lehnert, Detlev, and Klaus Megerle. "Problems of Identity and Consensus in a Fragmented Society: the Weimar Republic." In *Political Culture in Germany*, eds. Dirk Berg-Schlosser and Ralf Rytlewski. New York: St. Martin's Press, 1993.

Leopold, John A. *Alfred Hugenberg: The Radical Nationalist and the Campaign against the Weimar Republic*. New Haven: Yale University Press, 1977.

Lepsius, Mario Rainer. *Extremer Nationalismus. Strukturbedingungen vor der nationalsozialistischen Machtergreifung*. Stuttgart: W. Kohlhammer Verlag, 1966.

—— "Charismatic Leadership: Max Weber's Model and Its Applicability to the Rule of Hitler." In *Changing Conceptions of Leadership*, eds. Carl F. Graumann and Serge Moscovici. New York: Springer-Verlag, 1986.

—— "Parteiensystem und Sozialstuktur. Zum Problem der Demokratisierung der deutschen Gesellschaft." Chap. in *Demokratie in Deutschland. Soziologisch-historische Konstellationsanalysen. Ausgewählte Aufsätze*. Göttingen: Vandenhoeck & Ruprecht, 1993.

Lerman, Katherine Anne. *The Chancellor as Courtier: Bernhard von Bülow and the Governance of Germany 1900–1909*. Cambridge: Cambridge University Press, 1990.

Ley, Michael and Julius H. Schoeps, eds. *Der Nationalsozialismus als politische Religion*. Bodenheim: Philo Verlagsgesellschaft mbH, 1997.

Lidtke, Vernon. *The Alternative Culture: Socialist Labor in Imperial Germany*. New York: Oxford University Press, 1985.

Lohalm, Uwe. *Völkischer Radikalismus. Die Geschichte des Deutschvölkischen Schutz- und Trutz-Bundes 1919–1923*. Hamburg: Leibniz-Verlag, 1970.

McGuire, Michael. "Bismarck in Walhalla: the cult of Bismarck and the politics of national identity in Imperial Germany, 1890–1915." Ph.D. diss., University of Pennsylvania, 1993.

Machtan, Lothar. "Bismarck-Kult und deutscher National-Mythos 1890 bis 1940." In *Bismarck und der deutsche National-Mythos*, ed. Lothar Machtan. Bremen: Temmen, 1994.

—— *Bismarcks Tod und Deutschlands Tränen. Reportage einer Tragödie*. Munich: Wilhelm Goldman Verlag, 1998.

Madsen, Douglas and Peter G. Snow. *The Charismatic Bond: Political Behavior in Time of Crisis*. Cambridge, Mass: Harvard University Press, 1991.

Marx, Karl, and Friedrich Engels. *Collected Works*, vol. 24 (New York: International Publishers, 1989).

Meinecke, Friedrich. *The German Catastrophe: Reflections and Recollections*. Translated by Sidney B. Fay. Boston: Beacon Press, 1963.

Mommsen, Hans. *The Rise and Fall of Weimar Democracy*. Translated by Elborg Forster and Larry Eugene Jones. Chapel Hill: The University of North Carolina Press, 1996.

Mommsen, Wilhelm. *Bismarcks Sturz und die Parteien*. Stuttgart: Deutsche Verlags-Anstalt, 1924.

Mommsen, Wolfgang. *Max Weber and German Politics 1890–1920*. Translated by Michael Steinberg. Chicago: The University of Chicago Press, 1984.

—— "The Spirit of 1914 and the Ideology of a German 'Sonderweg'." Chap. in *Imperial Germany 1867–1918: Politics, Culture, and Society in an Authoritarian State*. Translated by Richard Deveson. London: Arnold, 1995.

Mosse, George. *The Nationalization of the Masses: Political Symbolism and Mass Movements in Germany from the Napoleonic Wars through the Third Reich*. New York: Howard Fertig, 1975.

Müller-Koppe, Jens. "Die deutsche Sozialdemokratie und der Bismarck-Mythos." In *Bismarck und der deutsche National-Mythos*, ed. Lothar Machtan. Bremen: Temmen, 1994.

Nichols, J. Alden. *Germany after Bismarck: The Caprivi Era, 1890–1894*. New York: W. W. Norton & Company, 1958.

Nipperdey, Thomas. "Nationalidee und Nationaldenkmal in Deutschland im 19. Jahrhundert." Chap. in *Gesellschaft, Kultur, Theorie. Gesammelte Aufsätze zur neueren Geschichte*. Göttingen: Vandenhoeck & Ruprecht, 1976.

Ozouf, Mona. *Festivals and the French Revolution*. Translated by Alan Sheridan. Cambridge, Mass: Harvard University Press, 1988.

Payne, Stanley G. *A History of Fascism, 1914–1945*. Madison: University of Wisconsin Press, 1995.

Peterson, Merrill. *Lincoln in American Memory*. New York: Oxford University Press, 1994.

Peukert, Detlev. *Die Edelweißpiraten. Protestbewegungen jugendlicher Arbeiter im Dritten Reich. Eine Dokumentation*. Cologne: Bund Verlag, 1980.

—— *The Weimar Republic: The Crisis of Classical Modernity*. Translated by Richard Deveson. New York: Hill and Wang, 1992.

Pflanze, Otto. "Bismarck and German Nationalism." *American Historical Review* LX (April 1955): 548–566.

—— *Bismarck and the Development of Modern Germany. Vol. I, The Period of Unification, 1815–1871*. Princeton: Princeton University Press, 1963.

—— *Bismarck and the Development of Modern Germany. Vol. II, The Period of Consolidation, 1871–1880*. Princeton: Princeton University Press, 1992.

—— *Bismarck and the Development of Modern Germany. Vol. III, The Period of Fortification, 1880–1898*. Princeton: Princeton University Press, 1992.

—— "Bismarck's *Gedanken und Erinnerungen*." In *Political Memoir: Essays on the Politics of Memory*, ed. George Egerton, 28–61. London: Frank Cass & Co. Ltd., 1994.

Pohl, Karl Heinrich. "Gustav Stresemann – Überlegungen zu einer neuen Biographie." Chap. in Karl Heinrich Pohl, ed., *Politiker und Bürger: Gustav Stresemann und seine Zeit*. Göttingen: Vandenhoeck & Ruprecht, 2002.

Pöls, Werner. "Bismarckverehrung und Bismarcklegende als innen-politisches Problem der Wilhelminischen Zeit." *Jahrbuch für die Geschichte Mittel- und Ostdeutschlands* 20 (1971): 183–201.

Puhle, Hans-Jürgen. *Agrarische Interessenpolitik und preußischer Konservatismus im wilhelminischen Reich (1893–1914). Ein Beitrag zur Analyse des National-ismus in Deutschland am Beispiel des Bundes der Landwirte und der Deutsch-Konservativen Partei*. Hannover: Verlag für Literatur und Zeitgeschehen, 1966.

Retallack, James N. "Conservatives contra Chancellor: Official Responses to the Spectre of Conservative Demagoguery from Bismarck to Bülow." *Canadian Journal of History* XX (August 1985).

——— *Notables of the Right: The Conservative Party and Political Mobilization in Germany, 1876–1918*. Boston: Unwin Hyman, 1988.

——— *Germany in the Age of Kaiser Wilhelm II*. New York: St. Martin's Press, 1996.

Rich, Norman. *Friedrich von Holstein: Politics and Diplomacy in the Era of Bismarck and Wilhelm II*. Vol. 1. Cambridge: Cambridge University Press, 1965.

Ringer, Fritz. *The Decline of the German Mandarins: The German Academic Community, 1890–1933*. Cambridge: Harvard University Press, 1969.

Rogge, Helmuth. *Holstein und Harden. Politisch-publizistisches Zusammenspiel zweier Außenseiter des Wilhelminischen Reichs*. Munich: C. H. Beck Verlag, 1959.

Rohe, Karl. "German Elections and Party Systems in Historical and Regional Perspective: an Introduction." In *Elections, Parties and Political Traditions: Social Foundations of German Parties and Party Systems, 1867–1987*, ed. Karl Rohe. New York: Berg, 1990.

——— *Wahlen und Wählertraditionen in Deutschland. Kulturelle Grundlagen deutscher Parteien und Parteiensysteme im 19. und 20. Jahrhundert*. Frankfurt am Main: Suhrkamp Verlag, 1992.

Röhl, John C. G. "The emperor's new clothes: a character sketch of Kaiser Wilhelm II." In *Kaiser Wilhelm II: New Interpretations, the Corfu Papers*, eds. John C. G. Röhl and Nicolaus Sombart. Cambridge: Cambridge University Press, 1982.

Rose, Detlev. *Die Thule-Gesellschaft. Legende – Mythos – Wirklichkeit*. Tübingen: Grabert Verlag, 1994.

Ross, Ronald J. *Beleaguered Tower: The Dilemma of Political Catholicism in Wilhelmine Germany*. Notre Dame: Notre Dame University Press, 1976.

Rothfels, Hans. "Problems of a Bismarck Biography." *The Review of Politics* 9(3) (July 1947): 362–380.

Scheck, Raffael. *Alfred von Tirpitz and German Right-Wing Politics, 1914–1930*. New Jersey: Humanities Press, 1998.

Schellack, Fritz. "Sedan- und Kaisergeburtstagsfeste." In *Öffentliche Festkultur: Politische Feste in Deutschland von der Aufklärung bis zum Ersten Weltkrieg*, eds. Dieter Düding, Peter Friedemann, Paul Münch. Hamburg: Rowohlt, 1988.

Sheehan, James J. *German Liberalism in the Nineteenth Century*. Chicago: The University of Chicago Press, 1978.

Shevin Coetzee, Marilyn. *The German Army League: Popular Nationalism in Wilhelmine Germany*. New York: Oxford University Press, 1990.

Smith, Jeffrey. "The Monarchy versus the Nation: the 'Festive Year' 1913 in Wilhelmine Germany." *German Studies Review* XXIII (May 2000).

Sontheimer, Kurt. *Antidemokratisches Denken in der Weimarer Republik: Die politischen Ideen des deutschen Nationalismus zwischen 1918 und 1933*. Munich: Deutscher Taschenbuch Verlag, 1968.

—— *Deutschlands Politische Kultur*. Munich: Serie Piper, 1990.

Stegmann, Dirk. *Die Erben Bismarcks. Parteien und Verbände in der Spätphase des Wilhelminischen Deutschlands. Sammlungspolitik 1897–1918*. Cologne: Kiepenheuer & Witsch, 1970.

—— "Between Economic Interests and Radical Nationalism: Attempts to Found a New Right-Wing Party in Imperial Germany, 1887–1894." In *Between Reform, Reaction, and Resistance: Studies in the History of German Conservatism from 1789 to 1945*, eds. Larry Eugene Jones and James Retallack. Providence: Berg, 1993.

Stribrny, Wolfgang. *Bismarck und die deutsche Politik nach seiner Entlassung (1890–1898)*. Paderborn: Ferdinand Schöningh, 1977.

Struve, Walter. *Elites against Democracy: Leadership Ideals in Bourgeois Political Thought in Germany, 1890–1933*. Princeton: Princeton University Press, 1973.

Tauber, Kurt P. *Beyond Eagle and Swastika: German Nationalism since 1945*, 2 vols. Connecticut: Wesleyan University Press, 1967.

Thimme, Annelise. *Flucht in den Mythos: Die Deutschnationale Volkspartei und die Niederlage von 1918*. Göttingen: Vandenhoeck & Ruprecht, 1969.

Tims, Richard Wonser. *Germanizing Prussian Poland: The H-K-T Society and the Struggle for the Eastern Marches in the German Empire, 1894–1919*. New York: Columbia University Press, 1941.

Tumarkin, Nina. *Lenin Lives! The Lenin Cult in Soviet Russia*. Cambridge, Mass: Harvard University Press, 1983.

Turner, Bryan S. "Nietzsche, Weber and the Devaluation of Politics: The Problem of State Legitimacy." Chap. in *Max Weber: From History to Modernity*. London: Routledge, 1992.

Turner, Henry Ashby Jr. *Stresemann and the Politics of the Weimar Republic*. Princeton, New Jersey: Princeton University Press, 1963.

Urbach, Karina. "Between Saviour and Villain: 100 Years of Bismarck Biographies," *The Historical Journal* 41(4) (Dec. 1998): 1141–1160.

Vascik, George. "Agrarian Conservatism in Wilhelmine Germany: Diederich Hahn and the Agrarian League." In *Between Reform, Reaction, and Resistance: Studies in the History of German Conservatism from 1789 to 1945*, eds. Larry Eugene Jones and James Retallack, 229–260. Providence: Berg, 1993.

Verhey, Jeffrey. *The Spirit of 1914: Militarism, Myth, and Mobilization in Germany*. Cambridge: Cambridge University Press, 2000.

Weber, Marianne. *Max Weber: A Biography*. Translated by Harry Zohn. New York: John Wiley & Sons, 1975.

Weber, Max. *On Charisma and Institution Building: Selected Papers*, ed. S. N. Eisenstadt. Chicago: University of Chicago Press, 1968.

—— *Economy and Society: An Outline of Interpretive Sociology*, eds. Guenther Roth and Claus Wittich. New York: Bedminster Press, 1968.

—— *From Max Weber: Essays in Sociology*, eds. H. H. Gerth and C. Wright Mills. London: Routledge, 1991.

Wegner-Korfes, Sigrid. *Otto von Bismarck und Rußland. Des Reichskanzlers Rußlandpolitik und sein realpolitisches Erbe in der Interpretation bürgerlicher Politiker (1918–1945)*. Berlin: Dietz Verlag, 1990.

Wehler, Hans-Ulrich. *Bismarck und der Imperialismus*. Cologne: Kiepenheuer & Witsch, 1969.

—— *The German Empire, 1871–1918*. Translated by Kim Traynor. New York: Berg, 1985.

—— *Deutsche Gesellschaftsgeschichte. Bd. 4. Vom Beginn des Ersten Weltkriegs bis zur Gründung der beiden deutschen Staaten 1914–1949*. Munich: C. H. Beck, 2003.

Weinberg, Gerhard L. "Reflections on Two Unifications." *German Studies Review* XXI (February 1998): 13–25.

Weller, B. Uwe. *Maximilian Harden und die "Zukunft"*. Bremen: Schünemann Universitätsverlag, 1970.

Wernecke, Klaus. *Der Wille zur Weltgeltung. Außenpolitik und Öffentlichkeit im Kaiserreich am Vorabend des Ersten Weltkrieges*. Düsseldorf: Droste Verlag, 1970.

Wright, Jonathan. *Gustav Stresemann: Weimar's Greatest Statesman*. New York: Oxford University Press, 2002.

Young, Harry. *Maximilian Harden, Censor Germaniae: The Critic in Opposition from Bismarck to the Rise of Nazism*. The Hague: Martinus Nijhoff, 1959.

Index

Adenauer, Konrad, 181
Agrarian League (Bund der
    Landwirte), 31, 40–1, 60, 76, 78,
    96, 97, 189
Anschluss, 169–70, 195
Austria-Hungary, 21, 22, 31, 32, 93,
    169–70, 195

Bang, Paul, 108, 138
Bassermann, Ernst, 68, 74, 77, 96, 134
Bethmann Hollweg, Theobald von,
    77–8, 132, 175, 185, 187–8, 190,
    193
    compared to Bismarck, 88, 112
    and German Right, 71–2, 74, 78,
        94–7
    view and/or use of Bismarck, 73,
        74, 78
    and war aims, 92, 94
'Bismarck', Battleship, 171–2
Bismarck-Bund, 58
Bismarck, Herbert, 31, 51
Bismarck Monuments, 8, 22, 56–8, 63,
    87–8, 90, 142, 145, 171
Bismarck, Otto von, 1, 4, 12–14, 19
    against democracy, 75, 102–3, 113,
        143
    and Agrarian League, 40–1
    and annexations, 91–4, 187
    and Anschluss, 169–70
    and anti-Nazi Resistance, 173–5
    and anti-Semitism, 173

birthday celebrations, 7–8, 13, 22, 26,
    32–3, 73, 90–2, 99, 137, 143, 167
'Bismarck to Hitler' connection, 3,
    165–70, 194–6
and charisma, 11, 19–20, 190–6
and 'Day of Potsdam', 166
death, 6, 8, 49–54, 60–1
declines in relation to Hitler, 170–1,
    173
and defining the nation, 2, 10, 20,
    22, 50, 54, 130
dismissal, 7, 20, 28–9, 31, 33–4, 38
dismissal of Tirpitz compared to
    that of, 96
and First World War, 88–99
'Fronde', 34, 39
and German academics, 52–3, 90,
    166–7
and German middle classes, 6, 54,
    159
honored, 7–8, 21–4
Huldigungsfahrten, 32
ignored/downplayed by Wilhelm II,
    55
indeterminate image of in Weimar,
    115, 189
inspires fear/concern in government,
    35, 39
inspires formation of Fatherland
    Party, 97
inspires opposition to Weimar
    Republic, 103, 106–11

217